CONTEMPORARY DYSTOPIAN FICTION FOR YOUNG ADULTS

From the jaded, wired teenagers of M.T. Anderson's *Feed* to the spirited young rebels of Suzanne Collins's *The Hunger Games* trilogy, the protagonists of Young Adult dystopias are introducing a new generation of readers to the pleasures and challenges of dystopian imaginings. As the dark universes of YA dystopias continue to flood the market, *Contemporary Dystopian Fiction for Young Adults: Brave New Teenagers* offers a critical evaluation of the literary and political potentials of this widespread publishing phenomenon. With its capacity to frighten and warn, dystopian writing powerfully engages with our pressing global concerns: liberty and self-determination, environmental destruction and looming catastrophe, questions of identity and justice, and the increasingly fragile boundaries between technology and the self. When directed at young readers, these dystopian warnings are distilled into exciting adventures with gripping plots and accessible messages that may have the potential to motivate a generation on the cusp of adulthood. This collection enacts a lively debate about the goals and efficacy of YA dystopias, with three major areas of contention: do these texts reinscribe an old didacticism or offer an exciting new frontier in children's literature? Do their political critiques represent conservative or radical ideologies? And finally, are these novels high-minded attempts to educate the young or simply bids to cash in on a formula for commercial success? This collection represents a prismatic and evolving understanding of the genre, illuminating its relevance to children's literature and our wider culture.

Balaka Basu holds a Ph.D. in English from The Graduate Center, City University of New York, US.

Katherine R. Broad holds a Ph.D. in English from The Graduate Center, City University of New York, US.

Carrie Hintz is Associate Professor of English at Queens College and The Graduate Center, City University of New York, US.

Children's Literature and Culture
Philip Nel, *Series Editor*

For a complete series list, please go to
routledge.com

Once Upon a Time in a Different World
*Issues and Ideas in African American
Children's Literature*
Neal A. Lester

The Gothic in Children's Literature
Haunting the Borders
Edited by Anna Jackson, Karen Coats,
and Roderick McGillis

Reading Victorian Schoolrooms
*Childhood and Education in
Nineteenth-Century Fiction*
Elizabeth Gargano

Soon Come Home to This Island
West Indians in British Children's Literature
Karen Sands-O'Connor

Boys in Children's Literature and
Popular Culture
*Masculinity, Abjection, and the
Fictional Child*
Annette Wannamaker

Into the Closet
*Cross-dressing and the Gendered Body
in Children's Literature*
Victoria Flanagan

Russian Children's Literature and Culture
Edited by Marina Balina and
Larissa Rudova

The Outside Child In and Out of
the Book
Christine Wilkie-Stibbs

Representing Africa in Children's Literature
Old and New Ways of Seeing
Vivian Yenika-Agbaw

The Fantasy of Family
*Nineteenth-Century Children's Literature
and the Myth of the Domestic Ideal*
Liz Thiel

From Nursery Rhymes to Nationhood
*Children's Literature and the Construction
of Canadian Identity*
Elizabeth A. Galway

The Family in English Children's Literature
Ann Alston

Enterprising Youth
*Social Values and Acculturation in
Nineteenth-Century American
Children's Literature*
Monika Elbert

Constructing Adolescence in
Fantastic Realism
Alison Waller

Crossover Fiction
Global and Historical Perspectives
Sandra L. Beckett

The Crossover Novel
*Contemporary Children's Fiction and Its
Adult Readership*
Rachel Falconer

Shakespeare in Children's Literature
Gender and Cultural Capital
Erica Hateley

Critical Approaches to Food in
Children's Literature
Edited by Kara K. Keeling and
Scott T. Pollard

Neo-Imperialism in Children's Literature
About Africa
A Study of Contemporary Fiction
Yulisa Amadu Maddy and Donnarae
MacCann

Death, Gender and Sexuality in
Contemporary Adolescent Literature
Kathryn James

Fundamental Concepts of Children's
Literature Research
Literary and Sociological Approaches
Hans-Heino Ewers

Children's Fiction about 9/11
Ethnic, Heroic and National Identities
Jo Lampert

The Place of Lewis Carroll in Children's
Literature
Jan Susina

Power, Voice and Subjectivity in Literature
for Young Readers
Maria Nikolajeva

"Juvenile" Literature and British Society,
1850–1950
The Age of Adolescence
Charles Ferrall and Anna Jackson

Picturing the Wolf in Children's Literature
Debra Mitts-Smith

New Directions in Picturebook Research
Edited by Teresa Colomer, Bettina
Kümmerling-Meibauer, Cecilia Silva-Díaz

The Role of Translators in Children's
Literature
Invisible Storytellers
Gillian Lathey

The Children's Book Business
Lessons from the Long Eighteenth Century
Lissa Paul

Humor in Contemporary Junior Literature
Julie Cross

Innocence, Heterosexuality, and the
Queerness of Children's Literature
Tison Pugh

Reading the Adolescent Romance
*Sweet Valley and the Popular Young Adult
Romance Novel*
Amy S. Pattee

Irish Children's Literature and Culture
New Perspectives on Contemporary Writing
Edited by Valerie Coghlan and
Keith O'Sullivan

Beyond Pippi Longstocking
*Intermedial and International Perspectives
on Astrid Lindgren's Work s*
Edited by Bettina Kümmerling-Meibauer
and Astrid Surmatz

Contemporary English-Language
Indian Children's Literature:
*Representations of Nation, Culture,
and the New Indian Girl*
Michelle Superle

Re-visioning Historical Fiction
The Past through Modern Eyes
Kim Wilson

The Myth of Persephone in Girls'
Fantasy Literature
Holly Virginia Blackford

Pinocchio, Puppets and Modernity
The Mechanical Body
Edited by Katia Pizzi

Crossover Picturebooks
A Genre for All Ages
Sandra L. Beckett

Peter Pan's Shadows in the Literary
Imagination
Kirsten Stirling

Landscape in Children's Literature
Jane Suzanne Carroll

Colonial India in Children's Literature
Supriya Goswami

Children's Culture and the Avant-Garde
Painting in Paris, 1890–1915
Marilynn Olson

Textual Transformations in Children's
Literature
Adaptations, Translations, Reconsiderations
Edited by Benjamin Lefebvre

The Nation in Children's Literature
Nations of Childhood
Edited by Kit Kelen and Björn Sundmark

Subjectivity in Asian Children's Literature
and Film
Global Theories and Implications
Edited by John Stephens

Children's Literature, Domestication, and
Social Foundation
Narratives of Civilization and Wilderness
Layla AbdelRahim

Charles Dickens and the Victorian Child
*Romanticizing and Socializing the Imperfect
Child*
Amberyl Malkovich

Second-Generation Memory and
Contemporary Children's Literature
Ghost Images
Anastasia Ulanowicz

Contemporary Dystopian Fiction for
Young Adults
Brave New Teenagers
Edited by Balaka Basu, Katherine R. Broad,
and Carrie Hintz

CONTEMPORARY DYSTOPIAN FICTION FOR YOUNG ADULTS

Brave New Teenagers

EDITED BY
BALAKA BASU,
KATHERINE R. BROAD,
AND CARRIE HINTZ

NEW YORK AND LONDON

First published 2013
by Routledge
711 Third Avenue, New York, NY 10017
Simultaneously published in the UK
by Routledge
2 Park Square, Milton Park, Abingdon, Oxfordshire OX14 4RN

First issued in paperback 2014

Routledge is an imprint of the Taylor and Francis Group, an informa business

© 2013 Taylor & Francis

The right of Balaka Basu, Katherine R. Broad, and Carrie Hintz to be identified as
the authors of the editorial material, and of the authors for their individual chapters,
has been asserted in accordance with sections 77 and 78 of the Copyright, Designs
and Patents Act 1988.

All rights reserved. No part of this book may be reprinted or reproduced or
utilised in any form or by any electronic, mechanical, or other means, now known
or hereafter invented, including photocopying and recording, or in any information
storage or retrieval system, without permission in writing from the publishers.

Trademark Notice: Product or corporate names may be trademarks or registered
trademarks, and are used only for identification and explanation without intent
to infringe.

Library of Congress Cataloging in Publication Data

Contemporary dystopian fiction for young adults : brave new teenagers / edited by
   Balaka Basu, Katherine R. Broad, Carrie Hintz.
      pages cm. — (Children's Literature and Culture ; 93)
   Includes bibliographical references and index.
  1. Young adult fiction, American—21st century—History and criticism.
2. Dystopias in literature.   3. Postmodernism (Literature)   I. Basu, Balaka,
editor of compilation.   II. Broad, Katherine R., editor of compilation.
III. Hintz, Carrie, 1970– editor of compilation.
   PS374.Y57C66 2013
   813'.6099283—dc23
   2012048128

ISBN 978-0-415-63693-3 (hbk)
ISBN 978-1-138-92192-4 (pbk)
ISBN 978-0-203-08493-9 (ebk)

Typeset in Minion
by IBT Global.

Contents

Series Editor's Foreword	ix
Acknowledgments	xi
Introduction	1
BALAKA BASU, KATHERINE R. BROAD, AND CARRIE HINTZ	

PART I
Freedom and Constraint: Adolescent Liberty and Self-Determination

Chapter 1	What Faction Are You In? The Pleasure of Being Sorted in Veronica Roth's *Divergent* BALAKA BASU	19
Chapter 2	Coming of Age in Dystopia: Reading Genre in Holly Black's Curse Workers Series EMILY LAUER	35
Chapter 3	Embodying the Postmetropolis in Catherine Fisher's *Incarceron* and *Sapphique* CARISSA TURNER SMITH	51

PART II
Society and Environment: Building a Better World

Chapter 4	Hope in Dark Times: Climate Change and the World Risk Society in Saci Lloyd's *The Carbon Diaries 2015* and *2017* ALEXA WEIK VON MOSSNER	69

viii • Contents

| Chapter 5 | Educating Desire, Choosing Justice? Susan Beth Pfeffer's Last Survivors Series and Julie Bertagna's *Exodus* | 85 |

CLAIRE P. CURTIS

| Chapter 6 | On the Brink: The Role of Young Adult Culture in Environmental Degradation | 101 |

ELAINE OSTRY

PART III
Radical or Conservative? Polemics of the Future

| Chapter 7 | "The Dandelion in the Spring": Utopia as Romance in Suzanne Collins's *The Hunger Games* Trilogy | 117 |

KATHERINE R. BROAD

| Chapter 8 | The Future Is Pale: Race in Contemporary Young Adult Dystopian Novels | 131 |

MARY J. COUZELIS

| Chapter 9 | Technology and Models of Literacy in Young Adult Dystopian Fiction | 145 |

KRISTI MCDUFFIE

PART IV
Biotechnologies of the Self: Humanity in a Posthuman Age

| Chapter 10 | Dystopian Sacrifice, Scapegoats, and Neal Shusterman's *Unwind* | 159 |

SUSAN LOUISE STEWART

| Chapter 11 | The Soul of the Clone: Coming of Age as a Posthuman in Nancy Farmer's *The House of the Scorpion* | 175 |

ERIN T. NEWCOMB

| Chapter 12 | Parables for the Postmodern, Post-9/11, and Posthuman World: Carrie Ryan's Forest of Hands and Teeth Books, M.T. Anderson's *Feed*, and Mary E. Pearson's *The Adoration of Jenna Fox* | 189 |

THOMAS J. MORRISSEY

Contributors   203

Index   207

Series Editor's Foreword

The Children's Literature and Culture series is dedicated to promoting original research in children's literature, children's culture, and childhood studies. We use the term "children" in the broadest sense, spanning from earliest childhood up through adolescence. The already capacious term "culture" encompasses media (radio, film, television, video games, blogs, websites, social networking sites), material culture (toys, games, products), acculturation (processes of socialization), and of course literature, including all types of crossover works. Since children's literature is defined by its audience, this series seeks to foster scholarship on the full range of children's literature's many genres and subgenres: fairy tales, folk tales, comics, graphic novels, picture books, novels, poetry, didactic tales, nonsense, fantasy, realism, mystery, horror, fan fiction, and others.

Founded by Jack Zipes in 1994, Routledge's Children's Literature and Culture is the longest-running series devoted to the study of children's literature and culture from a national and international perspective. In 2011, expanding its focus to include childhood studies, the series also seeks to explore the legal, historical, and philosophical conditions of different childhoods. An advocate for scholarship from around the globe, the series recognizes innovation and encourages interdisciplinarity. In Zipes' words, "the goal of the Children's Literature and Culture series is to enhance research in this field and, at the same time, point to new directions that bring together the best scholarly work throughout the world."

Philip Nel

Acknowledgments

We would like to thank all of our contributors for their compelling ideas, hard work, patience, and consummate professionalism over the two years it took to produce *Contemporary Dystopian Fiction for Young Adults: Brave New Teenagers*. As well, thanks go to Liz Levine, Julie Ganz, and Catherine Tung at Routledge, and to series editor Philip Nel for his helpful feedback on our initial proposal and the manuscript itself; they have all been a pleasure to work with.

We owe a special debt of gratitude to the Center for Humanities at the CUNY Graduate Center for supporting our Humanities Seminar "Possible Worlds, Alternative Futures: Utopianism in Theory and Practice." They provided us with a wonderful forum to develop and share our scholarship on YA dystopias. We are particularly grateful to Sampson Starkweather, Katherine Carl, and Aoibheann Sweeney for their leadership and vision. We are grateful for the support of all of our colleagues at CUNY, especially Mario DiGangi, Nancy Silverman, Jason Tougaw, Ammiel Alcalay, Rich McCoy, and Rachel Brownstein. We thank Dale Ireland and Meira Levinson for their efficient and timely research assistance.

At the Society for Utopian Studies, we thank Philip Wegner, Jennifer Wagner-Lawlor, Peter Fitting, Alex Macdonald, Naomi Jacobs, Rebecca Totaro, Claire Curtis, Jill Belli, Lyman Tower Sargent, Tom Moylan, Brian Greenspan, and Peter Sands for many years of discussion about the field of utopian studies. Many individuals at the Children's Literature Association Conference were a source of inspiration and insight, and we would like to express particular appreciation to Eric Tribunella, David P. McKay, and Sara Day.

Putting together this collection has been made infinitely more rewarding by the support of our families and friends. We would like to express our personal gratitude to Sumita and Dipak Basu, Daniel Clark, Robert Farrell, Eve Goodman, Peter Hamilton, Graham and Frances Hamilton, Carol and Art Hintz, Tamara Johnson, Katherine Knight-Lascoutx, and Edie Nugent. We also thank Michael Broad and Grace Massey for their generous hospitality in June 2012 and for their encouragement of our project.

Introduction

Balaka Basu, Katherine R. Broad, and Carrie Hintz

In 2008, the *New York Times Sunday Book Review* featured a piece titled "Scary New World" that took notice of a growing trend in the children's publishing marketplace: the recent explosion of dystopian fiction for young adults. The reviewer, young adult novelist John Green, began his article by remarking on the notable fertility of the field, saying, "The past year has seen the publication of more than a dozen postapocalyptic young adult novels that explore what the future could look like once our unsustainable lifestyles cease to be sustained. (Spoiler alert: It's gonna be bad)."[1] His review identified two particular texts to focus on: Susan Beth Pfeffer's *The Dead and the Gone* and Suzanne Collins's *The Hunger Games*. The second of these, Collins's trilogy, neatly outstripped all of its competitors and ensured that its genre would be the latest publishing phenomenon in a post-Potter, post-*Twilight* market—a market which, having been surprised (once or twice) by the extraordinary success and market power that a YA franchise can offer, now always seems to be looking for the Next Big Thing. With the highly anticipated film release of *The Hunger Games* in 2012, YA dystopias have indisputably become just that, and have not yet been superseded.[2]

With its capacity to frighten and warn, dystopian writing engages with pressing global concerns: liberty and self-determination, environmental destruction and looming catastrophe, questions of identity, and the increasingly fragile boundaries between technology and the self. When directed at young readers, who are trying to understand the world and their place in it, these dystopian warnings are distilled into exciting adventures with gripping plots. Their narrative techniques often place us close to the action, with first-person narration, engaging dialogue, or even diary entries imparting accessible messages that may have the potential to motivate a generation on the cusp of adulthood.

2 • Balaka Basu, Katherine R. Broad, and Carrie Hintz

Chris Crowe and Roberta Seelinger Trites outline a tradition of gritty YA novels popular with younger readers, beginning with texts such as S.E. Hinton's *The Outsiders* (1967).[3] Due to its apparent darkness, contemporary dystopian fiction for young adults may be read as part of this tradition, but this recent explosion of texts cannot be explained away as simply the natural progression of the YA genre. Lois Lowry's *The Giver* (1993) was a popular dystopia for younger readers, but it wasn't until the 2000s that readers started to find a plethora of dystopias lining the bookshelves of the YA section, with titles like M.T. Anderson's *Feed* (2002), Julie Bertagna's *Exodus* (2002), Meg Rosoff's *How I Live Now* (2004), Scott Westerfeld's *Uglies* (2005), Cory Doctorow's *Little Brother* (2008), Lauren Oliver's *Delirium* (2011), and many more. That readers "can't seem to get enough of fiction that suggests the future may be worse than the present" raises the question of why it holds such appeal.[4] As adult commentators begin to wonder whether YA fiction is "too dark" for their children to read,[5] these same children are diving deeper into the dystopian well, finding a sense of pleasure in texts that display an increasingly gloomy vision of the world they are to inherit.

Scholars as well as popular critics have remarked upon the genre's presence in the wider field of children's and young adult literature—and its overwhelming attraction for young audiences—but are just beginning to talk about the aesthetic qualities and political valences of these texts. *Contemporary Dystopian Fiction for Young Adults: Brave New Teenagers* enters a lively debate about the goals and efficacy of YA dystopias, with three major areas of contention. First, how do these texts balance didacticism with pleasure? Second, do these texts espouse radical political change, or do their progressive exteriors mask an inner conservatism? And finally, do they offer their readers hope or despair? While YA books often unflinchingly engage with the problems of adolescents, they are nonetheless tied to the broader tradition of children's literature, which stresses hope. YA dystopias can uphold that tradition of optimism, embrace a more cynical vision, or oscillate between the two. All these questions underscore the negotiation between often conflicting literary influences, political ideologies, and intended audiences that these texts must undertake.

Forms of Dystopian Imagining

Dystopian fiction describes non-existent societies intended to be read as "considerably worse" than the reader's own.[6] Yet dystopia is a tensely vexed term. Orthographically speaking, it seems like it ought to be the reverse of a utopia, the non-existent society "considerably better" than the current world.[7] But instead, the dystopia often functions as a rhetorical *reductio ad absurdum* of a utopian philosophy, extending a utopia to its most extreme ends in order to caution against the destructive politics and culture of the author's present. It generally differs from the utopia in that its prescription is negative, rather

Introduction • 3

than positive: it tells us not how to build a better world, but how to perhaps avoid continuing to mess up the one we've got. Although more traditional dystopias such as George Orwell's *1984* (1949) were largely "an extrapolation from the present that involved a warning,"[8] more recent examples, especially for young people, are expressly concerned with how to use this warning to create new possibilities for utopian hope within the space of the text.[9] The dystopian worlds are bleak not because they are meant to stand as mere cautionary tales, but because they are designed to display—in sharp relief—the possibility of utopian change even in the darkest of circumstances.

Each YA dystopia has its own aesthetic and political orientation; however, we can trace thematic threads in the genre that reflect how the central fears and concerns of the contemporary world are grafted onto a dystopian landscape. One major preoccupation of the dystopian imagination is the threat of environmental destruction. Novels like Saci Lloyd's *The Carbon Diaries 2015* (2009), Julie Bertagna's *Exodus* (2002) and *Zenith* (2007), and Paolo Bacigalupi's *Ship Breaker* (2010) envision the world as it has been damaged by global warming and other scenarios of ecological destruction. Rising sea levels, storms, drought, and the end of fossil fuels create social, political, and economic nightmares that sensitize readers to the dangers of environmental ruin at the same time that they depict young protagonists learning to adapt and survive in altered times.

The postapocalyptic dystopia can be distinguished from the environmental dystopia by its emphasis on a variety of other huge world-changing events, such as plague, World War III, cataclysmic asteroid crashes, or even zombies. These contemporary novels are prefigured by texts dating from the Cold War, such as Robert C. O'Brien's *Z for Zachariah* (1973) and Jean Ure's *Plague 99* (1989). In the twenty-first century, the production of postapocalyptic fiction seems if anything to have accelerated. Nuclear holocaust in Philip Reeve's *Mortal Engines* (2001), war in Meg Rosoff's *How I Live Now* (2004), and the outbreak of an unexplained rash of zombies in Carrie Ryan's *The Forest of Hands and Teeth* (2009) all function to destroy civilization as it once stood, leaving small bands of survivors struggling to exist in a world forever changed. One result of the apocalyptic event is that it can turn existing communities into dystopias marked by secrecy, fear, and control, as those in power use violence and repression to maintain what little social structure remains.

Another major theme in YA dystopias is conformity, which is often exaggerated for dramatic effect. Lowry's *The Giver* (1993), for instance, presents a world of stifling "sameness" devoid of color, emotion, and memory, while her *Gathering Blue* (2000) depicts a society where artists are kept under strict social control. Often such conformist societies embrace their uniformity out of a fear that diversity breeds conflict. In Scott Westerfeld's Uglies series (2005–2007), Veronica Roth's *Divergent* (2011), and Ally Condie's *Matched* (2011), government authorities have initiated strict policies to

4 • Balaka Basu, Katherine R. Broad, and Carrie Hintz

manage personalities, choices, and appearances, ostensibly eliminating the discord said to threaten communal well being. As they depict the struggle between adolescent protagonists and oppressive governments, these novels attempt to tease out the appropriate balance between personal freedom and social harmony.

The YA dystopia's rigid and repressive regimes are often enforced through the enslavement and silencing of citizens, and several methods are used to achieve this. The escalating wars in Patrick Ness's Chaos Walking trilogy (2008–2010) are as much about physical enslavement as psychological control. *Little Brother*'s state-sponsored detentions and the implanted devices that audit and control people's thoughts in Elana Johnson's *Possession* (2011) demonstrate physical and mental imprisonment respectively, whereas Catherine Fisher's *Incarceron* (2007) and *Sapphique* (2008) feature both kinds of constraint. Other forms of enslavement—economic, affective, or technological—can be equally powerful. In Collins's *The Hunger Games*, the districts are kept in firm check by grinding poverty and near starvation, as well as by the ruthless show of power demonstrated when young tributes are forced to fight for the Capitol's amusement. Governments in *Uglies*, *Delirium*, and *Matched* rely on mind-altering surgeries and psychological tampering to maintain a predetermined and restricted life for each citizen. In each case, the protagonist's rebellion involves a bid for freedom from the enslaving forces of the dystopian regime, often representative of monolithic adult authority that has abrogated its responsibility to the young people it rules.

Additionally, YA dystopias are sensitive registers to the explosion of information that characterizes contemporary society, and to the atmosphere of conspiracy that pervades popular political discourse. Many novels feature an awakening, sudden or gradual, to the truth of what has really been going on. Jonas in *The Giver* learns that adults in his society can lie; Tally in *Uglies* discovers that the surgery that makes her friends pretty also damages their brains; Marcus in *Little Brother* uncovers the truth about his government's actions; and Titus in *Feed* comes to at least a transient awareness of the human costs of the profit motive. In books like *Delirium* and *Matched*, protagonists are often manipulated and lied to in order to keep society running smoothly, yet they eventually find out and rebel. Access to information is often dangerous, but is repeatedly presented as the only way to become free.

Whether they depict a postapocalyptic struggle for survival or a valiant attempt to retain individuality in a totalitarian world, YA dystopias are marked by their ambitious treatment of serious themes. Yet the far-fetched concepts they employ may create a buffer between reader and text, perhaps allowing them to be read ultimately as flights of fancy rather than projections of a possible future. However, their wildly fantastic premises may provide young people with an entry point into real-world problems,

Introduction • 5

encouraging them to think about social and political issues in new ways, or even for the first time.

Didacticism and Escape: The Complicated Allure of YA Dystopias

As YA dystopias engage with contemporary political and social questions, they revolve around two contrasting poles: education and escape. The novels simultaneously seek to teach serious lessons about the issues faced by humanity, and to offer readers a pleasurable retreat from their quotidian experience. Writing for young people tends to balance the desire to please and instruct, *dulce et utile*, and this tension is particularly marked in YA dystopias. With their prescriptive qualities and unveiled moral messages, YA dystopian writing can seem preachy and even old-fashioned. However edgy the covers of these novels may appear, with burned-out landscapes and hip warriors, the didacticism of their content is reminiscent of that of Victorian novels for children. One of the most beloved of these, Charles Kingsley's *The Water Babies* (1862–1863), combines what Louisa May Alcott described as "moral pap for the young" with fantastic or fairy tale settings and political commentary on pressing issues of the day, such as child labor: a mélange of ideas, methods, and agendas that would probably seem familiar to readers of YA dystopian fiction today.[10]

Perhaps one of the strongest sources of appeal for young adult dystopias, then, is the unequivocal clarity of their message. *The Hunger Games*, for instance, comments on a dominant culture wedded to violence and control and it makes that critique in an obvious way: by centering the plot of the trilogy on a giant reality TV arena. For Stephen King, "Reading *The Hunger Games* is as addictive (and as violently simple) as playing one of those shoot-it-if-it-moves videogames in the lobby of the local eightplex; you know it's not real, but you keep plugging in quarters anyway."[11] In a work like *Feed*, the targets are also abundantly clear: intellectual laziness, consumerism, and hedonistic youth culture. This blatant didacticism signals to readers the problems with society while offering something like a training manual on how to overcome the dilemma, reverse the damage, and start anew. The YA dystopia presumes that adolescents should be idealists, offering a gratifying view of adolescent readers as budding political activists—a portrayal that flatters adolescents and reassures adults that they are more than apathetic youth. However, the easily digestible prescriptions suggested by many of these novels may allow young readers to avoid probing the nuances, ambiguities, and complexities of social ills and concerns too deeply.

For all their overt didacticism, YA dystopias can also indulge a very different, and seemingly contradictory, impulse: escape from the strictures of social convention—surely an adolescent's dream. Scott Westerfeld reads

6 • Balaka Basu, Katherine R. Broad, and Carrie Hintz

YA dystopias and postapocalyptic fiction as a release from the overscheduled pressures of contemporary adolescent lives:

> The other side of the boom in dystopian teen novels is a boom in postapocalyptic tales. The system is asking a lot from teenagers and not giving them much respect in return, so it's no wonder that stories about that system exploding, breaking down under its own contradictions, or simply being overrun by zombies are also beloved of teenagers.
>
> What is the apocalypse but an everlasting snow day? An excuse to tear up all those college applications, which suddenly aren't going to determine the rest of your life?[12]

The dystopian snow day arguably demands a different kind of survival kit than the world many adolescents inhabit, and the result can be a gleeful sense of liberation. Furthermore, the dismantled structures of the dystopian world might possess a particular magnetism for readers who feel ostracized or otherwise alienated from current society. YA dystopias provide an island where misfit toys can shine, after traditional weights and measures of success have been discarded.

Both didacticism and escape have a role to play in the reception and impact of the YA dystopian genre. Although they may seem opposed, both elements have value on their own and in conjunction. Together they speak to the possibility that adolescents can at once fit themselves to better meet society's demands *and* shape society to better reflect their own desires and goals, creating the world they need, the world they want, and the world that they deserve.

YA Dystopias and Popular Forms

The YA dystopian genre belongs to the wider traditions of utopian/dystopian literature, science fiction, and children's literature. It also draws on a number of familiar, enduring, and popular plots and narrative forms, including the *Bildungsroman*, the adventure story, and the romance. Viewed cynically, the prominence of these recognizable elements and familiar plots may simply demonstrate the lucrative rewards of the dystopian label; placing a story of whatever genre in a dystopian setting seems to be a good way to raise sales. Yet there may be some aesthetic value to this mixture: if readers are already primed to respond to conventions they recognize from other works, they may find the new genre more resonant and accessible. At the same time, it's important to note that some readers, particularly new readers, may well be encountering these fundamental narrative structures for the first time within these texts, potentially breathing new life into older forms. As Laura Miller notes,

Introduction • 7

"An advantage to having young readers is that most of this stuff is fresh to them . . . To thrill them, a story doesn't have to be unprecedented. It just has to be harrowing."[13] But while the literary possibilities of this generic commingling seem evident, it's also possible that the political potentials of YA dystopias have been foreclosed by this association with more traditional narrative structures.

In emphasizing the trials of adolescents, YA dystopias recapitulate the conventions of the classic *Bildungsroman*, using political strife, environmental disaster, or other forms of turmoil as the catalyst for achieving adulthood. The novels detail how the conditions of the dystopian society force protagonists to fall from innocence and achieve maturity as they realize the dystopian realities in which they live. Raffaella Baccolini and Tom Moylan in their introduction to *Dark Horizons: Science Fiction and the Dystopian Imagination* (2003) remark on the ways in which "the dystopian citizen moves from apparent contentment into an experience of alienation and resistance."[14] Uncovering the failures of the dystopia often means leaving aside childhood and confronting the harsh truths of the adult world. As we discussed above, this awakening often includes a realization of how ruined the adult world has become: kids learn adults are lying, their parents have problems, the system can't protect them, they have to take care of themselves, and so on.

The confrontation with the realities of the adult world may lead to a standoff between adolescents and adults that empowers young people to turn against the system as it stands and change the world in ways adults cannot, locating the utopian potential of dystopian scenarios within YA protagonists themselves. The use of the *Bildungsroman* form, however, may also create ambivalence about the role of rebellion in facilitating growth. As young people stand up and fight the system, they also learn their own limitations. While the political awakening that YA dystopias associate with coming of age might inspire rebellion against a stultifying status quo, it also might teach their protagonists to strike a compromise between change and acceptance: to come to terms with an imperfect world. The ability of the protagonist to really envision something new might therefore be circumscribed by the conventions and forms of the *Bildungsroman* itself.

Another popular form on which the YA dystopia draws is the adventure genre, which found its apogee in the nineteenth and early twentieth centuries.[15] Contemporary YA dystopias could in fact be seen as a reinvention of the adventure tradition, tapping into the appeal that popular adventure stories had and continue to have for their readers. In *Adventure, Mystery, and Romance: Formula Stories as Art and Popular Culture* (1976), John G. Cawelti defines adventure as the story "of the hero—individual or group—overcoming obstacles and dangers and accomplishing some important and moral mission."[16] If, as Martin Burgess Green writes, "adventure is the name for

8 · Balaka Basu, Katherine R. Broad, and Carrie Hintz

experience beyond the law, or on the very frontier of civilization,"[17] the breakdown of society in YA dystopias creates the "frontier" setting as well as the conditions for adventure. This experience beyond the law typically allows for a degree of wish fulfillment. YA dystopias likewise allow readers to imagine, for instance, the danger and the thrill of standing up to a tyrannical government in *Little Brother*, surviving off the land in *The Hunger Games*, or charting new territory in *Exodus*. However, many protagonists of YA dystopias are overwhelmed by the exigencies and stresses of their adventures, and attempt to reinstate the law in reaction to them. Also, as the heroes undergo a series of trials, they often seek to restore a lost, comforting safety and security to their lives, turning from futurity to embrace a nostalgic past.

Meanwhile, as adolescent protagonists confront the dangers of the dystopian future, they often also find love, making the romance plot an important element of the YA dystopian genre. While many dystopian novels contain romance narratives, the connection seems especially pronounced in YA dystopias, which may capitalize on teenagers' preoccupations with courtship to compel their interest in the dystopian world. As one adolescent reviewer writes about Scott Westerfeld's *Extras* (2007), "I like this book because it's action packed, full of adventure . . . and, oh, she meets this guy, who wouldn't like that?"[18] But the romance plot often does more than simply provide appeal. In Patrick Ness's Chaos Walking trilogy, romantic feelings steer the adolescent lovers to stand up to dystopian forces in order to create a better world for each other. In a recent spate of YA dystopias focused on teenage girls and reproduction, such as *Matched* and Megan McCafferty's *Bumped* (2011), the fight for a better world is itself a fight for love, as dystopian forces keep teenagers from choosing their own mates. Romance, then, can play a key role in shaping the dystopian narrative and the possibilities for social change enacted in the novel.

The impact of the romance on the dystopian narrative varies. Romance may advance the political aims of the narrative when a new boyfriend or girlfriend encourages the protagonist to develop a new perspective or embark on a new experience. But romance is historically a conservative genre and just as often serves to affirm traditional norms, advancing the primacy of heterosexual couples while associating such relationships with growing up and finding a place in the world. Very few YA dystopias include queer relationships as a central focus, suggesting a reluctance to subvert dominant mores. As Paulo Bacigalupi has noted, "There's a strange dearth of GLBTQ characters simply living their lives, defying Big Brother or fighting off the zombie apocalypse."[19] Moreover, YA dystopias that end in romantic fulfillment tend to include a retreat from society into an insular relationship, turning away from the social and political involvement that motivated the narrative in the first place. Regardless of the ways in which the dystopian narrative imports romantic conventions, however, it is hard to imagine a YA dystopian novel without the particular insecurities and excitement of budding love.

Introduction • 9

To contend with the intersections between traditional literary forms and the more recent YA dystopias, then, it is necessary to ask whether this genre as a whole charts new territory, remains rooted in old conventional forms, or reflects a combination of both past and future. The tension between allegiances to the past and the future can be further illuminated by looking at the YA dystopia's positioning within the larger tradition of science fiction. YA dystopias, though largely set in science fictional futures, often look backward for both their pleasures and their answers. The Hunger Games series, for instance, uses the classical themes of tributes and gladiatorial combat to great effect, calling to mind Theseus and the Labyrinth, as well as the ancient Roman arena. In *Archaeologies of the Future: The Desire Called Utopia and Other Science Fictions* (2007), Fredric Jameson suggests that science fiction, with its "continuing technological bias" and its "built environment," is at its core a genre of futurity, unlike fantasy, which he believes to be almost always the product of an "imaginary regression to the past" and to nature.[20] But the distinction is not so clear in YA dystopias. For example, Westerfeld's sophisticated science fiction novel *Uglies* argues to some degree for a return to an organic, pretechnological state, where protagonists need to resist interference with their bodies and accept their natural appearances. An examination of these novels indicates, then, that by juxtaposing the YA dystopia with older forms, authors are able to imagine the future as an invocation of the past.

Brave New Teenagers: Questions and Debates

The aim of *Contemporary Dystopian Fiction for Young Adults: Brave New Teenagers* is to enable a prismatic understanding of the genre as a political, cultural, and aesthetic phenomenon. The first section of the collection, "Freedom and Constraint: Adolescent Liberty and Self-Determination," considers how the generic conventions of YA, dystopian, and utopian literature impact the construction of the adolescent self in relation to the social collective. For Balaka Basu, the tensions between utopia and dystopia reinforce contradictory messages about identity formation: the adolescent protagonist aspires to break the strictures of dystopia, but she also longs to fit in. Basu's "What Faction Are You In? The Pleasure of Being Sorted in Veronica Roth's *Divergent*" addresses how the impulse to categorize identities into definitive groups reflects *both* a utopian and a dystopian desire, and how such inflexible structures can limit independence and undermine social and political critique. Basu reads in the novel "a reluctance to commit fully to the necessary upheaval," but Emily Lauer argues, in contrast, that there may be radical potential in an adolescent's inability to transcend dystopian classifications. In "Coming of Age in Dystopia: Reading Genre in Holly Black's Curse Workers Series," Lauer describes a dystopian world that "is not destined to be overthrown, but rather negotiated." Characters find a place for their diverse

10 · Balaka Basu, Katherine R. Broad, and Carrie Hintz

abilities within an oppressive regime, suggesting an alternate model for how to grow up amidst constrained choices.

Carissa Turner Smith mediates between these two views by addressing the limitations of prescribed social roles—as Basu does—while advocating "an acceptance of messy, imperfect, embodied communal life" that resonates with Lauer's approach. In "Embodying the Postmetropolis in Catherine Fisher's *Incarceron* and *Sapphique*," Smith reminds us of the body's role in shaping possibilities for liberty within and against conformist dystopian worlds. Reading Edward Soja's postmetropolis as "a theoretical framework for understanding the spatiality of YA dystopias and . . . the development of the individual in a regimented society," Smith breaks down the binaries between utopia and dystopia and shows how these spaces are inhabited in two coextensive carceral worlds. By addressing the myriad factors that contribute to the adolescent's capacity for self-determination, together these essays suggest ways that the complex and hybrid nature of the YA dystopian genre shapes the construction of the self by reinforcing social, cultural, political, and personal limitations—while sometimes positing liberating possibilities in unexpected ways.

Our second section, "Society and Environment: Building a Better World," offers three readings of critical eco-dystopias or postapocalyptic texts. Alexa Weik von Mossner's "Hope in Dark Times: Climate Change and the World Risk Society in Saci Lloyd's *The Carbon Diaries 2015* and *2017*" considers Lloyd's near-future eco-critical dystopias in the light of Ulrich Beck's idea of the "world risk society," where catastrophic events and crises reach beyond national and geographical boundaries. When Lloyd's adolescent protagonist Laura Brown faces the abrupt end of her "normal" lifestyle due to Britain's strict rationing of carbon emissions and by the harsh weather caused by global warming, she channels her anger and frustration into political activism: "She begins to understand that life in the world risk society can only get better if she and others around the world take the challenges seriously without falling into despair." Examining further the impulse toward political engagement, Claire P. Curtis's "Educating Desire, Choosing Justice? Susan Beth Pfeffer's Last Survivors Series and Julie Bertagna's *Exodus*" considers two contrasting postapocalyptic novels for young adults, both of which contemplate life after a disaster. The first and third books of Pfeffer's series focus on the survival of protagonist Miranda and her family when a cataclysmic asteroid strike shifts the moon's orbit closer to earth, resulting in earthquakes, tsunamis, volcanic eruptions, and drastic climate change. Miranda and some members of her family ultimately find refuge in one of the "safe towns" available only to the rich and well-connected, which Curtis argues is part of the novel's presentation of "a narrow world of stingy pseudo-safety." In Bertagna's *Exodus*, global sea rise threatens the home of the protagonist Mara: the isolated island of Wing. Mara initiates a journey to the dazzling sky city of New Mungo. Finding only a privileged society blinded by the virtual pleasures of the cyberworld, she decides to lead a diverse group of people to a new settlement in

Greenland. As Curtis notes, Bertagna's portrayal of "an expansive, often frightening world of possibilities and uncertainty" offers a genuinely utopian portrayal of a young protagonist who "will always strive to move forward toward something better" by recognizing and combatting injustice and thinking beyond the welfare of her own family. Elaine Ostry's essay, "On the Brink: The Role of Young Adult Culture in Environmental Degradation," also engages with the political and personal development of adolescents, examining how novels by Anderson, Bertagna, and Westerfeld promote environmental awareness. Technological utopias echo youth culture's "love for technology, consumption, and distraction" while the ecological utopia promotes a more salutary maturity "with its emphasis on self-reliance, self-restraint, hard work, decision-making, and community." At the same time, the books acknowledge that nature often needs technology to survive, an acknowledgement that encourages young readers to think about environmental problems in more complex ways. Ostry ends with a meditation on the ambivalent endings of the books, "where the future of their worlds remains uncertain." While these endings may offer despair, they can also "honor the ability of readers to realize that there are no easy answers to the problems we face, particularly those of the environment."

Rebellion against the status quo is a common feature of YA dystopian fiction, especially if such rebellion promises to redeem the world from postapocalyptic collapse. But the essays in our third section, "Radical or Conservative? Polemics of the Future," suggest the genre has a more complex relationship with social critique and activism. In "'The Dandelion in the Spring': Utopia as Romance in Suzanne Collins's The Hunger Games Trilogy," Katherine R. Broad examines the courtship narrative that comprises such a popular part of Collins's series. Although its heroine, Katniss, is perceived by many readers to be a groundbreaking "feminist icon," the narrative is limited in the ways it disrupts patriarchal gender roles. Broad reads the conclusion of the series—which ends with a vision of Katniss's "safe, stable, and highly insular heterosexual reproductive union"—as the foreclosure of alternative possibilities for female futures. Considering the depiction of racial identity, Mary J. Couzelis's "The Future Is Pale: Race in Contemporary Young Adult Dystopian Novels" illuminates how insidiously whiteness may become the default state even in the utopian imaginings of novels such as Lois Lowry's The Giver, Scott Westerfeld's Uglies, and Collins's The Hunger Games, perpetuating—however unconsciously—racial hierarchies and an "often unacknowledged white privilege ideology." Addressing the construction of race and gender in the future society, Broad and Couzelis both suggest that issues related to personal identity, normativity, and the perpetuation of traditional hierarchies may keep some novels from fulfilling the radical aims of dystopian rebellion.

In contrast, Kristi McDuffie's "Technology and Models of Literacy in Young Adult Dystopian Fiction" takes a more hopeful view of the progressive possibilities offered by the YA dystopian form. McDuffie begins by showing how novels such as M.T. Anderson's *Feed*, Ally Condie's *Matched*, and West-erfeld's *Uglies* demonstrate adult fears of literacy loss among adolescents by privileging old-fashioned methods of reading and writing. Pitting these nostalgic forms against technologies that apparently corrupt and have themselves been corrupted, these novels choose to valorize the traditional. "Overall," McDuffie writes, "technology functions as a mechanism of control" in texts such as these, "while print literacy, including canonical literature and writing, is a mechanism for knowledge and rebellion." She concludes, however, with an examination of Cory Doctorow's *Little Brother*, a novel that wholly embraces the potential for alternative and digital multiliteracies to fuel rather than inhibit radical new forms of resistance.

Dystopian fiction frequently imagines the consequences of new developments in science and technology, often evincing a profound unease over how biotechnology destabilizes conceptions of humanity and the boundaries of the human body. The final section of this collection, "Biotechnologies of the Self: Humanity in a Posthuman Age," explores the impact of biotechnology on adolescents. Susan Louise Stewart's "Dystopian Sacrifice, Scapegoats, and Neal Shusterman's *Unwind*" illustrates how biotechnology victimizes children and threatens to undermine human life altogether. Stewart reads the enforced organ donation in *Unwind* as a reframing of Mosaic Law's "burnt offerings" in a contemporary holocaust narrative in which "children become sacrifices and scapegoats and are eventually cannibalized through their whole body 'donations.'" Erin T. Newcomb suggests, however, that attention to the theological can help mediate such anxieties over the effects of biotechnology. In "The Soul of the Clone: Coming of Age as a Posthuman in Nancy Farmer's *The House of the Scorpion*," Newcomb describes the transition from child to adult as one characterized by the soul, not just the body. According to Newcomb, "The only cure for the inhumanity of the posthuman condition, Farmer's text suggests, is to balance biotechnology with a philosophy that asserts the *de facto* value of all life."

It is this reimagining of human life that Thomas J. Morrissey takes up in "Parables for the Postmodern, Post-9/11, and Posthuman World: Carrie Ryan's Forest of Hands and Teeth Books, M.T. Anderson's *Feed*, and Mary E. Pearson's *The Adoration of Jenna Fox*." Whereas Newcomb and Stewart address ways in which biotechnology threatens to appropriate children's bodies in future worlds dominated by highly dubious political and social structures, Morrissey counters that biotechnology also offers productive ways of imagining how humanity can thrive in a posthuman world. "The question of whether and how humans will survive and prosper in centuries to come is inextricably tied to the question of who or even *what* we will become," Morrissey writes. Exploring how biotechnology leads to new views of ourselves as a species, he suggests that technological innovations may offer hope for the future, even as they raise political, spiritual, and ethical questions about the meaning of human life in a new age.

Introduction • 13

YA dystopias are a vivid snapshot of contemporary cultural anxieties: what individuals and even the human species as a whole might have to fear in the future. As we edited this collection, we were struck by how so many of our contributors returned to questions of hope and despair and reflected on the issue of whether young people, with enough encouragement and inspiration, can in fact create a better world. Ultimately, our contributors are divided about whether they see the YA dystopian genre as inspiring change, or whether they feel that the genre has fallen short of its potential. This is a critical debate that is just beginning. In their fascinating mix of genres and sometimes contradictory appeals, these novels are hard to pin down, but so rewarding to read and to analyze critically. We offer this collection as an early exploration of some of the central issues raised by this resurgent genre, and we look forward to the evolving conversation.

Notes

1   John Green, "Scary New World," *The New York Times,* November 7, 2008, http://www.nytimes.com/2008/11/09/books/review/Green-t.html.
2   See Diane Roback and John A. Sellers, "Bologna 2012: Trends of the Show," *Publishers Weekly,* March 29, 2012, http://www.publishersweekly.com/pw/ by-topic/childrens/childrens-industry-news/article/51290-bologna-2012-trends-of-the-show.html. Roback and Sellers remark that although it may be "overall . . . getting harder to sell new dystopian projects," this seems to be because there are already "so many out or in the pipeline." Indeed, at the time of writing, The Hunger Games series remained the top selling children's series, while dystopian novels (*Divergent* [2011] and *Insurgent* [2012]), accounted for two slots in the top five bestselling children's books of the week.
3   See Chris Crowe, "Young Adult Literature: What Is Young Adult Literature?" *The English Journal* 88.1 (1998): 120–122 and Roberta Seelinger Trites, "Theories and Possibilities of Adolescent Literature," *Children's Literature Association Quarterly* 21.1 (1996): 2–3.
4   "Scholastic Experts Issue List of 'Ten Trends in Children's Books from 2010,'" *Scholastic,* December 8, 2010, http://mediaroom.scholastic.com/node/404.
5   See, for instance, Meghan Cox Gurdon, "Darkness Too Visible," *The Wall Street Journal,* June 4, 2011, http://online.wsj.com/article/ SB10001424052702303365740457 6357622592697038.html.
6   Lyman Tower Sargent, "The Three Faces of Utopianism Revisited," *Utopian Studies* 5.1 (1994): 9.
7   Ibid.
8   Ibid., 8.
9   See Raffaella Baccolini, "The Persistence of Hope in Dystopian Science Fiction," *PMLA* 119.3 (2004): 520.

14 · Balaka Basu, Katherine R. Broad, and Carrie Hintz

10 Louisa May Alcott, *The Journals of Louisa May Alcott*, ed. Joel Myerson, Daniel Shealy, and Madeleine B. Stern (Boston: Little, Brown, 1989), 204.

11 Stephen King, "The Hunger Games," *Entertainment Weekly*, September 12, 2008, http://www.ew.com/ew/article/0,,20419951_20223443,00.html.

12 Scott Westerfeld, "The Dark Side of Young Adult Fiction: Breaking Down the 'System,'" *The New York Times*, December 27, 2010, http://www.nytimes.com/roomfordebate/2010/12/26/the-dark-side-of-young-adult-fiction/breaking-down-the-system.

13 Laura Miller, "Fresh Hell: What's Behind the Boom in Dystopian Fiction for Young Adults?" *The New Yorker*, June 14, 2010, http://www.newyorker.com/arts/critics/atlarge/2010/06/14/100614crat_atlarge_miller.

14 Raffaella Baccolini and Tom Moylan, "Introduction: Utopia and Histories," in *Dark Horizons: Science Fiction and the Dystopian Imagination*, ed. Raffaella Baccolini and Tom Moylan (New York: Routledge, 2003), 5.

15 After the success that Defoe, Scott, and Cooper had with young audiences, adventure novels such as *The Swiss Family Robinson* (1812) began to be written specifically for children in the nineteenth century. The genre continued to develop exponentially through the Victorian era and the twentieth century; representative texts include: *Children of the New Forest* (1847), *Treasure Island* (1883), *We Didn't Mean to Go to Sea* (1937), and *Johnny Tremain* (1947). See *Children's Literature: An Illustrated History*, ed. Peter Hunt et al. (Oxford: Oxford University Press, 1995), 98–100; 149–50.

16 John G. Cawelti, *Adventure, Mystery, and Romance: Formula Stories as Art and Popular Culture* (Chicago: University of Chicago Press, 1976), 39.

17 Martin Burgess Green, *Seven Types of Adventure Tale: An Etiology of a Major Genre* (University Park: The Penn State University Press, 1991), 3.

18 Samantha Correa, "Just My Opinion!: On *Extras*, by Scott Westerfeld," in *Books for the Teen Age*, ed. The Office of Young Adult Services (New York: The New York Public Library, 2008), 14.

19 Paulo Bacigalupi, "Straight-Laced Dystopias," *Kirkus Reviews*, April 4, 2012, http://www.kirkusreviews.com/blog/young-adult/straight-laced-dystopias/.

20 Fredric Jameson, *Archeologies of the Future: The Desire Called Utopia and Other Science Fictions* (New York: Verso, 2007), 64.

Works Cited

Alcott, Louisa May. *The Journals of Louisa May Alcott*, edited by Joel Myerson, Daniel Shealy, and Madeleine B. Stern. Boston: Little, Brown, 1989.

Baccolini, Raffaella. "The Persistence of Hope in Dystopian Science Fiction." *PMLA* 119.3 (2004): 518–521.

———— and Tom Moylan. "Introduction: Utopia and Histories." In *Dark Horizons: Science Fiction and the Dystopian Imagination*, edited by Raffaella Baccolini and Tom Moylan, 1–12. New York: Routledge, 2003.

Bacigalupi, Paulo. "Straight-Laced Dystopias," *Kirkus Reviews*, April 4, 2012. http://www.kirkusreviews.com/blog/young-adult/straight-laced-dystopias/.

Correa, Samantha. "Just My Opinion!: On Extras, by Scott Westerfeld." In *Books for the Teen Age*, edited by the Office of Young Adult Services. New York: The New York Public Library, 2008.

Crowe, Chris. "Young Adult Literature: What Is Young Adult Literature?" *The English Journal* 88.1 (1998): 120–122.

Cawelti, John G. *Adventure, Mystery, and Romance: Formula Stories as Art and Popular Culture.* Chicago: University of Chicago Press, 1976.

Green, John. "Scary New World." *The New York Times*, November 7, 2008. http://www.nytimes.com/2008/11/09/books/review/Green-t.html.

Green, Martin Burgess. *Seven Types of Adventure Tale: An Etiology of a Major Genre.* University Park: The Penn State University Press, 1991.

Gurdon, Meghan Cox. "Darkness Too Visible." *The Wall Street Journal*, June 4, 2011. http://online.wsj.com/article/SB10001424052702303657404576357622592697038.html.

Hunt, Peter, ed. *Children's Literature: An Illustrated History.* Oxford: Oxford University Press, 1995.

Jameson, Fredric. *Archaeologies of the Future: The Desire Called Utopia and Other Science Fictions.* New York: Verso, 2005.

King, Stephen. "The Hunger Games." *Entertainment Weekly*, September 12, 2008. http://www.ew.com/ew/article/0,,20419951_20223443,00.html.

Miller, Laura. "Fresh Hell: What's Behind the Boom in Dystopian Fiction for Young Adults?" *The New Yorker*, June 14, 2010. http://www.newyorker.com/arts/critics/atlarge/2010/06/14/100614crat_atlarge_miller.

Roback, Diane and John A. Sellers, "Bologna 2012: Trends of the Show." *Publishers Weekly*, March 29, 2012. http://www.publishersweekly.com/pw/by-topic/childrens/childrens-industry-news/article/51290-bologna-2012-trends-of-the-show.html.

Sargent, Lyman Tower. "The Three Faces of Utopianism Revisited." *Utopian Studies* 5.1 (1994): 1–37.

"Scholastic Experts Issue List of 'Ten Trends in Children's Books from 2010.'" *Scholastic*, December 8, 2010. http://mediaroom.scholastic.com/node/404.

Trites, Roberta Seelinger. "Theories and Possibilities of Adolescent Literature." *Children's Literature Association Quarterly* 21.1 (1996): 2–3.

Westerfeld, Scott. "The Dark Side of Young Adult Fiction." *The New York Times*, December 27, 2010. http://www.nytimes.com/roomfordebate/2010/12/26/the-dark-side-of-young-adult-fiction/breaking-down-the-system.

Part One

Freedom and Constraint

Adolescent Liberty and Self-Determination

Chapter One
What Faction Are You in?
The Pleasure of Being Sorted in Veronica Roth's *Divergent*

Balaka Basu

Whatever else they may do, all heroes of young adult fiction—and by extension, their readers—are eventually asked to consider the two great questions of adolescence: "Who am I now? And who do I want to be when I grow up?" As they do so, they inevitably embark upon a quest for identity, an apparently innocuous pursuit that lies at the very core of the genre. Consistently featured in these novels, this search for a tangible identity seems so natural that it has almost entirely escaped interrogation. It is perhaps all the more unsettling to realize, then, that at the end of their quests, the heroes of YA narratives tend to find not an individual identity but a collective one, defined mainly by membership in a particular group. Forming an adult identity is not understood by these novels as forging a unique, never-before-seen, and thus ultimately unclassifiable self, but instead as fitting in with an already extant *type* of self. Perhaps nowhere is this better encapsulated than in Veronica Roth's *Divergent* (2011), a recent and immensely popular "high concept" entry into the YA dystopian arena that seeks to critique this troubling understanding of identity but succeeds only in perpetuating and celebrating it.

A high concept narrative has a premise that is both "striking" and "easily reducible" to a single sentence, which too succinctly represents the experience conveyed by the entire text.[1] When this term is applied to a YA dystopia, the result is generally a narrative that centers around a totalitarian regime dedicated solely to the enforcement of this one-sentence premise and a spunky adolescent hero/heroine's resistance against said regime. *Divergent*'s high concept—what if society divided itself into rigid groups, each dedicated to

20 · Balaka Basu

the cultivation of a single virtue, whose adherents are identified through a personality test?—overtly equates forging a personal identity for oneself with fitting into a pre-existing identity type, a slippage previously gestured towards by many of the novel's predecessors in YA fiction. While a dystopian novel might be expected to caution against the dangers of such a slippage, *Divergent*'s narrative and rhetoric instead subtly endorse it.

Roth's novel appears to be positioned as a warning against the seductive pleasures of being categorized and classified: the truly admirable people in the story are "Divergent" and possess multiple virtues, making it difficult (though not impossible) to group them successfully. Beneath this surface message, however, the novel tacitly promotes the ideals of classification that have shaped its society, suggesting that its dystopia is the result of correctable corruption, not the product of a fundamentally misconceived idea. To be categorized is comforting and so, with a past nostalgically alluded to in her narrative, Roth suggests that a society explicitly organized by such categorization was at one point successful and possibly could be again. *Divergent*'s attraction lies in its ability to define its protagonists, offering readers the hope of being similarly defined—the enchanting possibility of a world where their own interior minds can be "read" and essentialized, and in which their identities may no longer be so alarmingly fluid.

Reading Identity through Labels in YA Literature

High concept narratives like *Divergent* are often a "replication and combination of previously successful narratives"[2] or, in other words, a collage of pre-existing texts; thus, in order to fully understand *Divergent*'s perspective on identity, it will be helpful to examine the textual strands it incorporates and combines to construct its own narrative. These strands, I have suggested, are culled from a long tradition within YA literature, a tradition that begins with the need to make character and identity instantly decipherable and then goes on to conflate the resulting group label with personal identity itself.

Maude Hines remarks that the need to associate character with immediately and clearly comprehensible emblems

> recalls earlier European and American responses to anxieties about "true" character that proliferated in the late nineteenth and early twentieth centuries. These anxieties, produced in the wake of growing industrialization and urbanization, were reflected in fears of confidence men in the city, the merit badges of the Boy Scouts, and pseudosciences like phrenology and physiognomy.[3]

She notes how as early as in *The Master Key: A Fable of Electricity* (1901), L. Frank Baum invents the device of the "character marker," spectacles that reveal the character of the person observed through the placement of a letter on the forehead: G for good, E for evil, W for wise, F for foolish, K for kind, C for cruel. Yet in Baum's novella, the main character, Rob, resists this knowledge: he is uncomfortable with the idea of using the character marker on his friends and family and eventually becomes hesitant about the ethical valence of using it on other people, deciding that anyone "who would take advantage of such a sneaking invention as that would be worse than a thief!"[4] While the reasons for his discomfort are not fully explored in the novella and seem to relate to the unfair advantage over others that the spectacles bestow, it is evident that character, distilled into simple and visible signs of group membership, is likely to transform into the symbol of that membership itself rather than reflecting the complex interplay of traits that make up authentic personality. Identity under this rubric therefore begins to equal membership in the group, distinguished by a single marker of difference continually and disproportionately stressed.

Novels whose central focus is not on issues of identity, such as Philip Pullman's *His Dark Materials* (1995–2000), are nevertheless popular in large part because of the readability of identity that they offer. As with Baum's novella, one of the most memorable aspects of Pullman's series is the method through which his characters' souls are made immediately legible. In lieu of a letter on the forehead, in Pullman's parallel universe human characters possess a daemon: an autonomous manifestation of the person's spirit in animal form that makes their personality immediately visible "to others as well as themselves."[5] While the daemons of children are constantly in flux, changing form from one moment to the next, adulthood in Pullman's world is marked by the daemon's "settling" into a single, unchanging form, stilling the mercurial identity of a child into a defined and static shape.

The villains of *His Dark Materials* claim to oppose the daemons' settling, and so it seems as if Pullman wants his audience to support it; indeed, Pullman's young heroine, Lyra, as well as her readers, seem to look forward to the fixing of identity with a fervent anxiety that generates a great deal of excitement and driving curiosity, perhaps because the child's desire to know the ultimate form of their daemon is paired by Pullman with the development of sexual desire. In fact, the antagonists' wish to prevent the daemons' settling is merely a byproduct of their efforts to curb this burgeoning sexuality and the growth of experience, efforts which are seen by the narrative universe to be in error. However, one wonders why exactly Pullman sees the rigid fixing of identity as a central part of growing up and sexual maturity in the first place: why do the daemons need to settle so finally? While adolescents might hope that puberty is the last moment of change and instability in a person's life, it seems somewhat invidious to claim that this is so.

Regardless, Pullman's narrative presents the fixing of the daemon's form into a specific animal as an essential aspect of entering adulthood. This fixing need not necessarily imply the complete erasure of individuality: after all, the

22 • Balaka Basu

animal world is probably diverse enough to offer each character its own "type" of soul. However, daemons explicitly function as markers of group identity as well. While Lyra, as the main protagonist, is delineated finely and precisely, as is her daemon, Pantalaimon, Pullman's minor characters fare less well: many of their daemons operate not just as a marker of personality, but also of position within society. For instance, the daemons of all witches are birds, while those of all servants are dogs. While a goose or beagle daemon may be a marker of individual personality, the encompassing classification of "bird" or "dog" is what utterly determines the person's role in life, thus subsuming his or her personal identity to their group membership. As Hines points out:

> The form of the daemon is also an important key to character and even to class position . . . The natural place of servants (among themselves and as servants) is obvious, observable, through the dog shape of their daemons. Servant is not merely a profession, but ontology: the figure of the daemon naturalizes the rigidity of the class system in Lyra's world. While not all people with dog daemons are necessarily servants, the fact that all servants have dog daemons belies the infinite possibility the daemon represents before puberty.[6]

This "infinite possibility" creates an unstable identity that cannot be categorized, due to its multiplicity. Growing up in Pullman's world, then, means the stabilization of this identity into a single entity that will fit into a rigid system of classification.

In a recent study, Melanie D. Koss and William H. Teale performed a content analysis of current trends in the YA genre, and discovered that although

> YA novels have the reputation of being hard and edgy, filled with harsh social issues such as sex, violence, drugs, and the like . . . the most frequent subjects were not so much the hard and gritty, but rather, again, related to the idea of fitting in. . . . Overall trends in subject matter included a shift away from coming-of-age stories to a focus on books with themes of fitting in, finding oneself, and dealing with major life changes.[7]

Their work further underscores the popularity of Pullman's suggestion that growing up is congruent with fitting in. Put another way, understanding oneself means discovering how to describe one's identity within the context of pre-existing categories.

A consideration of the elements which coalesce to form *Divergent*'s perspective on identity would not be complete without a discussion of Harry Potter. In fact, one could easily describe *Divergent* as what happens when Harry Potter meets *The Hunger Games* (2008): an adventure-*cum*-romance set in a dystopian society based around the wizarding world's Sorting Hat. In J.K. Rowling's world, all the students of witchcraft and wizardry at Hogwarts are divided by this magical Sorting Hat into four distinct groups—Gryffindor (the brave), Slytherin (the ambitious), Ravenclaw (the smart), or Hufflepuff (the loyal)—based on their current personality at the age of eleven as well as what they consider to be important in life. This system is clearly, whether consciously or unconsciously, the source for Roth's factions. Though problematized in Rowling's text, the House system is never completely overthrown: when a character's complexity is discovered to be inadequately represented by his House allegiance, the novel's readers are told "sometimes . . . we Sort too soon,"[8] not that in the final analysis, perhaps people can't or shouldn't be so easily sorted. It may be this very rigidity that audiences find so attractive and comforting; in any event, much like Pullman's daemons, the conceit of Hogwarts's four Houses endures as one of the most popular and compelling aspects of Rowling's fantasy world.

Indeed, legions of devoted readers continue to ask themselves what kind of animal their daemon would be and which House they ought to be in. As they do so, they encounter a plethora of fan sites that provide the option to take an online quiz to "get sorted" and find out who they are and where they belong. In her essay "Safe as Houses: Sorting and School Houses at Hogwarts" (2003), Chantel Lavoie catalogs a number of such sites, which she sees as reflecting competing interpretations of Rowling's text.[9] Regardless of their interpretations, however, the proliferation of these quizzes reveals adolescents' enormous interest in being sorted—especially by an external force that can make one's inner mind legible. Considering the number of online personality quizzes that have been based on fictional systems of identity categorization, it was probably only a matter of time until *Divergent* appeared: a book whose entire narrative is based around a personality quiz, a book which has of course in turn *also* produced its own "real world" online quiz.

Categorizing Divergence

Divergent takes place in a dystopian future Chicago that ironically believes it is still a utopia; its society has divided itself into factions, each of which is dedicated to the cultivation of the single virtue felt by its members to be the fundamental element in the eradication of war and other societal evils. Each faction is responsible for a specific function: the government is run by Abnegation (the selfless); the law by Candor (the honest); education and invention by Erudite (the intelligent); caretaking and social services by Amity (the kind); and defense and security by Dauntless (the brave). Children are raised in their parents' factions until the age of sixteen, at which point they undergo an aptitude test that determines which faction they are suitable for. It is during this testing process that Roth's heroine, Beatrice Prior, discovers that her question does not have the easy answer she is looking for; instead of having a definite result as most people in her world do, her test reveals that she is "Divergent,"

24 · Balaka Basu

possessing traits and aptitudes that belong to multiple factions. By making her heroine Divergent, Roth appears to want to indicate that such classification into categories is itself problematic, but this thesis is subtly undercut throughout the narrative, as well as flatly contradicted by its marketing, both of which continue to offer the promise of categorization to the novel's readers, a promise that they render eminently desirable.[10]

In the novel, the aptitude test is administered through a controlled hallucination produced by the injection of a mind-altering serum. Within the subsequent reality simulation, the subject is faced with a series of choices between two oppositional items or actions. In the first of these, Beatrice is given a choice between a basket containing a piece of cheese or a long knife that could presumably be used as a weapon; later in the test, she must decide whether to intervene when a vicious dog is about to attack a small girl and whether to tell a lie to save herself or someone else from "something awful."[11] When offered the initial choice between the knife and the cheese, she refuses to be dictated to by the test's parameters, stubbornly forcing the simulation to progress to the next scenario without successfully obtaining the data that would be provided by her selection. Even in successive scenarios, where she actually *does* take decisions—choosing to protect the little girl from the dog, but not to tell the truth even to save a life—Beatrice's responses display a variety of character traits instead of just one. Thus after the simulation ends she is told that although "normally, the simulation progresses in a linear fashion, isolating one faction while ruling out the rest," *her* results are "inconclusive" and indicate that she apparently has "equal aptitude" for Abnegation, the faction in which she has been raised; Erudite, the faction which houses the apparent villains of the piece; and Dauntless, the faction which she ultimately chooses (21).

Beatrice is warned that Divergence is an "extremely dangerous" condition and that telling anyone about it may result in her death (23). However, the threats to her safety concern her less than the uncertainty about her identity, which she expected the aptitude test to end. She is disappointed because she doesn't want to choose a faction herself; instead, she wants the choice to have been made clearly for her by the aptitude test, so she can finally know who she is and where she belongs. Divergence is not an identity that she is willing to accept, because it does not satisfy this desire. While she is loath to assign herself a faction, she eventually does so because she cannot bear the thought of being without one, saying, "To live factionless is not just to live in poverty and discomfort; it is to live divorced from society, separated from the most important thing in life: community" (20). It is evident that group membership—successfully fitting into a community—is the most desirable thing in the world to Beatrice, and her Divergence also worries her because she is afraid it will make her incompatible with the faction of her choice. Since she thinks that expulsion from the faction system is a fate worse than death, after she joins the Dauntless, she completely predicates her identity on the

What Faction Are You in? • 25

group membership she so desperately craves, even changing her name from "Beatrice" to "Tris" to better fit in with her new faction and signal that she has left her previous persona behind.

While at first it seems that Divergence is an unconstructed and permeable identity that resists classification, as the novel progresses it begins to contradict this idea. For instance, Roth clearly draws a correlation between free-thinking and Divergence. During the aptitude test, it is hinted that it is Tris's Divergence which allows her to resist the mind-altering drug's control, empowering her *not* to choose either the knife or the cheese. This hint is later made fully explicit when Tris is undergoing the next round of trials that will ensure her acceptance into the ranks of the Dauntless. This process, called Initiation in the novel, involves not just the testing of physical courage and prowess—as measured by initiates' performance in a series of duels, obstacle courses, and war games—but also more drug-induced simulated reality sessions that supposedly test emotional and mental courage by pitting Dauntless initiates against their worst fears. Tris and her Dauntless trainer/romantic interest Four—who is of course also Divergent—particularly excel at the tests involving the serum. When Tris investigates her unusual ability to withstand the serum's compulsion, she is told that her resistance to it is directly related to her Divergence; in other words that someone who is Divergent is "someone who is aware, when they are in a simulation, that what they are experiencing is not real . . . Someone who can then manipulate the situation or shut it down" (257). Divergence can be read, then, as the ability to overcome externally imposed control through the exercise of free will.

When Tris realizes that she "must be awake because [she is] Divergent" (419), she is referring to her ability to elude the serum's control, but the rhetorical construction of the sentence implies that non-Divergent people are, in some sense, oblivious to what is going on around them. This idea is amplified a few pages later when Tris's mother (naturally also secretly Divergent) presents the novel's ostensible message in her description of the condition, saying,

> Every faction conditions its members to think and act a certain way. And most people do it. . . . But our minds move in a dozen different directions. We can't be confined to one way of thinking, and that terrifies our leaders. It means we can't be controlled (441–442).

Belonging to a single faction is clearly connected here with qualities that Roth seems to find contemptible: susceptibility to conditioning, brainwashing, and passivity. As the reverse, Divergence is the literal embodiment of resistance to the dystopia of totalitarian classification she has built.

It's interesting to note, however, that Roth construes this resistance as a single virtue—much like the ones that define her factions. If the Dauntless are the brave, it appears that the Divergent are the independent, who cannot

26 · Balaka Basu

be told what to do or controlled by authority. They may even be successfully discovered by the aptitude test, if not entirely in the way that the makers of the test had in mind, making it very difficult to read Divergence as anything other than just another category in the system.

While the novel clearly maintains that Divergence is optimal, by choosing a single faction to spawn most of the Divergent, Roth further supports the ideal of categorization, since the system doesn't even need to be refined in order to accurately evaluate and categorize people and their potential. We are told by Jeanine (the Erudite villain responsible for the development of the serum, who is using its mind-controlling power to turn the Dauntless into a mindless army of automatons in a bid for societal control) that "most of the Divergent" are "weak-willed, God-fearing nobodies from *Abnegation*, of all factions" (429, italics original). While it is evident that Jeanine is wrong to say that the Divergent are weak-willed, since it has been clearly demonstrated that they are the reverse, she doesn't appear to be incorrect about their tendency to be "God-fearing" since throughout the novel, Abnegation has been painted as the most explicitly religious faction. In fact, Four—born to Abnegation, but choosing Dauntless for his faction like Tris—has the phrase "Fear God Alone" emblazoned on his wall, a sentiment clearly regarded with admiration by Tris and by the novel's general tenor. Additionally, Tris herself—whose heroic qualities are, after all, the primary focus of the novel—feels that "Abnegation is what I am. It is what I am when I'm not thinking about what I'm doing. It is what I am when I am put to the test. It is what I am even when I appear to be brave" and goes so far as to wonder, "Am I in the wrong faction?" (379). If most of the Divergent have an aptitude for Abnegation, as seems to be the case, it is a strong argument for the condition being classifiable, and not the free and indefinable quality it claims to be.

Four says at one point that "the aptitude test tells you nothing" and that he thinks "we've made a mistake . . . We've all started to put down the virtues of the other factions in the process of bolstering our own. I don't want to do that. I want to be brave, and selfless, *and* smart, *and* kind, *and* honest" (405, italics original). However, Four's assurances of plurality and fluidity to Tris would be much more convincing if he were right that "the aptitude test tells you nothing"; that is, if faction were truly irrelevant to Divergence. Instead it does tell us two things: one, that those who can resist the serum are Divergent, and two, that those with a tendency toward Abnegation are more likely to be Divergent. Consider for instance one of the story's villains, Eric, who is a sadistic trainer in Dauntless. Towards the end of the novel, Tris realizes his true nature, saying, "I recognize Eric for what he is: an Erudite disguised as a Dauntless, a genius as well as a sadist, a hunter of the Divergent" (362). It's difficult to see how someone who is both Erudite and Dauntless isn't himself Divergent, but apparently Divergence is not a possibility in Roth's narrative universe for those who aren't also good—in other words, those who lack Abnegation. Divergence then is not simply the aptitude for multiple factions but a faction itself, with identifiable traits like any other.

The novel ends by shattering the two factions Tris has close ties with, Dauntless and Abnegation, leaving their erstwhile members basically faction-less. Tris has no alternative at this point but to embrace her Divergence, concluding that with "no home, no path, and no certainty" she is "no longer Tris, the selfless, or Tris, the brave" and "must become more than either" (487). Unfortunately, it would be easier to believe in this statement if her language up to this point had displayed a firm purpose of amendment in patterns of thought. Instead, even after her mindset theoretically changes, by which time Tris has already been encouraged to think of her Divergence as a gift, and of the factions as a poor idea, she continues to label both her actions and the people she meets in just these terms, saying for example, "Because I am Dauntless, it's my duty to lead now" (451). Her wildly fluctuating rhetoric—first embracing factional labels, then Divergence, then factionlessness—does not encourage readers to buy into the breakdown of the society's structure of categorization, especially since the factional labels have been used throughout the majority of the novel as unproblematic descriptors, by both Tris and Four, our protagonists and narrators.

Nostalgia for a Mythical Utopia

Dystopias are often read as advocating social change, but, as I've shown, the rhetoric of Tris's narration communicates a reluctance to commit fully to the necessary upheaval that begins to take place in the final pages of the novel. It's possible to read this as a sign of the YA dystopia's innate conservatism. In an article on the recent explosion of dystopian writing for young adults, novelist Philip Reeve writes:

> Dystopian fiction, while appearing to offer a radical criticism of modern society, is often deeply conservative. Portraying our civilization as doomed, it looks to the past for answers—to the rugged individualism of the frontier spirit, or a meek retreat to preindustrial ways of life.[12]

However, while *Divergent* does look to our own past, with its concerns regarding illegible identity dating back to the early twentieth century at least, Roth's universe is inflected not as much by our real history, as it is by her fictional one. Its conservatism, though pervasive, is for the zenith of her own invented system rather than the frontier or other preindustrial modes of existence.

When initially introducing the faction concept, Roth relates its history as part of the Choosing Ceremony, when the new crop of sixteen-year-olds determines their adult allegiance. The leader of Abnegation, Marcus, gives the following speech:

28 · Balaka Basu

> Decades ago our ancestors . . . divided into factions that sought to eradicate those qualities they believed responsible for the world's disarray . . . Those who blamed aggression formed Amity . . . Those who blamed ignorance became the Erudite . . . Those who blamed duplicity created Candor . . . Those who blamed selfishness made Abnegation . . . And those who blamed cowardice were the Dauntless (41–43).

It turns out that Marcus is also Four's abusive father, making anything he says deeply suspect. Even before we learn about Marcus's villainy though, Tris questions this history to some degree, as well as the whole concept of choosing a faction, momentarily recognizing that instead of getting to choose their own way, they are actually choosing from "five predetermined ways"—an entirely different matter (42).

Nevertheless, the novel continues to reflect nostalgically upon this historical narrative. Thus, instead of aspiring to break down the system, Tris wants to return to when it was allegedly working, observing:

> Maybe Dauntless was formed with good intentions . . . But it has strayed far from them. . . . Despite the depravity I see in Dauntless . . . in the brief moment that I have loved it here, I saw a faction worth saving. Maybe we can become brave and honorable again (206–207).

Regardless of how the system has been corrupted, Tris and therefore the reader envision a past to which her present can aspire, where the categorization is untainted, operates as intended, and furthermore, is the only feasible alternative to an "isolation . . . worse than death" (207).

Whenever characters express dissatisfaction with the faction system, they almost always qualify it with a nostalgic longing. When Four says, "I've always felt that I don't quite belong among the Dauntless," he is quick to follow it with, "Not the way they are now, anyway," implying that they have been a different way in the past, when he might have fit in with them better (335). Similarly, even after Tris has been sexually assaulted, beaten, and otherwise punished by the Dauntless cadre, she is still willing to believe in their ideals. For instance, when she hears Eric, one of her most sadistic opponents, recount the Dauntless code of faith, her reaction is to think: "No matter how badly the leaders have warped the Dauntless ideals, those ideals can still belong to me" (412). Even Tris's mother, who turns into the most vocal critic of the faction system by the end of the novel, qualifies her statement "I don't care about the factions" with, "Look where they got us. Human beings as a whole cannot be good for long before the bad creeps back in and poisons us again" (441). The rhetoric of her statement, however disappointed, clearly implies that the faction system was once "good" before the "bad" crept back in.

This blind faith in the system's utopian possibility illustrates what Oona Eisenstadt reads in a strand of Emmanuel Levinas's discussion of Anti-Utopia:

we ought to mistrust utopia at least partially because of the "idea that Utopian aspirations result in dystopia, or that an attempt to found an ideal regime results in monstrosity."[13] It seems clear that Roth's system will necessarily produce dystopia, but the novel's resistance to change seems to indicate that reform not revolution is required. This tension between the utopia of the past that Roth imagines and the dystopia of the present that it has transmuted into seems to understand neither utopia nor dystopia as a mechanism for social change, but instead as a society whose ideals and philosophy remain the same, believing that only its practice has become corrupted and reversibly so, at that.

Rob McAlear's new rhetorical model of dystopia, which diagrams this area of speculative thought in a semiotic square, may help us better describe Roth's novel. Rather than setting up "utopia" in opposition to "dystopia," McAlear suggests that we need four terms—Utopia and Anti-Utopia; Dystopia and Anti-Dystopia—to understand the genre. If a utopia uses an appeal to hope to imagine systemic change, and a dystopia uses an appeal to fear to do the same, then we need two classifications within the genre that embrace conservatism and complacency rather than revolution and resistance. He writes:

> Dystopias use fear in order to open up the possibility of change; that is, they warn in order to promote resistance. Under this model, Dystopia becomes not so much a mediating term between Utopia and Anti-Utopia, rather it becomes Utopia's complement ... The politics of social change require both positive representations of change, Utopia, and the raising of awareness and resistance to current historical trends, Dystopia. Likewise, the maintenance of ideological systems requires both opposition to other systems, Anti-Utopia, and complacency, Anti-Dystopia.[14]

Using this model, *Divergent*'s past where the faction system is said to have worked, alluded to nostalgically in the novel, exemplifies an Anti-Dystopia of complacency that has transformed over time into an Anti-Utopia that opposes all other methodologies. It never achieves the possibility of social change that either a true utopia would offer through hope or a true dystopia would offer through an appeal to fear, because it never interrogates its own axiom that classification is an aspirational possibility.

A Dystopia of the Online Personality Quiz

Unfortunately, through the novel's marketing, this lack of interrogation extends from Roth's fiction back into the real world. Visitors to *Divergent*'s Facebook page, for instance, have the opportunity to take an online version of the aptitude test themselves. Blogger Phoebe North describes her experience with the quiz a few weeks before the novel's debut:

30 • Balaka Basu

> Last night, I stumbled across a Facebook quiz where you can "discover your faction" a la Veronica Roth's upcoming debut *Divergent*. It was a clever piece of marketing and design, where you select options in a brief thought experiment until your single true faction becomes clear . . . That little test distilled what is, perhaps, the greatest selling point of Roth's book, the simple hook which asks you to consider your own values and traits and categorize yourself according to them. I found myself doing so several times throughout *Divergent* . . . But despite the attractiveness of this premise, it never rang true for me even at the outset. Oh, sure, younger teens might buy it without question (in a rare display of Candor-like candor, my husband quipped, "Factions? Teens eat that shit up!").[15]

While North's assessment here is apt, it's extraordinary to note that neither she nor anyone else seem to notice that the aptitude test on Facebook, though resembling the test described in the novel's pages fairly closely, fails to duplicate it on one crucial point: there is no way for the reader to be marked Divergent.

Just as in the novel, the first question in the Facebook version of the aptitude test asks the subject to choose between the knife and the cheese, but Beatrice's refusal to choose isn't an option; if it has to, the online quiz, unlike Beatrice's tester, will wait forever for subjects to make their decision. Regardless of how many conflicting attributes the quiz-taker's answers display, the test will still result in the assignment of a single faction, making Divergence impossible. Since as North notes, the test "distills" the essential pleasure of the book—the question of what faction the reader would be in, if they lived in Roth's world—it says something that even the novel's problematic attempt at a fluid categorization of identity is here arrested and made even more rigid. While this can't really be ascribed to Roth, who probably did not design the online quiz, the fact that none of the novel's fans seem to have noticed this discrepancy suggests that the pleasure to be found in Roth's universe is in her fixing of identity, not in the possibility that categorization is dangerous.

It's clear that the insidious pleasure we take in categorizing and in being categorized obscures the dystopian nature of such categories, however much we might claim otherwise. In an interview with Amazon.com, Roth describes the impulse behind her novel's premise:

> I think we all secretly love and hate categories—love to get a firm hold on our identities, but hate to be confined—and I never loved and hated them more than when I was a teenager. That said: Though we hear a lot about high school cliques, I believe that adults categorize each other just as often, just in subtler ways. It is a dangerous tendency of ours. And it begins in adolescence.[16]

While Roth seems here to be questioning the concept of categorization, her words are telling: she hates to be constrained, but simultaneously wants to get

What Faction Are You in? • 31

a "firm hold on . . . identity." This desire seems extraordinarily conservative in a post-Foucauldian age that purports to read identity as fluid and unfixed, shaped by circumstance and social context, and ultimately impermanent. Nevertheless, just like her characters, Roth's every attempt at critique of a system of classification, and its conflation of group membership with individual identity, simultaneously becomes celebration. *Divergent*'s incredible popularity—it was optioned for film months before it even hit bookshelves—shows that the pleasures to be found in "loving categories" apparently far outweigh their dangers for Roth's readers as well.

Notes

1 See Justin Wyatt, *High Concept: Movies and Marketing in Hollywood* (Austin: University of Texas Press, 1994), 13. The recent film *Cowboys and Aliens* (2011) is an example of a high concept, where the entire experience—what would happen if cowboys had to fight aliens?—is adequately condensed into the title. Conversely, the premise of *Lord of the Rings* (1954–1955) reduced to a single sentence—nine people go on a quest to destroy a magical ring of evil in a volcano—would probably not give an accurate representation of the whole narrative.

2 Ibid.

3 Maude Hines, "Second Nature: Daemons and Ideology in *The Golden Compass*," in *His Dark Materials Illuminated: Critical Essays on Philip Pullman's Trilogy*, ed. Millicent Lenz and Carole Scott (Detroit: Wayne State University Press, 2005), 39.

4 L. Frank Baum, *The Master Key* (New York: Bowen-Merrill, 1901), http://www.gutenberg.org/ files/436/436-h/436-h.htm.

5 Hines, "Second Nature," 38.

6 Ibid., 39.

7 Melanie D. Koss and William H. Teale, "What's Happening in YA Literature? Trends in Books for Adolescents," *Journal of Adolescent and Adult Literacy* 52.7 (2009): 567–569.

8 J.K. Rowling, *Harry Potter and the Deathly Hallows* (New York: Arthur A. Levine Books, 2007), 680.

9 Chantel Lavoie, "Safe as Houses: Sorting and School Houses at Hogwarts," in *Reading Harry Potter: Critical Essays*, ed. Giselle Liza Anatol (Westport, CT: Greenwood, 2003), 40. Lavoie reads one site, which asks visitors to think "really hard" about their identity as it spits forth a random House assignment, as capturing the effect of desire on the Sorting Hat's assessment; another site, which specifically aligns Slytherin House with selfishness, Lavoie understands as making explicit what was implied only subtextually in Rowling's text, where Slytherin is said to be aligned with the more neutral trait of ambition.

32 • Balaka Basu

10 *Divergent* is the first novel in Roth's projected trilogy, and at the time of writing, was the only installment available. By the time of publication, however, the second novel of the series, *Insurgent* (2012), had been released. Although no claims can be made about the third novel, which hasn't yet been written, and a full examination of *Insurgent* is beyond the scope of this essay, it seems relevant to touch upon the implications of Roth's second novel for the argument laid out here. Briefly, then, *Insurgent* completes the "world tour" of the fictional universe by focusing on the two factions that are not fully explored in *Divergent*, Amity and Candor. The novel closes with the suggestion that the whole faction system has been a carefully constructed social experiment, closed off from the rest of the world and designed to solve its problems. Despite the clear intention of the trilogy to eventually break down the faction system at least somewhat, it continues to read the "sorting" of people as a utopian possibility, since this is the method by which the world will presumably be saved. As well, factional allegiances remain adequate descriptors of identity: Beatrice/Tris continues to embody Dauntless; her parents continue to embody Abnegation. My contention remains that the series thus far uses the allure of categorization to appeal to readers, never fully interrogating the desire for a collective identity and group membership that so imbues it.

11 Veronica Roth, *Divergent* (New York: Katherine Tegen Books, 2011), 17. Subsequent references will be cited parenthetically in the text.

12 Philip Reeve, "The Worst Is Yet to Come," *School Library Journal* 57.8 (2011): 36.

13 Oona Eisenstadt, "Anti-Utopianism Revisited," *Shofar: An Interdisciplinary Journal of Jewish Studies* 26.4 (2008): 125–126.

14 Rob McAlear, "The Value of Fear: Toward a Rhetorical Model of Dystopia," *Interdisciplinary Humanities* 27.2 (2010): 36.

15 Phoebe North, "Review: *Divergent* by Veronica Roth," *Phoebe North* (blog), April 20, 2011, http://www.phoebenorth.com/2011/04/20/review-divergent-by-veronica-roth/.

16 "A Q&A with Veronica Roth," http://www.amazon.com/Divergent-Trilogy-Veronica-Roth/dp/0062024027/ref=sr_1_1?s=books&ie=UTF8&qid=1302981501&sr=1–1.

Works Cited

"A Q&A with Veronica Roth." http://www.amazon.com/Divergent-Trilogy-Veronica-Roth/dp/0062024027/ref=sr_1_1?s=books&ie=UTF8&qid=1302981501&sr=1–1.

Baum, L. Frank. *The Master Key.* New York: Bowen-Merrill, 1901. http://www.gutenberg.org/files/436/436-h/436-h.htm.

Eisenstadt, Oona. "Anti-Utopianism Revisited." *Shofar: An Interdisciplinary Journal of Jewish Studies* 26.4 (2008): 120–138.

Hines, Maude. "Second Nature: Daemons and Ideology in *The Golden Compass.*" In *His Dark Materials Illuminated: Critical Essays on Philip Pullman's Trilogy,* edited by Millicent Lenz and Carole Scott, 37–47. Detroit: Wayne State University Press, 2005.

Koss, Melanie D. and William H. Teale. "What's Happening in YA Literature? Trends in Books for Adolescents." *Journal of Adolescent and Adult Literacy* 52.7 (2009): 563–572.

Lavoie, Chantel. "Safe as Houses: Sorting and School Houses at Hogwarts." In *Reading Harry Potter: Critical Essays*, edited by Giselle Liza Anatol, 35–50. Westport, CT: Greenwood, 2003.

McAlear, Rob. "The Value of Fear: Toward a Rhetorical Model of Dystopia." *Interdisciplinary Humanities* 27.2 (2010): 24–42.

North, Phoebe. "Review: *Divergent* by Veronica Roth." *Phoebe North* (blog), April 20, 2011. http://www.phoebenorth.com/2011/04/20/review-divergent-by-veronica-roth/.

Reeve, Philip. "The Worst Is Yet to Come," *School Library Journal* 57.8 (2011): 34–36.

Roth, Veronica. *Divergent*. New York: Katherine Tegen Books, 2011.

———. *Insurgent*. New York: Katherine Tegen Books, 2011.

Rowling, J.K. *Harry Potter and the Deathly Hallows*. New York: Arthur A. Levine Books, 2007.

Wyatt, Justin. *High Concept: Movies and Marketing in Hollywood*. Austin: University of Texas Press, 1994.

Chapter Two
Coming of Age in Dystopia
Reading Genre in Holly Black's Curse Workers Series

Emily Lauer

When the Pixar film *The Incredibles* was released in 2004, viewers and reviewers alike were able to recognize its similarities to an objectivist parable because it contains, among other things, an anti-regulation plot. As A.O. Scott's review noted, when the film opens, "Various do-gooders, meddlers and bureaucrats ... have driven the world's once-admired superheroes underground, into lives of bland split-level normalcy."[1] The government in *The Incredibles* creates a right-wing dystopia of a kind generally associated with Ayn Rand's ideas: an oppressive regulatory regime is presented in order to glorify a utopian "free" capitalist economy in contrast. In the article "Utopia Beyond Our Ideals: The Dilemma of the Right-Wing Utopia" (1991), Peter Fitting describes a libertarian utopia as one that embraces the "premise that too much government regulation and interference" have created a real-world crisis that needs to be addressed as dystopian.[2] Fitting uses Ayn Rand's novel *Atlas Shrugged* (1957) as an example of this kind of utopia. The objectivist dystopia in *The Incredibles*, like that in Rand's novels, implies a contrasting objectivist utopia where the "problem" of government regulation does not exist.

In *The Incredibles*, those "who manifest superiority in some area are viewed as a reproach to those who are mediocre" and their specialness is policed in order to placate the mediocre.[3] *The Incredibles* "is not subtle in announcing its central theme. Some people have powers that others do not, and to deny them the right to exercise those powers, or the privileges that accompany them, is misguided, cruel, and socially destructive."[4] In other words, regulating ability creates dystopian conditions for the naturally elite. The audience is led

36 • Emily Lauer

to sympathize with the "supers" rather than the meddling regulators. The regulators claim that their decree against the supers is meant to eradicate the expensive destruction of property perpetrated whenever the supers battle. However, audiences are led to see that in fact, petty envy and the need to feel special are the motivating factors behind the regulation. At the end of the film, the regulators decide to lift the restrictions on the supers because they discover that the destruction they wreak is a small price to pay for the sense of security they offer from villains; the supers then triumphantly return to their former elite status.

Holly Black's young adult Curse Workers series (2010–2012) seems to begin with similar conditions. In the world of the Curse Workers series, some people have the ability to perform acts of persuasive magic by touching each other with their hands, which is called "curse working." In this world, magic has been outlawed. At first glance, the oppressive government in Black's series seems familiar, not just because the world is like our own in many ways, but also because it exhibits a recognizable anxiety about what happens in a culture when those with elite, unusual abilities are not allowed to excel in them. However, while some of the premise in the Curse Workers series is indeed similar to that of *The Incredibles* or *Atlas Shrugged*, the plot is not. In the three books that make up this series, readers follow Cassel Sharpe, a teenager from a family of con artists and curse workers, as he makes discoveries and decisions about what his place in the world will be. His family, curse workers (and therefore criminals) all, use their abilities to manipulate the emotions, health, and memories of those around them in order to con people, including Cassel, out of money and valuables. Cassel's grandfather is both a kind, loving force in Cassel's life and a death worker: a successful hit man for the Zacharov crime family.

The characters in the world of the Curse Workers series attempt to find a balance between cultivating individual specialness (even though some forms of specialness are forbidden) and living under an enforced equality. While the government restrictions placed on curse working (and the societal taboos that go along with those restrictions) create dystopian conditions for Cassel, the removal of those restrictions would not create utopian conditions. This dystopia is not destined to be overthrown, but rather negotiated. Instead of being a Randian tale as is *The Incredibles*, championing the struggle of a born leader as petty minds attempt to hold him back, the Curse Workers series unfolds as a story about negotiating allegiances: Cassel learns how to fit into an imperfect world as best as possible. His task is to figure out how to reject his government's and culture's decrees about his worth and discover his own sense of self, rather than to cure his society's ills.

In that way the Curse Workers series is as much a *Bildungsroman* as it is a YA dystopia, since it presents a young man finding his place in society as he learns to negotiate the world around him. This genre designation has political implications: if the Curse Workers series is a *Bildungsroman* set in a dystopia

Coming of Age in Dystopia · 37

(an idea I will explore in this chapter), perhaps we need to rethink what it means to come of age under dystopian conditions. By presenting a character arc of successful self-discovery in a troubled world, Black's trilogy proves it is possible to be politically progressive in a dystopian setting even if the government bugbear you are facing down happens to be one envisioned to scare right-wing children rather than left-wing ones. The culmination of this trilogy suggests that many stories of young adult maturation may require an acceptance of dystopian conditions.

Policing Specialness

Holly Black's Curse Workers series is comprised of the young adult novels *White Cat* (2010), *Red Glove* (2011), and *Black Heart* (2012). In these novels' version of the U.S., a flourishing underworld has developed because "the thing about curse magic being illegal is that it turns everyone who uses it into a criminal. And criminals stick together."[5] High school history lessons include the fact that the ban on curse work in the U.S. was enacted soon after the prohibition of alcohol and then "the big six worker families came into power all down the East Coast in the thirties and have remained that way ever since. Nonomura. Goldbloom. Volpe. Rice. Brennan. Zacharov. They control everything."[6]

In stories of policing the special, it is clear that somewhere, wishes for equality have gone awry. The people in charge of these societies believe, as Lyman Tower Sargent says in "The Three Faces of Utopianism Revisited" (1994), "Life in a perfect society is best even for imperfect people because they will accept it as better or law (force) will impose it."[7] In the Curse Workers series, the sought-after perfection is a kind of purity: the lack of an ability to curse work. Laws that regulate ability, however, end up oppressing the able to a disproportionate degree such that force leads to freedom of a kind for only those in the dis-abled but dominant group.

The illegality of curse working puts the burden of policing the special on the government, but social mores also serve to enforce restrictions on curse working. For instance, citizens wear gloves at all times to keep their hands off each other and thus wearing gloves is considered part of common decency. Because social mores help enforce the government's specialness legislation, it is rude as well as dangerous to talk about curse working; as curse working is illegal, it can be neither regulated nor studied. The fear of working in Black's world is born partly out of the ignorance and secrecy in which working must occur. While the government may be testing workers secretly, sharing practical knowledge about curse working is illegal. Just as the restrictions on women's freedom in *The Handmaid's Tale* (1985) or *Persepolis* (2000) do not actually keep women safe, it is also true that in the Curse Workers series, the wearing of gloves and outlawing of curse work do not keep people safe from

38 · Emily Lauer

being worked, or keep workers safe from the crippling "blowback" that occurs after some curses. Workers are not taught how to use their powers safely, and curse working generally happens under dangerous conditions. In this way, the use of the word "workers" as short for "curse workers," which occurs throughout the trilogy, echoes a need in our own world for safe working conditions. Since safety is not ensured by the regulations against curse working, it seems possible that they are enforced only to maintain a power relationship in which the dis-abled group is dominant.

Additionally, the Curse Workers series presents a world in which many people assume others' worth based on whether or not they are curse workers. A campaigning politician asks his constituents, "Did you know that no one requires testing of applicants to government jobs to determine who among us are potentially dangerous criminals? . . . We must root all workers out of our government! How can we expect our legislators to be safe when their staffers, their aides, even their constituents could be seeking to undermine policies directed at bringing these sinister predators to light, because those policies would inconvenience them" (*Black*, 67). This politician is a fear monger, using hatred of a disadvantaged minority to bolster his chances at election.

He is not, however, alone in the Curse Workers series for espousing the idea that ability shapes worth. Throughout the trilogy we are given more and more evidence that making assumptions about people's worth based on this single category of ability is faulty and impractical. Growing up, Cassel "knew that there were regular people and there were workers, and workers were better than regular people. That's what everyone in Carney believed, or it's at least what they told" him (*Black*, 169). While workers break the law explicitly, non-workers can exploit their legal and perceived moral ascendancy over workers in problematic ways. They have official privilege and social privilege but also fear the innate privilege of workers. In Black's world, the correctness of policing specialness is up for debate rather than condemned outright because although the illegality of curse working discourages moral uses of these powers, the ability to work curses actually has no bearing on moral integrity: what individuals will do with their powers is unpredictable. While some characters believe that workers are inferior, and others believe that workers are superior, neither view is entirely correct.

Despite the U.S. government's role in policing specialness in this world, the workers' situation is not even contained by national borders. Cassel is shown images of workers in other countries who have had their hands removed in order to stop them from working curses. He is informed that "violence against [workers] isn't taken seriously." Cassel is not surprised to hear this, because he finds it difficult "to take violence seriously when workers are the ones with all the advantages" (*White*, 160). But even as he thinks this, his "eyes keep stopping on the brutal, jagged flesh, healed dark and probably burned" in a picture of a worker whose hand was removed (*White*, 160). Removing workers' hands

Coming of Age in Dystopia • 39

is understood to be removing an unfair advantage, like giving one runner a "handicap" in a race.

Exploring the Dystopian in the Curse Workers Series

In the Curse Workers series the world is dystopian because a minority is systematically denied the ability to reach its potential. As political theorist Robert E. Lane argues in "Quality of Life and Quality of Persons: A New Role for Government?" (1994), a society needs to provide people with the means of achieving their own potential. Lane claims that "it is not what is given ('resourcism') but what people *do* with what is given that is essential to my conception of a high quality of life."[8] He argues that the idea of "quality of life" should be based not only on the access that people have to a high "quality of conditions" such as education, housing, etc., but rather "the *relation* between quality of conditions" and the ability that individuals have to appreciate and enjoy these conditions, an ability that Lane calls "quality of persons." He explains, "I employ the concept of a better *quality of person* to mean development of nine qualities derived from studies of mental health: capacity for enjoying life, cognitive complexity, a sense of autonomy and effectiveness, self-knowledge, self-esteem, ease of interpersonal relations, an ethical orientation, personality integration, and, to take advantage of opportunities for work and income, a productivity orientation."[9]

By making working illegal, the U.S. government as it appears in the Curse Workers series has systematically denied workers a high quality of life by denying them the ability to realize many of these nine factors. Fundamentally, it is the systematic deprivation of the "productivity orientation" for a whole group of people that makes the world a dystopia, especially since this deprivation hinders workers' ability to develop in other ways. Regardless of the cognitive complexity and the sense of autonomy and effectiveness that their talents may bestow, workers who are criminalized as a result of their innate and involuntary abilities are limited in their self-esteem, their potential to enjoy life, and their ethical development. Furthermore, because any lawful presentation of the self requires that these individuals must constantly lie, this society must also necessarily limit workers' personality integration and ease of interpersonal relations.

It is these limitations to workers' quality of life, as imposed by the dystopian elements of Cassel's world, that cause many of his personal problems, both directly and indirectly. Cassel is caught between a government that tells him he is in the wrong simply for having specific abilities, a public that rightly fears those abilities, and a family who wants to exploit those abilities because they are part of a criminal underworld that is enabled by the outlawing of working. These conditions have a negative impact on Cassel's sense of self-worth, and he begins the trilogy full of shame and confusion. On the one hand, the

40 · Emily Lauer

governmental policies' effect on Cassel can be read as an indication of genre. As Carrie Hintz has noted in her article "Monica Hughes, Lois Lowry, and Young Adult Dystopias" (2002), a "marker of the young adult utopia or dystopia, one intimately bound with its political message, is the frequent presence of shame and confusion for the protagonist."[10]

However, the trilogy departs from more typical YA dystopias in that Cassel shows no signs of wanting to eradicate this shame by becoming a Harry Potter-like savior for his subculture. As it turns out, the responsibility for overcoming his shame will be placed on personal growth, rather than systemic changes. In *White Cat*, the first book of the trilogy, repressive governmental policies toward curse working are part of the background. They must be introduced to account for the organized crime system around curse working, but beyond that they do not enter the action much. Cassel tells his school friend Daneca, who is recruiting for a curse workers' rights organization, "I'm not a worker, and I don't care if you are. Find someone else to recruit or save or whatever it is you are trying to do" (*White*, 20). Even though Cassel does not want to participate in politics, arguments about workers' rights shape the world around him. For instance, even when his mind is on other things, Cassel still registers what is on television: "On the news I see Governor Patton, who has been a big proponent of proposition two, the thing that's supposed to force everybody to get tested to ascertain who's a worker and who's not. Patton is going on and on about how he believes that workers should come forward in support of his proposition so that they can let the world know that they are the good, law-abiding citizens they claim to be" (*White*, 137–138). Immediately after acknowledging distrust of Patton, Cassel goes to a high school party where he kisses his ex-girlfriend, gets in a fight with her current boyfriend, and then drives his drunk roommate home. Patton is on his television, but not in the forefront of his mind.

In *Red Glove*, the second book, the government's policies begin to influence Cassel's actions directly even though he still resists involvement in politics. Daneca convinces him to attend a rally protesting proposition two, which will require all New Jersey citizens to be tested for the gene that indicates the ability to curse work. Daneca tells him, "If proposition two passes, then workers are going to be tested. Everyone will be."[11] Cassel protests that he already knows what she's telling him, and that "no matter how much the government of New Jersey says it is going to keep that information anonymous, it's not. Soon workers are going to be refused jobs, denied housing, and locked up for the crime of being born with a power they didn't ask for" (*Red*, 24). They go to the rally, Daneca bringing along her love interest, Sam, and Cassel bringing along his love interest, Lila, in a kind of double date. They arrive too late to truly join any of the activities and are rounded up and arrested merely for being on the outskirts of the protest. Eventually they are released from jail and go back to school. Cassel remarks: "By lights-out

Coming of Age in Dystopia · 41

it's as if the whole thing never happened" (*Red*, 160). Cassel is aware of political affairs, but he holds himself removed from decisions and events that have the potential to shape his future.

While their participation in traditional political protest is stunted, the characters' reactions to the experience are noteworthy, as they illuminate some intersections between curse working and socioeconomic class. Even before the protest, Cassel tries to explain to Daneca that workers may not believe "anything's going to get better" for them even if they were to strive for a better world (*Red*, 141). Daneca does not understand this kind of pessimism about effecting change through established channels. After their experience at the protest, she continues to pressure Cassel and others to get politically involved. Much of her lack of cynicism is due to the socioeconomic privilege she has always enjoyed, a contrast to Cassel's own upbringing that leaves him less sure about conventional avenues of change.

Daneca's mother, Mrs. Wasserman, is a shining beacon of hope in this series. She is a curse worker, but privileged in other ways—she is wealthy, healthy, well-situated, and well-educated, all of which allow her to be an advocate for workers' rights in relative safety. Mrs. Wasserman is famous in the world of the Curse Workers series for a speech "filmed sitting in the office of her brick house in Princeton" in which she publicly explored the ways in which "it benefited crime families to prevent workers from finding ways to use their talents legally. She admitted to being a worker herself. It was an impressive speech. A dangerous speech" (*White*, 20). After making a speech declaring the safety of some curse working and the benevolence of some curse workers, Mrs. Wasserman's role *had* to become that of a positive example of what legalized working could mean for law-abiding citizens. She was able to fulfill this role because of her socioeconomic security and comfort.

As Sargent defines utopianism, Mrs. Wasserman is a utopian. Sargent asserts that "if we are frustrated by something in our society, we dream of a society in which it is corrected. Often we dream even though we, personally, are well fed and sexually fulfilled. We still dream at least in part because, content, we are capable of recognizing that others are not and feel that others should also be fulfilled. At its root, then, utopianism is the result of the human propensity to dream while both asleep and awake."[12] Mrs. Wasserman dreams of a better world, and lives publicly the kind of life she advocates for all workers. It is the life she believes all workers could have, if working were to be legalized. In this way she serves as a foil to Cassel's family and the other characters who use curse working in ways that indicate that legalizing curse working might cause more problems than it solves. Cassel acknowledges that "there are workers who aren't con artists, workers who don't want anything to do with organized crime. But when Daneca thinks of workers, she thinks of her mother. When I think of workers, I think of mine" (*Red*, 25). Cassel's mother, an active curse worker and a con artist, could not have made the speech for which Mrs. Wasserman is known.

42 · Emily Lauer

Cassel recognizes that Mrs. Wasserman lives the life she advocates, and that this makes her reliable in a world full of people on whom Cassel cannot rely. When Cassel must weigh his options with the Zacharov crime family, the Brennan crime family, and the Feds, all of whom are trying to recruit him, he feels he can't trust any one, including himself. In this situation, he calls Mrs. Wasserman (*Red*, 294). He trusts her because she is honest and open about her attempts to change the world into a better place—what she thinks the world should be. She is trustworthy because she not only dreams, but also lives and acts by the strictures of those dreams.

Mrs. Wasserman is vocal about how her dreams shape her actions. In warning Cassel about working for the government, she explains that the Feds have a Licensed Minority Division—that is, a government agency that employs workers to track down and prosecute other workers, "sometimes for legitimately terrible crimes, sometimes for minor infractions . . . And I'm sure that some kids wind up with fine, upstanding government jobs. I just want us to live in a world where worker kids don't have to play cops or robbers." In response to this, Cassel thinks, "I can't imagine that world. I don't think I'd fit in there" (*Red*, 181). Cassel cannot see himself becoming a part of Mrs. Wasserman's ideal world. In fact, he cannot see himself belonging in the world she already lives in, either. A page later he thinks, "I always feel awkward in Daneca's house. I can't help casing the joint" because the Wassermans' comfortable wealth and privilege are so different from Cassel's own upbringing (*Red*, 182). Even as he reaches out to Mrs. Wasserman, then, Cassel holds himself removed from her utopian vision and her ideas about change.

The Ethics of Choosing Dystopia

Cassel's feeling of awkwardness is not limited to the Wassermans' house. He has trouble fitting in generally. At the beginning of the trilogy, he is caught between the underworld of curse working and the legitimate world of his fancy private school, Wallingford. He wants to fit into both, but does not trust his own ability to do so. He narrates, "I spend most of my time at school faking and lying. It takes a lot of effort to pretend you're something you're not. I don't think about what music I like; I think about what music I should like" (*White*, 9). He tells his roommate, "It's hard to be a good person. . . . Because I already know I'm not" (*White*, 29). Cassel struggles to be part of the legitimate world that creates dystopian conditions for workers like him, at the same time that he knows he will never belong.

His inability to feel at home in either world is due to his conviction that he is both a bad person and a bad criminal. His self-esteem improves as he realizes neither part of that conviction is true: he is not the only non-worker in a family of workers, but is rather a powerful transformation worker. Furthermore, he did not (as he had been cursed to misremember) kill his best friend

Coming of Age in Dystopia · 43

as a child but rather rescued her from an assassination attempt the best way he knew how. Realizations of his power and innocence allow him to make informed decisions about his life. For instance, when he mouths off to his brother, Cassel feels a pang of worry but then realizes, "I'm not Cassel Sharpe, kid brother and general disappointment, anymore. I'm one of the most powerful practitioners of one of the rarest curses. . . . They should be afraid of me" (*White*, 210).

However, even as his self-knowledge grows, throughout much of the series he is obsessed with determining whether or not he is a good or bad person. He has thoughts such as, "I don't want to be a monster, but maybe it's too late to be anything else" (*White*, 237) and tells Daneca, "I can't be trusted" (*Red*, 277). Is he a good guy if he works for the government? Agent Jones tells Cassel in *Red Glove*, "You could be on the right side of the law. You don't have to protect these people, Cassel." Cassel thinks "*I am these people* . . . but his words make me fantasize for a moment about what it would be like to be a good guy, with a badge and a stainless reputation" (130, italics original). To work on the side of the government would mean betraying his family and friends—the people Jones refers to so disdainfully as "these people." Plus, it later turns out the Feds play dirty. So, is he a good guy if he helps his mother and brothers with their criminal enterprises instead? That usually means conning innocent people. Is he a bad guy for being able to work curses at all? Is he a good guy if he does what he's told? Cassel's uncertainties about his own value and the nature of goodness indicate layers of inherent contradiction in the way his society equates ability with morality.

In *Black Heart*, the third book of the trilogy, he is plunged into direct political action. He allows the government to recruit him, which he rationalizes by thinking, "If I don't trust my own instincts toward right and wrong, I have to trust someone's. That's why I wanted to join the government, right? So that if I was going to do bad things, it would at least be in the service of good people" (95). In some ways, the resolution of the trilogy overall is enabled by Cassel extricating himself successfully from this involvement and this way of thinking. As his worlds of school, family, and government recruiters begin to merge, Cassel realizes that the "good guy" option is not available to him. He discovers that the government planned to frame him for the murder of a right-wing fear-mongering politician. They "wanted to get rid of Patton, but [they] also wanted proposition two to pass. So [they] decided to make a martyr out of [Patton]. Two birds, one stone" (*Black*, 283). Disgusted and disillusioned, Cassel manages to discredit Patton without hurting him, ensuring proposition two will not pass and he himself cannot be framed for murder. "I hold up one gloved hand. 'Just spare me the justifications. I thought you were the good guys, but there are no good guys,'" he tells one of the government agents who planned to betray him (*Black*, 282).

Cassel's choice will not be between good and bad, but rather just how he wants to fit into the world. By the end of the trilogy, he comes to terms with

44 • Emily Lauer

his role in his dystopian society. Early in the second book, he thinks, "Daneca used to annoy me with all her bleeding-heart crap. I figured there was no point in changing a world that didn't want to be changed. But I don't think that Sam would appreciate me saying that out loud. And I don't even know if I believe it anymore" (*Red*, 22). Cassel grudgingly acknowledges that the possibility for change in the world exists, but he still decides not to throw his whole being into working for it. Cassel does not join Mrs. Wasserman in her utopian dreams or activities. He trusts her, but does not follow her because he does not have the kind of socioeconomic privilege that she does, which allows her to assert her worker status and still live comfortably. Also, he does not have evidence that working within the system can change the system; Mrs. Wasserman's utopianism therefore does not seem viable to him. He notes, "The problem with people like Mrs. Wasserman is exactly this. She's *kind*. She's *good*. . . . It's easy to take advantage of her optimism, her faith in how the world should work" (*Black*, 133, italics original). He couldn't even envision himself fitting into her perfect world, so he chooses instead to do what will allow him to live the life he wants to live in his imperfect world.

To be truly self-actualized, Cassel must negotiate his role in dystopia rather than seeking to overthrow it. At the end of the trilogy, after foiling the Feds' attempt to frame him for murder, he leaves the area with his love interest, Lila, who will come into her inheritance as head of a crime family. He is fulfilling his society's expectations for him. A powerful worker, raised in a family of con artists with ties to organized crime, he drops out of school and turns down a government job, not to become a spokesperson for worker rights or a vigilante hero, but instead to take his "rightful" place at the side of a powerful mob boss. This is not, however, a tragic ending in which our protagonist fails to break away from society's expectations of him. Rather, it is a triumphant ending, in which Cassel has clearly finally figured out, after close to a thousand pages of wondering, what life choices will afford him the most happiness and satisfaction. Not only has he figured it out, he is acting positively to achieve that life rather than reacting passively or defensively as others attempt to manipulate him.

As Hintz has noted, "Young adult utopias take on some of the elements of the *Bildungsroman*, adding an exploration of the political life of the individual."[13] And as David H. Miles has noted, both Wilhelm Dilthey and Georg Wilhelm Friedrich Hegel assert that the "emphasis" of the *Bildungsroman* is "the conciliatory, conservative nature of the genre—the hero's ultimate assimilation into existing society."[14] Cassel explores his political options, then rejects his government's claims on his worth, but does not overthrow that government. His story is a *Bildungsroman* that takes place in a dystopia he cannot ameliorate significantly. He therefore gains those qualities of "capacity for enjoying life . . . self-knowledge, self-esteem, ease of interpersonal relations, an ethical orientation, personality integration, and, to take advantage of opportunities for work and income, a productivity orientation"[15] that Lane lists as integral to

Coming of Age in Dystopia • 45

a high quality of persons, within and despite his dystopian setting, by prioritizing his personal happiness, his love life, over the development of an ethical orientation that would surely lead him to nothing but misery. He eventually realizes, "I don't need [a semblance of normality] anymore. I'm okay with being a con artist and a grifter. With being a worker. With having friends who will hopefully forgive me for taking off on a mad road trip. With being in love" (*Black*, 295).

The Dystopian Genre and the *Bildungsroman*

In some ways, then, this trilogy fits the classic idea of a *Bildungsroman* at least as well as it fits the idea of a YA dystopia. As Susan L. Cocalis asserts in her article, "The Transformation of 'Bildung' from an Image to an Ideal" (1978), "There is no consensus on what constitutes that genre . . . [but] we have generally accepted Dilthey's broad formulation of *Bildung* as the process by which a young male hero discovers himself and his social role through the experience of love, friendship, and the hard realities of life."[16] All that certainly happens to Cassel: he discovers he is a transformation worker with the rare ability to change the substance of people and things at will, and that his family has been altering his memories to make him believe he is a murderer. He and Lila face a number of obstacles but end the series together. He overcomes his initially low self-esteem enough to develop true, lasting friendships with his classmates Sam and Daneca. After being forced to choose between working for the government or working for a crime family, he eventually faces the hard reality that neither his own family nor the government can be trusted and that he will be happiest in a social role that aligns him with Lila's crime family—that is, conservatively assimilating into his society's existing expectations for him.

In more traditional dystopian young adult fiction, there is often the subversive subtext that Alison Lurie treats at length in her essay collection *Don't Tell the Grown-ups* (1990): things are so wrong in society that children are better able to set the world right than are adults; or, at least, children and/or teens cannot rely on the adults already in power. However, Cassel, unlike traditional heroes of dystopian YA fiction, is not closely following what Rebecca Carol Noël Totaro refers to as "the course from longing to hope and action charted by Bloch."[17] The protagonists who do follow this course go on to save or improve their troubled worlds. Cassel, however, has a different sort of trajectory. He ultimately takes his "right" role in his own dystopian society, which has distinct genre implications.

It is possible that more traditional protagonists of young adult fiction have an easier time of it. For instance, when Harry Potter must choose between allegiance with the problematic government of his wizarding world or the more pure option of standing by Dumbledore in the fight against Voldemort,

46 · Emily Lauer

he chooses the obviously right allegiance for his world. I am not saying that the world of Harry Potter is simplistic, but rather that Harry's choices are usually more clearly defined. It is easier for Harry's reader to know which choice is right, regardless of how difficult it may be for Harry to follow through on that choice. Cassel's choices are less distinct. He is not choosing between the official line against evil and the better line against evil. He is not choosing between the easy way and the right way, or between good and evil at all, but rather between several problematic allegiances with various crime families, with his own family, with a utopian dreamer he trusts but does not believe will be effective, and with a government that he realizes operates like a crime family itself. Each choice has its own set of drawbacks and smaller set of perks. He must negotiate these choices rather than repudiate evil in all its forms. Mrs. Wasserman had not protected him as an infant, as Dumbledore did Harry, and he has no reason to expect her kind of activism to create the world he would want to live in. Therefore, Cassel must forge his own path, deciding the best of the options presented to him rather than steadfastly following a beloved teacher figure in a war between good and evil.

This does not make Cassel a traditional "good guy," but, as Lane notes in his discussion of quality of persons, "objective justice is unrecognizable without an ethical orientation."[18] Cassel has to invent his own ideas of ethics and justice because to embrace the official ones would be to cultivate self-hatred. As Hintz has noted, in young adult dystopias trust of the status quo is framed at least in part by adolescents' ability to trust adults. This is "a way of using the transition from adolescence to adulthood to focus on the need for political action and the exercise of political will within a democratic society."[19] This works in the other direction too. That is, young adult dystopia can provide a way to think about adolescence *through* thinking about politics, in addition to providing a way to think about politics *through* thinking about adolescence: in young adult dystopia, "adolescent heroes and heroines must take matters into their own hands" as they learn the adults in authority are not necessarily good or trustworthy,[20] which can serve as a symbol for ceasing the dependence we associate with childhood and assuming the responsibilities of adulthood.

Therefore, we can see Cassel's eventual awareness that he is shaping his own future as growth of agency from childhood to adulthood. Cassel takes on the responsibilities of adulthood by taking "matters into [his] own hands" in a very literal way. In *Red Glove*, the crime boss Zacharov tells Cassel that as a transformation worker, "with these hands . . . you will make the future. Be sure it is a future in which you want to live" (203). Cocalis asserts that such self-shaping forms part of the definition of the *Bildungsroman*: "The artist-hero of a *Bildungsroman* would have to be an earnest young man who finds himself in conscious opposition to existing forms of society or to his particular social class and who therefore embarks on a mission to ameliorate the situation after a period of passive exposure to the world."[21] After Cassel is exposed to his options, he ameliorates his own situation and forges the world he wants to live in by rejecting everyone else's demands on him. As he figures out how he wants to shape his future, he conserves society's expectations for him, which merges with other definitions of *Bildungsroman*.

Conclusion

This trilogy is a classic *Bildungsroman* in which an adolescent takes his rightful place in society and the form of that society is conserved. Yet it's also a progressive tale in which an initially mistrustful character makes friends he respects and they all help each other and celebrate their differences. However, one could also argue that this trilogy is classic *noir* (Cassel plays different corrupt factions off of each other, runs successful sting operations, and solves mysteries, some of which involve a femme fatale, usually while sleep deprived and often while in physical pain). A case could also be made for seeing the behavior of the curse workers in this world as an allegory for racial passing. And as discussed, the trilogy also presents a recognizable dystopian society of the kind that comments on governmental regulations of ability.

As is the case for the *Harry Potter* books, the ability to classify this series in multiple genres is part of what makes it successful. The story is not simply the inevitable course of action brought about by the world in which it takes place; the other elements cannot be ignored. It is not Cassel's role in this trilogy to overthrow the government, thus freeing curse workers from the oppression under which they suffer, but rather to choose among the many bad options that are presented to him. If one assumes that because Holly Black's Curse Workers series presents a government that wants to police specialness, then she must therefore agree with a repudiation of regulation as seen in objectivist dystopia, one would be incorrect. A reader who assumes that the plot will move from this kind of dystopia towards an objectivist utopia will be disappointed, possibly in a way that would not allow a reader to enjoy the trilogy on its own terms.

The shape of the dystopian element, in this case government policing the special, does not necessarily predict the plot of a story that takes place in that dystopia. Perhaps learning to live happily in a right-wing dystopia can even be as progressive as overthrowing a left-wing dystopia. In *The Incredibles*, two characters note (correctly, for that world) that when everybody is special, that means no one is. In the Curse Workers series, however, Cassel learns that judging specialness based on the ability to curse work is foolish—that there are all kinds of abilities and that none of them necessarily correspond to moral worth. As Sargent asks, "Can we make correct choices? This is the question raised by the dystopians."[22] Cassel, while he rejects a life of utopianism as represented by Mrs. Wasserman, eventually conforms to Sargent's idea of a dystopian. As he leaves the stage of wondering whether or not it is possible for him to be a good guy, Cassel muses, "But now I wonder—what if everyone

48 • Emily Lauer

is pretty much the same and it's just a thousand small choices that add up to the person you are? No good or evil, no black and white, no inner demons or angels whispering the right answers in our ears like it's some cosmic SAT test. Just us, hour by hour, minute by minute, day by day, making the best choices we can" (*Black*, 242).

Notes

1 A.O. Scott, "Being Super in Suburbia Is No Picnic," *New York Times*, November 5, 2004, http://www.nytimes.com/2004/11/05/movies/05incr. html.
2 Peter Fitting, "Utopias Beyond Our Ideals: The Dilemma of the Right-Wing Utopia," *Utopian Studies* 2.1 (1991): 98.
3 Wendy McElroy, "Movie Review: *The Incredibles*," *Lew Rockwell*, April 2, 2005, http://www.lewrockwell.com/ mcelroy/mcelroy68.html.
4 Scott, "Being Super."
5 Holly Black, *Black Heart* (New York: Margaret McElderry Books, 2012), 65. Subsequent references will be cited parenthetically in the text.
6 Holly Black, *White Cat* (New York: Margaret McElderry Books, 2010), 16, 35. Subsequent references will be cited parenthetically in the text.
7 Lyman Tower Sargent, "The Three Faces of Utopianism Revisited," *Utopian Studies* 5.1 (1994): 24.
8 Robert E. Lane, "Quality of Life and Quality of Persons: A New Role for Government?," *Political Theory* 22.2 (1994): 231, italics original.
9 Ibid., 220, 224, italics original.
10 Carrie Hintz, "Monica Hughes, Lois Lowry, and Young Adult Dystopias," *The Lion and the Unicorn* 26.2 (2002): 255–256.
11 Holly Black, *Red Glove* (New York: Margaret McElderry Books, 2011), 24. Subsequent references will be cited parenthetically in the text.
12 Sargent, "Three Faces," 4.
13 Hintz, "Monica Hughes," 255.
14 David H. Miles, "The Picaro's Journey to the Confessional: The Changing Image of the Hero in the German *Bildungsroman*," *PMLA* 89.5 (1974): 981.
15 Lane, "Quality," 224.
16 Susan L. Cocalis, "The Transformation of 'Bildung' from an Image to an Ideal," *Monatshefte* 70.4 (1978): 399.
17 Rebecca Carol Noël Totaro, "Suffering in Utopia: Testing the Limits in Young Adult Novels," in *Utopian and Dystopian Writing for Children and Young Adults*, ed. Carrie Hintz and Elaine Ostry (New York: Routledge, 2003), 135.
18 Lane, "Quality," 234.
19 Hintz, "Monica Hughes," 255.

20 Ibid., 260.

21 Cocalis, "Transformation," 408.

22 Sargent, "Three Faces," 26.

Works Cited

Bird, Brad. *The Incredibles.* DVD. Burbank, CA: Disney/Pixar, 2004.

Black, Holly. *Black Heart.* New York: Margaret McElderry Books, 2012.

———. *Red Glove.* New York: Margaret McElderry Books, 2011.

———. *White Cat.* New York: Margaret McElderry Books, 2010.

Cocalis, Susan L. "The Transformation of 'Bildung' from an Image to an Ideal." *Monatshefte* 70.4 (1978): 399–414.

Fitting, Peter. "Utopia Beyond Our Ideals: The Dilemma of the Right-Wing Utopias." *Utopian Studies* 2.1 (1991): 95–109.

Hintz, Carrie. "Monica Hughes, Lois Lowry, and Young Adult Dystopias." *The Lion and the Unicorn* 26.2 (2002): 254–264.

Lane, Robert E. "Quality of Life and Quality of Persons: A New Role for Government?" *Political Theory* 22.2 (1994): 219–252.

McElroy, Wendy. "Movie Review: *The Incredibles.*" Review of *The Incredibles* by Brad Bird. *Lew Rockwell,* April 2, 2005. http://www.lewrockwell.com/ mcelroy/mcelroy68.html.

Miles, David H. "The Picaro's Journey to the Confessional: The Changing Image of the Hero in the German *Bildungsroman.*" *PMLA* 89.5 (1974): 980–992.

Sargent, Lyman Tower. "The Three Faces of Utopianism Revisited." *Utopian Studies* 5.1 (1994): 1–37.

Scott, A.O. "Being Super in Suburbia Is No Picnic." Review of *The Incredibles* by Brad Bird. *New York Times,* November 5, 2004. http://www.nytimes.com/2004/11/05/movies/05incr.html.

Totaro, Rebecca Carol Noël. "Suffering in Utopia: Testing the Limits in Young Adult Novels." In *Utopian and Dystopian Writing for Children and Young Adults,* edited by Carrie Hintz and Elaine Ostry, 127–138. New York: Routledge, 2003.

Chapter Three
Embodying the Postmetropolis in Catherine Fisher's
Incarceron and *Sapphique*

Carissa Turner Smith

"Read Catherine Fisher's *Incarceron*, Become Instant Expert on Foucauldian Philosophy," promises the headline of a book review on *Examiner.com*.[1] Welsh author Catherine Fisher's young adult dystopian fantasy *Incarceron* (published in 2007 in the UK, 2010 in the U.S.) and its sequel *Sapphique* (published in 2008 in the UK, 2010 in the U.S.) have gained popularity not only with teen readers but also with adults eager to draw connections with poststructuralist theory. Kate Quealy-Gainer's review in the *Bulletin of the Center for Children's Books* (2010) hails *Incarceron* as "Foucault meets science fiction,"[2] while even blog reviews include commentary like, "Imagine Foucault wrote a speculative sci-fi fantasy novel. For kids."[3] As these examples suggest, the comparison to Foucault's history of the prison in *Discipline and Punish* (1975) is appealing, even for readers who are not professional academics. Incarceron is, after all, the name of an all-seeing prison, which almost begs the use of panopticism as a theoretical framework. In the novels, Incarceron was originally part of a utopian scheme to restore society after the Years of Rage, an apocalyptic struggle that destroyed the moon and its tides. In this postapocalyptic order, criminals and other undesirables are sent into Incarceron, a sentient prison in an undisclosed location, with no known entry or exit. The Prison itself sees to all its inmates' needs. Meanwhile, the non-incarcerated population, living in the Realm, is kept in order by the restoration of an earlier Era (corresponding to the eighteenth century). Ruled by period "Protocol"—costumes, manners, technology, etc.—the residents of the Realm begin to discover that their situation is not all that different from that of Incarceron's inmates, thus

52 · Carissa Turner Smith

illustrating Foucault's argument about the broader disciplining of society. As he asks, "Is it surprising that prisons resemble factories, schools, barracks, hospitals, which all resemble prisons?"[4]

While the Foucauldian notion of disciplinary societies proves somewhat fruitful as a framework for understanding the Realm in Fisher's work, the wholesale application of panopticism to Incarceron requires more nuance: there are significant differences in the spatial organizations of Incarceron and the panoptic prison. Fisher has said that *Incarceron* was partially inspired by Giovanni Battista Piranesi's *Carceri d'invenzione*, a series of eighteenth-century engravings depicting vast, dark, labyrinthine prisons.[5] In *Discipline and Punish*, Foucault explicitly contrasts the light, open, observable spaces of the panoptic prison with "the ruined prisons, littered with mechanisms of torture, to be seen in Piranese's [sic] engravings."[6] The space of Incarceron differs significantly from this panoptic prison. Most notably, centralization of space is essential to the functioning of the panoptic gaze: one of Jeremy Bentham's dictates was that, in the Panopticon, "the inmate will constantly have before his eyes the tall outline of the central tower from which he is spied upon."[7] Moreover, the Panopticon's "enclosed nature does not preclude a permanent presence from the outside . . . anyone may come and exercise in the central tower the functions of surveillance."[8] In Incarceron, by contrast, space is decentralized, and surveillance accomplished through a series of red eyes in every corridor and wing of the Prison. Though the Prison watches its inmates through these eyes, the only outside observer who has access to the images recorded through the eyes—or, indeed, access to the Prison at all—is the Warden.

Thus, Incarceron shares greater similarity with the centerless, private-surveillance-governed postmetropolis theorized by Edward Soja (who does draw considerably from Foucauldian theories of space and power) and M. Christine Boyer, among others. In *Postmetropolis* (2000), Soja presents six discourses describing the spatiality of postmodern urban life, two of which are particularly significant as a theoretical framework for dystopian YA literature in general and the Incarceron series in particular. First, in the discourse referred to as the "Carceral Archipelago," the postmetropolis is figured as "a collection of *carceral cities*, an archipelago of 'normalized enclosures' and fortified spaces that both voluntarily and involuntarily barricade individuals and communities in visible and not-so-visible urban islands, overseen by restructured forms of public and private power and authority."[9] While the Carceral Archipelago discourse focuses on "overt disciplinary techniques of surveillance, enclosure, incarceration, and policing space," the "Simcities" discourse "explores a different and more subtle form of social and spatial regulation, one that literally and figuratively 'plays with the mind,' manipulating civic consciousness and popular images of cityspace and urban life to maintain order."[10] In other words, the Simcity exerts control by destabilizing the boundary between reality and fantasy—or, the hyper-real. In *CyberCities: Visual Perception in the Age of Electronic Communication* (1997), Boyer further

Embodying the Postmetropolis · 53

explains the insufficiency of Foucauldian panoptic discipline to describe the operations of power-knowledge in the Simcity (or, as she calls it, the Cyber-City): "Gilles Deleuze has recently suggested that Michel Foucault's spaces of enclosure are increasingly strained. Thus the family, the factory, the school, the de-industrialized city, and certainly the process of city planning are in various stages of dissolution, reflective of the disciplinary breakdown that CyberCities entail. So, Deleuze maintains, disciplinary societies that molded behavior are being replaced by numerical societies of modulating control facilitated by computer technology."[11] *Incarceron* and *Sapphique* unite the two discourses of the Simcity and the Carceral Archipelago, tracing their inter-relation. Ultimately, Fisher's work implies that the healing of the fragmented, stratified, and disembodied space of the postmetropolis is achieved through embodied dwelling in historied space.

Fragmented Space: Breaking Down the Utopia/Dystopia Binary

The most notable spatial divide in the Incarceron series is between the Prison (Incarceron) and the Realm, a divide initially constructed as between dystopian space and utopian space. In this, Fisher's books share in the geography of other postmetropolitan works of literature and film, most notably the film *Blade Runner* (1982), in which, according to Boyer, "post-nuclear-holocaust Los Angeles" is "crowded with 'inferior' people abandoned long ago by most of the 'superior' beings, who moved to 'Off-Planet' colonies."[12] The geographical arrangement in *Blade Runner*, however, is more indicative of mid- to late-twentieth-century anxiety about white flight from the inner city—an urban jungle to be abandoned—and the resulting expansion of suburbia. The urban/suburban division relies upon the notion that the city has a center—a feature notably missing from the true *post*metropolis, which, due to both fragmentation and sprawl, is characterized by the instability of boundaries demarcating "inside" and "outside." Another difference between the Incarceron series and the geographies of dystopian works like *Blade Runner* is that, in the latter, we never see the Off-Planet colonies, while in the Incarceron series, both Realm and Prison are depicted. Moreover, in Fisher's novels, those who inhabit the supposedly idyllic Realm are not those who physically depart from the squalor of the lower classes, but rather those who expel the inmates of Incarceron from their midst (one might suggest a parallel to urban gentrification rather than suburban flight here).

In the Incarceron series, the divide between Prison and Realm, between Inside and Outside, is supposedly unbreachable. The Prison was sealed off and hidden, residents of the Realm were told, to prevent contamination of Incarceron's utopian experiment. Most denizens of the Realm truly believe that Incarceron is a utopia, which is one reason that sixteen-year-old Claudia, daughter of the Warden of Incarceron, is desperate to find a way in (the other reason is that her father forbids her from acquiring information about it, and in the tradition of YA

54 • Carissa Turner Smith

heroines, Claudia is drawn to prohibited knowledge). The records of the Realm's Court attest to the original utopian dreams behind Incarceron's creation: *"It was decided from the beginning that the location of Incarceron should be known only to the Warden. All criminals, undesirables, political extremists, degenerates, lunatics would be transported there. The Gate would be sealed and the Experiment commence. It was vital that nothing should disturb the delicate balance of Incarceron's programming, which would provide everything needed—education, balanced diet, exercise, spiritual welfare, and purposeful work—to create a paradise."*[13] Apparently the architects of Incarceron did not trust the Prison to provide everything without some guidance, for a number of Sapienti—highly respected scholars and teachers—also entered the Prison voluntarily, at the same time as the prisoners. The diary of the first prisoner, Lord Calliston (condemned to Incarceron for treason against the Realm), reveals that the early prisoners, too, shared the vision of Incarceron as a utopia: *"Everything was prepared for, every eventuality covered. We have nutritious food, free education, medical care better than Outside, now that the Protocol rules there. We have the discipline of the Prison, that invisible being that watches and punishes and rules"* (*Incarceron*, 311). However, when we meet the Prison's inmates, in the first chapter of the novel, it is apparent that dreams of utopia have long since ceased: life in Incarceron is a daily struggle for survival against competing bands of marauders and against the whims of the Prison itself. The prisoners desire nothing more than escape Outside, to see the stars, and throughout the centuries, they have passed down legends of the one man who escaped the Prison's confines: Sapphique.

The fact that residents of both the Realm and the Prison consider the space "outside" to be a utopia and that each can, from the reader's perspective, be classified as a dystopia is not a unique aspect of the Incarceron series. Many works of YA fiction have suggested the interrelation of utopia and dystopia, as noted by Jack Zipes: in YA fiction, "the pursuit of perfection, the perfect place and society, can also lead to rigid if not totalitarian societies."[14] When Sapphique appears in a vision and tells a character that, in essence, everywhere is a prison—"Whether it's Inside or Out, I've learned, is not really important. I fear they both may be the same"[15]—the reader feels little surprise. What is exceptional about the Incarceron series is the fact that *both* utopia and dystopia, Prison and Realm, are spaces that depend upon alienating their inhabitants from their physical surroundings and from their own bodies. In this, Fisher's work participates directly in Soja's discourses of the postmetropolis, connecting the Carceral Archipelago and the Simcity discourses.

Incarceron as Carceral City

When we first meet Finn, the male protagonist of *Incarceron*, he is a member of a band of thieves controlling one wing of the vast Prison. The band, known as the Comitatus (a term recalling small-scale medieval feudalism), under

Embodying the Postmetropolis · 55

their Winglord Jormanric, defend their territory and lead raids against rival groups within the Prison. The splitting of the inmates into competing factions is in fact one of the first signs of discord mentioned in Lord Calliston's diary:

> *Dissident groups are forming; territory is disputed. Marriages and feuds develop. Already two Sapienti have led their followers away to live in isolation, claiming they fear the murderers and thieves will never change, that a man has been killed, a child attacked. Last week two men came to blows over a woman. The Prison intervened. Since then neither of them has been seen.*
>
> *I believe they are dead and that Incarceron has integrated them into its systems. There was no provision for the death penalty, but the Prison is in charge now. It is thinking for itself* (Incarceron, 311, italics original).

With the division of the population into armed splinter groups, and with no central system of governance other than the Prison itself, Incarceron adopts increasingly totalitarian measures to control its population. As the inhabitants respond fearfully to the instability of their environment, the spatial ordering of Incarceron begins to resemble Soja's Carceral Archipelago. Soja describes the Carceral Archipelago as an "*ecology of fear* . . . filled with many different kinds of protected and fortified spaces, islands of enclosure and anticipated protection against the real and imagined dangers of daily life."[16] In the real-world postmetropolis, the carceral trend includes phenomena as diverse as well-to-do gated communities, middle-class HOAs, and the containment of Skid Row: the uniting factor is a decentralized geography, coupled with a zeit-geist of fear.

While there are small cities and towns within Incarceron—all of them possessing gates and guards—there is no capital city within the Prison. As Finn and his companions travel through Incarceron, seeking the way Out, they have little sense of physical destination.[17] Each area of the Prison is truly a world unto itself, possessing no reputation outside its own walls. It is merely an area to be passed through—and, hopefully, survived. The Prison heightens this sense of isolation and instability by constantly changing its own geography, moving tunnels and bridges to new locations, suggesting something of the impermanence of a shan-tytown or favela. The one constant within Incarceron's landscape is the presence of the red eyes through which the Prison observes all that happens within its confines. Finn and his companions discover that the images recorded through these eyes are kept in books, and that each prisoner has an entry with a series of video images chronicling his or her life under the gaze—an unsettling revelation, to be sure, but one with obvious parallels to CCTV methods of security surveillance (another feature of the Carceral Archipelago). The video surveillance gaze has some similarities with the panoptic gaze but also possesses an aura unique to postmetropolitan life. Boyer explains that, as "American society shifts away from the panopticon surveillance of bodies (that is, based on spatial organization) and becomes more reliant on the diffused observation techniques

56 · Carissa Turner Smith

provided by video monitoring, this sort of shorthand identification becomes handy for controlling the population: 'The more modest task of the monitor [is] to provide partial coverage of dangerous spaces, not to pretend to make surveillance perfect, but only to ensure that in protected zones defensive actions might be taken in response to invasions.'"[18] Similarly, though Incarceron theoretically is all-seeing, in practice its gaze seems to be restricted to certain areas. The Prison uses its eyes to respond to developing situations, launching Prisonquakes when it sees a behavior contrary to its own interests and goals—but in certain wings "the Prison rarely bothered itself to stir" (*Incarceron*, 28). This suggests the spatial stratification of postmetropolitan surveillance, with priority given to either extremely wealthy or extremely impoverished zones.[19]

The Prison would, of course, be a more perfect parallel to the privatized surveillance of the carceral postmetropolis if the individual Winglords, rather than the Prison itself, monitored the eyes. Even so, Incarceron's geography reflects many anxieties about urban space in the twenty-first century. The Realm's attempt to isolate itself from the threat of "undesirables" echoes the existence of hidden and deliberately forgotten spaces within the postmetropolis. Iain Chambers writes convincingly of the transformation of urban space "into aestheticized cityscapes (in architecture and art galleries, cultural and heritage centres, loft living and designer homes), while their previous populations, if they have no role to play in this act, are inserted into other discourses: ethnic communities, urban poverty, inner-city decay, industrial decline, drugs, organized crime."[20] Drawing from Chambers, Soja further opines that those "who have no role to play in the new metropolis are made virtually invisible."[21] In the Incarceron series, the Prison's inmates are so literally invisible to those in the Realm that they can be detected only with a powerful microscope. Shrunk to an infinitesimal size, the millions of prisoners within Incarceron are contained in a tiny silver ornament worn on the Warden's watch. Only very advanced technology could allow entry or egress from Incarceron—technology lacking to Incarceron's inmates, and forbidden to the Protocol-following inhabitants of the Realm. Technology has the power to unite the postmetropolitan landscape, but, in practice, enhances its divisions.

The Realm as Simcity

Meanwhile, the Realm, the "Outside" so desirable to Incarceron's inmates, seems like a stifling prison to those who dwell there. King Endor's Decree, the document that led to the establishment of the Realm and that appears in epigraphs at the beginnings of chapters in *Incarceron* and *Sapphique*, reveals that the primary means of population control in the Realm is the regulation of time, rather than space. In contrast to Incarceron, where time is unmonitored (another point of difference from the Foucauldian prison), the Realm depends upon the regulation of time.[22] The suppression of time is meant to create a utopia, according to King Endor: "*We will choose an Era from the past and re-create it. We will make a world free from the anxiety of change! It will be Paradise!"* (*Incarceron*, 15, italics original). Unsurprisingly, it is not. Even King Endor's Decree recognizes that there is a price to be paid for the apparent security of historylessness. First appealing to nostalgia, he ends by arguing that historical re-enactment is the only option for maintaining societal order: *"We must find a simpler way of life. We must retreat into the past, everyone and everything, in its place, in order. Freedom is a small price to pay for survival"* (*Incarceron*, 97, italics original). In contrast to the constantly shifting landscape of Incarceron, in the Realm, *"Time is forbidden. From now on nothing will change"* (*Incarceron*, 171, italics original). The Warden evaluates Claudia's household management based on whether it is true to Era or not. Even apparently insignificant details like period dress are revealed to be part of the elaborate discipline of this faux-eighteenth-century society.[23] Claudia, while trading her silk dress and petticoats for a non-Era jumpsuit, reflects, "Clothes changed you. Long ago, King Endor had known that. That was why he had stopped Time, imprisoned everyone in doublets and dresses, stifled them in conformity and stiffness" (*Incarceron*, 73). To Claudia, the Realm's Protocol is a prison—and a prison of the Foucauldian sort, in which the disciplines of corsets, crumpets, and curtsies operate to render "'docile' bodies."[24] (It is perhaps no coincidence that the Realm chooses to emulate the eighteenth century—the era when, according to Foucault, disciplinary regulation was perfected.) In this stratified society, however, the rich have the option of partial escape through technology—which is forbidden, but available anyway to those with means. Skinwands are liberally applied to erase the wrinkles of the women at Court. The Sapienti are allowed certain lenience with regard to Era norms, and they possess sophisticated computers at their Academy. For the rest of the Realm, however, this technology is inaccessible. As a member of a secret revolutionary society complains, "We are chained hand and foot by Protocol, enslaved to a static, empty world where men and women can't read, where the scientific advances of the ages are the preserve of the rich, where artists and poets are doomed to endless repetitions and sterile reworkings of past masterpieces. Nothing is new. New does not exist" (*Incarceron*, 243). Nor, in fact, does "old."

Aside from skinwands (tools erasing from the body evidence of history), one of the more common uses of non-Era technology seems to be for surveillance purposes—though, in the Realm, surveillance is accomplished through listening devices, as opposed to the video-camera-like eyes of Incarceron. In one particularly illustrative scene, Lord Evian and Claudia are near a pond, discussing a potential revolution, when suddenly Lord Evian notices a duck waddling towards him, flaps his arms, and chases it away. In explanation of his behavior, he reflects, "We never know where the listeners are . . . That is what the Havaarna [the monarchic dynasty to which King Endor belonged] have done to us, Claudia. They have riddled us with fear" (*Incarceron*, 163). Though Lord Evian does not say so, the fear prevalent in the Realm is not only the anxiety that, at any given moment, someone may be eavesdropping

58 · Carissa Turner Smith

on your conversation, but also the uncertainty about whether a duck is, in fact, a duck. No one is entirely sure what is real and what is virtual within the Realm. Weather is entirely manufactured: storms are scheduled for times when the members of the Court are not out hunting. In a key moment in *Sapphique*, Claudia begins to question the appearances around her more than she had dared to do previously: "She had no idea how much of this landscape was real—certainly some of the birds, and the hosts of butterflies . . . surely they were real. In truth, if they weren't, she didn't want to know. Why not accept the illusion, just for one day?" (188). Her tutor Jared, a Sapient, then warns her about the beguiling power of illusion, saying, "As a society we have lost the ability to tell the real from the fake. Most of the Court, at least, don't even care which is which. It concerns the Sapienti greatly" (188). The Realm, in other words, suffers from the cognitive dissonance produced by virtual reality.

However, while the Incarceron series addresses the postmodern concern of indistinguishable reality and illusion, it does not go as far as many postmodern theorists (Baudrillard, most notably) in suggesting that the simulacrum is the only reality.[25] In the Incarceron series, in fact, the true decay of the Realm is finally revealed. As Incarceron draws to itself all the strength necessary for an attempt to escape itself, it drains electrical power from the Realm, causing flashes of insight into the state of things behind the sumptuous façade: "The blue vase was cracked. Its marble pedestal was painted wood. The walls were a mess of wires and faded paint. Great damp patches soaked the ceiling; in one corner the plaster had fallen and drips cascaded in" (*Sapphique*, 248). When Finn first beholds one of these flashes, he thinks he is "back in the gray world of Incarceron" (*Sapphique*, 252). The Realm's virtual manipulation of reality is one of the tools it uses to deceive its subjects into believing that their world is utterly different from that of the Prison. Technology, though forbidden in the Realm, is actually the force upon which it is built. As Howard Rheingold suggests in *The Virtual Community* (1993), even the supposed democracy of virtual technology tends to be used to promote "disinformocracy": "While a few people [the Sapienti, in the Incarceron series] will get better information via high-bandwidth supernetworks, the majority of the population, if history is any guide, are likely to become more precisely befuddled, more exactly manipulated. Hyper-reality is what you get when a Panopticon evolves to the point where it can convince everyone that it doesn't exist; people continue to believe they are free, although their power has disappeared."[26] Incarceron unintentionally brings enlightenment to the Realm's subjects, ripping away the veil of technology and showing them the true nature of their world.

Embodying the Postmetropolis

Many theorists of the Simcity have explicitly connected virtual reality's disembodied experience to the "territorial unmooring of cityspace."[27] Boyer

Embodying the Postmetropolis • 59

explains, "In the bodily disenchantment that haunts our postmodern era, if the self is unstable, dephysicalized, and thus beginning to disappear, making projections from it ambiguous and unclear, then the image of the city as a normally functioning or healthy body also begins to be undermined."[28] Along similar lines, Celeste Olalquiaga uses the term psychasthenia to refer to the "state in which the space defined by the coordinates of the organism's own body is confused with represented [virtual, as opposed to physical] space."[29] According to Olalquiaga, "bodies are becoming like cities," because both are defined by "the topography of computer screens and video monitors."[30] Olalquiaga here links the virtual reality of the Simcity to the surveillance of the Carceral Archipelago, suggesting that each shares a common problem rooted in disembodiment.

Given that the Incarceron series addresses postmetropolitan anxieties, it is fitting that the solution to the problems of both Realm and Prison comes through embodiment. Jared, Claudia's tutor, suffers from a mysterious, lingering illness that will kill him within a few years—an illness for which there might have been a cure if the Realm had not restricted itself to the medical practices of the eighteenth century. For Jared, the body is a prison, and parallels between him and Incarceron are established early in the series. In one scene in *Incarceron*, the Prison speaks of its own corruption, brought about by the inescapable reality of human evil: *"There is no system that can stop that, no place that can wall out evil, because men bring it in with them, even in the children. Such men are beyond correction, and it is my task only to contain them. I hold them inside myself. I swallow them whole"* (260–261, italics original). Within a few pages, Jared refers to his body's illness in similar language: as he prepares to give himself his pain medicine, he reflects that "the pain that lived deep in his body seemed still to grow slowly, like a living thing; he sometimes thought that it devoured the drug, that he was feeding its appetite" (267). Like Jared, the Prison wants to escape itself, a desire that first occurred to it when Sapphique wore a magic glove that led him and the Prison to share "one mind" for the time he wore it. His desire to escape "infected" the Prison—as Jared tells Claudia, "desire can be a disease," infectious and all-consuming (*Sapphique*, 140). Yet the analogy of body and prison is not as simple as it seems, for Incarceron decides that, to escape itself, it must build a body, a body that will pass through the portal into the Realm. Using the Warden—now trapped inside—and other prisoners to do its bidding, Incarceron begins to assemble a body, using a statue of Sapphique as a base, and adding feathers, reminiscent of an Icarus-like tale told about Sapphique. In the book's climax, Jared dons the glove, which somehow renders him one with the statue, making it come to life. Voluntarily trapping himself within the Prison and the Prison's "body," he finds freedom not only for himself but also for the people within both the Realm and Incarceron.

Though how exactly Jared's crucial act functions remains something of a mystery within the novel, it seems to reverse the postmetropolitan

60 · Carissa Turner Smith

phenomenon of disembodiment. Within the Realm, Jared has been aware of his body in a way that other subjects have not, feeling his illness as "a tiny flaw in the Realm's perfection, a crack that could not be patched up or disguised" (*Sapphique*, 409–410). Because his pain constantly reminds him of his embodied condition, of the fact that time still exists and will, indeed, bring about his death, he remains particularly aware of the deceptive appearance of the Realm and is not as dismayed as the others when its true decay begins to be revealed: "Now everything was as marred as he was" (*Sapphique*, 410). Without their virtual façade, the residents of the Realm will have to find new ways of living in their bodies and their physical environment. Jared's act also reforms the disembodied gaze of surveillance in the Prison. In bringing embodied compassion to Incarceron, he renders its gaze a loving one, rather than a monitoring one. After Jared becomes Incarceron's body, Finn, left behind observing the goings-on via the monitors in the Warden's room, realizes that he is now watching events unfold through a particular set of eyes. Seeing Claudia through the monitors, Finn comprehends that he is "looking at her through someone else's eyes, eyes that were very slightly blurred, as if the Prison's gaze had tears in it" (*Sapphique*, 453). The Prison now not only sees, but can be seen. Speaking to Incarceron/Jared, the Warden says, "So, my old friend, you have found yourself a body after all . . . But you haven't Escaped." Jared/Incarceron replies, "*Ah, but I have. I've Escaped myself, but I won't be leaving. That is the paradox that is Sapphique*" (*Sapphique*, 455, italics original). In this paradox, the Incarceron series addresses the desire for escape that characterizes both the fortified spaces of the Carceral Archipelago and the hyper-reality of the Simcity, revealing this desire as misguided. "Escape," Sapphique tells Jared in a vision, "is not enough; it does not answer the questions. It is not Freedom" (*Sapphique*, 305).

In rewriting escape, Jared's act undoes the spatial divisions between Realm and Prison and, by extension, shows the potential for altering the spatial politics that characterize postmetropolitan life. Jared/Incarceron declares, "Now we're all together. Inside and Outside. . . . No one will need to Escape; I promise you that. But the door will be open, for those who wish to come and go." Jared/Incarceron then makes a door, easing the difficulty of traveling between Prison and Realm. Jared/Incarceron declares his intention to make the Prison a paradise, "just as it was supposed to be," and the book suggests that this time success may be possible, for the Prison now has a human heart and a body (*Sapphique*, 455). For those in the Realm, life will continue without illusion and without Protocol, but with hard work. Apparently, some hierarchy will remain—Claudia and Finn will serve as King and Queen, though the necessity of the monarchy and of their apparently loveless marriage remains unexplained—but the rigid class stratifications of the Era will end. Keiro and Attia, two of Finn's fellow former prisoners who have joined him in the Realm, offer hope for survival without the false comforts that have held up the Realm for 150 years. They also point to those in the Realm who already know

Embodying the Postmetropolis · **61**

how to survive without virtual reality, the former serfs of the Realm. Claudia, looking out across the ruined landscape, sees "the candlepoints of flame in the cottages of the poor, the hovels where the Prison's wrath and fury had brought no change" (*Sapphique*, 462). In the last lines of the novel, Finn says of these former serfs, "Those are the stars too" (*Sapphique*, 462). In both the Prison and the Realm, then, the power that overcomes the spatial divisions is the embrace of embodied living, bodies that suffer and age, but bodies that can cross through space and rebuild ruined worlds.

If, as with much dystopian YA fiction, *Incarceron* and *Sapphique* are meant to provide young readers with some guidance and inspiration for how to live rightly in the world, then what is this particular series' contribution? Unlike many other YA works, the Incarceron series does not really suggest individual solutions—read more books, or else this scary future will happen!—to social maladies. Fisher does, however, imply the value of physical suffering (disease, aging, hard work, etc.) as validation of the body's real existence in time and space. Indeed, one could read the Incarceron series as promoting a revised view of Foucauldian disciplines. For Foucault, the disciplines (the methods "which made possible the meticulous control of the operations of the body, which assured the constant subjection of its forces and imposed upon them a relation of docility-utility"[31]) possess a negative (if not explicitly condemned) connotation. However, Charles Taylor and others have suggested that this aspect of Foucault is merely an extension of the modern desire for the unconstrained "freedom and power of the self."[32] As we have seen, Fisher is more inclined to present the self, rather than society, as the prison from which we need to be freed. The Incarceron series posits "Sapphique"—the paradox of escape from the self, without disengagement from one's surroundings—as the solution to not only the divisions of the postmetropolis, but also to the constraining self. While some disciplines, like those of the Realm, exist to erase history and thus trap the self within itself, other disciplines, like that of work, can be a force freeing us from the self. There is no escape from the power of discipline, but it can be directed towards the end of creating, rather than repressing, history.

While teen readers of the Incarceron series are unlikely to have read Foucault, they are likely to have wrestled with the desire for freedom, and some of them may be discovering that the tyranny they want to escape is that of the self. In response to postmetropolitan fears, a wholly negative, Foucauldian reading of discipline proves insufficient. The Incarceron series addresses the escapism offered by the walled-off islands of the postmetropolis or the disembodiment of virtual reality, but promotes an acceptance of messy, imperfect, embodied communal life. Then, too, the series suggests that, even if embodied living eases some of the anxiety caused by the virtual reality of the Simcity, some questions about reality remain unanswered. Claudia, at the end of *Sapphique*, still wants to know whether Finn really is Prince Giles, the disappeared heir to the Realm's throne. "Does it matter?" the Warden asks her (*Sapphique*,

62 • Carissa Turner Smith

458). "Yes!" shouts the chorus of frustrated readers, both teen and adult. This frustration, however, educates readers about acceptance of the ambiguities of life lived in any era. Similarly, readers may be frustrated with the series' lack of resolution on the question of whether Sapphique truly existed. We are left only with Jared's reflections after Sapphique appears to him in what may be a vision, dream, or hallucination: "As he urged the horse to a gallop, he thought about the power of vision; whether Sapphique had been an aspect of his own mind, or a real being. None of it was that simple. There were whole shelves of texts back in the Library discussing the powers of the visionary imagination, of memory and dreams ... For him it had happened. That was what mattered" (*Sapphique*, 332). While in some ways Jared's conclusion threatens to reinscribe the self as the arbiter of reality, Fisher is more focused on how Jared's acceptance of ambiguity inspires embodied action. The very next sentence in *Sapphique* reads, "He rode hard. By midday he was in the lands of the Wardenry, tired, but surprising himself by his endurance. At a farm he climbed down a little stiffly and was given milk and cheese by the farmer" (332). Jared's vision does not divorce him from physical reality, but rather spurs him on to embodied action in the world. His body bears signs of stiffness and tiredness, it receives the nourishment of food, and it moves through space towards a goal. His body experiences both time and space, and Fisher implies that this has the power to transcend social stratification as well, linking Sapient and farmer.

The Incarceron series suggests that both bodies and cities should show their age, the record of their involvement in time and space. As mentioned previously, Catherine Fisher has stated that Piranesi's *Carceri d'invenzione* engravings were part of the inspiration for *Incarceron*. However, Piranesi is also famous for his etchings of Rome, a fact mentioned by Boyer in *Cyber-Cities*. Boyer draws from Barbara Stafford's argument that Piranesi's depictions of the city deliberately employ "the physiognomic method of anatomical drawings."[33] Piranesi "allowed the decaying bodies of his ruins to remain suffering surfaces, aging with dirt;"[34] according to Stafford, he "thus helped his contemporaries to recontextualize the ruins of the past into the living organism of modern urban Rome."[35] The implication for both the fictional world of the Incarceron series and the inhabitants of postmetropolitan reality is that both the body and the city should show evidence of their particular histories. The history-bearing body and city cannot be easily divided into utopian and dystopian spaces, for they are transformed into *place*—storied space. As a reading of the Incarceron series through the framework of the postmetropolis suggests, Fisher's novels reflect the social anxieties caused by stratified, yet unstable geographies, including the geography of the body. While Fisher points to no easy solutions, the Incarceron series suggests that recontextualizing the ruins of the past—in other words, allowing city-places and body-places to tell stories—plays a significant role in remedying the ills of the Carceral Archipelago and the Simcity.

Notes

1   Tracy Bealer, "Read Catherine Fisher's *Incarceron*, Become Instant Expert on Foucauldian Philosophy," *Examiner.com*, July 8, 2010, http://www.examiner.com/speculative-fiction-in-raleigh/read-catherine-fisher-s-incarceron-become-instant-expert-on-foucauldian-philosophy.

2   Kate Quealy-Gainer, review of *Incarceron*, *Bulletin of the Center for Children's Books* 63.6 (2010): 245.

3   "*Incarceron* (and *Sapphique*) by Catherine Fisher," *Gob Wrote a Book*, March 3, 2010, http://gobwroteabook.blogspot.com/2010/03/incarceron-and-sapphique-by-catherine.html.

4   Michel Foucault, *Discipline and Punish: The Birth of the Prison*, trans. Alan Sheridan (New York: Pantheon Books, 1977), 228.

5   E.I. Johnson, "Interview: Catherine Fisher—*New York Times* Bestseller and Award-Winning Welsh Children's Fantasy Author of *Incarceron*," *Up Close & Personal*, May 5, 2010, www.fictionforyoungadults.blogspot.com/2010/03/upcoming-interview-catherine-fisher-new.html.

6   Foucault, *Discipline and Punish*, 205.

7   Ibid., 201.

8   Ibid., 207.

9   Edward W. Soja, *Postmetropolis: Critical Studies of Cities and Regions* (Malden, MA, and Oxford: Blackwell, 2000), 299, italics original. While Foucault does mention carceral cities and even "the carceral archipelago" in *Discipline and Punish*, his use of this phrase is very different from the direction in which Soja takes it. See Foucault, *Discipline and Punish*, 296–308.

10 Soja, *Postmetropolis*, 324.

11 M. Christine Boyer, *CyberCities: Visual Perception in the Age of Electronic Communication* (New York: Princeton Architectural Press, 1997), 18.

12 Ibid., 110.

13 Catherine Fisher, *Incarceron* (New York: Dial Books, 2010), 68, italics original. Subsequent references will be cited parenthetically in the text.

14 Jack Zipes, "Foreword: Utopia, Dystopia, and the Quest for Hope," in *Utopian and Dystopian Writing for Children and Young Adults*, ed. Carrie Hintz and Elaine Ostry (New York and London: Routledge, 2003), xi.

15 Catherine Fisher, *Sapphique* (New York: Dial Books, 2010), 303. Subsequent references will be cited parenthetically in the text.

16 Soja, *Postmetropolis*, 299, italics original.

17 This could also share in some features of the Simcity discourse, as it bears some resemblance to non-linear, hyperlink-driven "travel" on the web. Boyer describes movement in the CyberCity thus: "The relays of references, the inversion of orders of precedence, the endless lists of texts all present the chaotic effects of randomness and indeterminacy, generating neither options nor choices. Being constantly on the move in order to escape the repressive machines of disciplinary societies or to fully exploit

64 · Carissa Turner Smith

the uncertain voyages of complexities in societies of control offers us no foundation on which to stand, to criticize, to remember the past, or to plan the future." Boyer, *CyberCities*, 31.

18 Boyer, *CyberCities*, 125–126, quoting Thomas L. Dunn, "The New Enclosures," in *Reading Rodney King/Reading Urban Uprising*, ed. Robert Gooding-Williams (New York: Routledge, 1993), 186.

19 Even when the Prison is watching, its intermittent inaction frustrates the prisoners. Finn, who is more aware of the Prison's gaze than most, becomes irate when he realizes that Incarceron will *not* intervene to prevent a dangerous situation: "In that moment, through all its stairs and galleries and thousands of labyrinthine chambers he knew that Incarceron had sensed his peril ... that the Prison watched him and would not interfere." Fisher, *Incarceron*, 8.

20 Iain Chambers, *Border Dialogues: Journeys in Postmodernity* (London and New York: Routledge, 1990), 53.

21 Soja, *Postmetropolis*, 151.

22 Fisher leaves unreconciled the conflict between the Realm's belief that Incarceron was founded a mere 150 years ago and the prisoners' belief that it began centuries ago. If time does pass differently in the two worlds, it does not cause any disjuncture when characters travel in-between. Another possibility is that time is perceived differently in each world.

23 In this connection of detailed discipline to power, *Incarceron* most strongly echoes Foucault: "A meticulous observation of detail, and at the same time a political awareness of these small things, for the control and use of men, emerge through the classical age bearing with them a whole set of techniques, a whole corpus of methods and knowledge, descriptions, plans and data. And from such trifles, no doubt, the man of modern humanism was born." Foucault, *Discipline and Punish*, 141.

24 Ibid., 138.

25 Jean Baudrillard, *Simulacra and Simulation*, trans. Sheila Faria Glaser (Ann Arbor: University of Michigan Press, 1994).

26 Howard Rheingold, *The Virtual Community: Homesteading on the Electronic Frontier* (Reading, MA: Addison-Wesley, 1993), 297.

27 Soja, *Postmetropolis*, 150.

28 Boyer, *CyberCities*, 80.

29 Celeste Olalquiaga, *Megalopolis: Contemporary Cultural Sensibilities* (Minneapolis: University of Minnesota Press, 1992), 1–2.

30 Ibid., 17. Also qtd. in Soja, *Postmetropolis*, 151.

31 Foucault, *Discipline and Punish*, 137.

32 Charles Taylor, *Sources of the Self: The Making of the Modern Identity* (Cambridge, MA: Harvard University Press, 1989), 488.

33 Boyer, *CyberCities*, 93.

34 Ibid.

35 Barbara Stafford, *Body Criticism: Imaging the Unseen in Enlightenment Art and Medicine* (Boston: MIT Press, 1991), 70. Also qtd. in Boyer, *CyberCities*, 94.

Works Cited

Baudrillard, Jean. *Simulacra and Simulation*. Translated by Sheila Faria Glaser. Ann Arbor: University of Michigan Press, 1995.

Bealer, Tracy. "Read Catherine Fisher's *Incarceron*, Become Instant Expert on Foucauldian Philosophy." *Examiner.com*, July 8, 2010. http://www.examiner.com/speculative-fiction-in-raleigh/read-catherine-fisher-s-incarceron-become-instant-expert-on-foucauldian-philosophy.

Boyer, M. Christine. *CyberCities: Visual Perception in the Age of Electronic Communication*. New York: Princeton Architectural Press, 1996.

Chambers, Iain. *Border Dialogues: Journeys in Postmodernity*. London and New York: Routledge, 1990.

Fisher, Catherine. *Incarceron*. New York: Dial Books, 2010.

———. *Sapphique*. London: Hodder Children's Books, 2008.

Foucault, Michel. *Discipline and Punish: The Birth of the Prison*. Translated by Alan Sheridan. New York: Pantheon Books, 1977.

"*Incarceron* (and *Sapphique*) by Catherine Fisher." *Gob Wrote a Book*, March 3, 2010. http://gobwroteabook.blogspot.com/2010/03/incarceron-and-sapphique-by-catherine.html.

Johnson, E.I. "Interview: Catherine Fisher—*New York Times* Bestseller and Award-Winning Welsh Children's Fantasy Author of *Incarceron*." *Totally YA*, May 5, 2010. www.fictionforyoungadults.blogspot.com/2010/03/upcoming-interview-catherine-fisher-new.html.

Olalquiaga, Celeste. *Megalopolis*. Minneapolis: University of Minnesota Press, 1992.

Quealy-Gainer, Kate. Review of *Incarceron*. *Bulletin of the Center for Children's Books* 63.6 (2010): 245.

Rheingold, Howard. *The Virtual Community: Homesteading on the Electronic Frontier*. Reading, MA: Addison-Wesley, 1993.

Soja, Edward. *Postmetropolis: Critical Studies of Cities and Regions*. Malden, MA and Oxford: Blackwell, 2000.

Stafford, Barbara. *Body Criticism: Imaging the Unseen in Enlightenment Art and Medicine*. Boston: MIT Press, 1991.

Taylor, Charles. *Sources of the Self: The Making of the Modern Identity*. Cambridge, MA: Harvard University Press, 1989.

Zipes, Jack. "Foreword: Utopia, Dystopia, and the Quest for Hope." In *Utopian and Dystopian Writing for Children and Young Adults*, edited by Carrie Hintz and Elaine Ostry, ix–xi. New York and London: Routledge, 2003.

Part Two

Society and Environment

Building a Better World

Chapter Four
Hope in Dark Times
Climate Change and the World Risk Society in Saci Lloyd's *The Carbon Diaries 2015* and *2017*

Alexa Weik Von Mossner

We live in troubled times. According to the United Nations, climate change is among the most serious and far-reaching threats to human life on earth. The UN Global Issues website states: "By the middle of the 20th century, it was becoming clear that . . . the process of 'global warming' was accelerating. Today, nearly all scientists agree that we must stop and reverse this process now—or face a devastating cascade of natural disasters that will change life on earth as we know it."[1] Scientists have also sent out dire warnings. NASA climatologist James Hansen writes in *Storms of My Grandchildren* (2009) that we now have clear evidence that "the continued exploitation of all fossil fuels on Earth threatens not only the other millions of species on the planet but also the survival of humanity itself—and the timetable is shorter than we thought."[2] In his 2011 *Eaarth: Making Life on a Tough New Planet*, the internationally renowned environmentalist Bill McKibben even claims that we should give our planet a new name (*Eaarth*), because the life-friendly habitat we used to call "earth" is already on its way to becoming an inhospitable place, "with melting poles and dying forests and a heaving, corrosive sea, raked by winds, strafed by storms, scorched by heat."[3]

It is little wonder that these dark prospects have made their way into the pages of young adult dystopian fiction. Saci Lloyd's *The Carbon Diaries 2015* (2008) and its sequel *The Carbon Diaries 2017* (2009) take us into a near-future London and, as Vanessa Thorpe puts it, "into a frightening era where climate change is busily altering all the norms of modern existence."[4] Through the eyes of sixteen-year-old Laura Brown, they give us a glimpse of what might be in store for us in what German sociologist Ulrich Beck has called the *world risk society*: a transnational, global community that is connected by shared ecological and economic risks and in which one cannot help but be affected by potential or actual devastation that happens elsewhere. For Beck, the knowledge and anticipation of such repercussions and their potentially catastrophic effects marks "the end of the other" because they collapse the distance between those who are victims and those who are privileged and safe.[5] Lloyd shows us what such collapse could look like in the heart of England, in a near future that, at least at the outset, seems a direct extension of our present everyday lives. This dystopian scenario is eerily related to what we hear today from climatologists, sociologists, and political scientists concerned with the possible future effects of climate change and resource depletion.

However, despite their gloomy atmosphere and their serious engagement with pressing social and ecological concerns, *The Carbon Diaries* never become too depressing or overbearing. Cleverly mixing the dystopian with the utopian, they leave a space for hope that makes them bearable and indeed enjoyable for young readers. The German philosopher Ernst Bloch saw the "principle of hope" at the heart of the utopian endeavor, which he located not only in literary texts but also in political practice and common daydreaming.[6] And while Ruth Levitas has argued in *The Concept of Utopia* (1990) that "the essential element in utopia is not hope, but desire . . . for a better way of being,"[7] scholars and writers tend to agree that in the case of the young adult dystopian text, one cannot in fact do *without* at least a glimmer of hope. The young reader expects—and needs—stories that are gripping but nevertheless offer at least a promise that a better world will be possible. *The Carbon Diaries 2015* and *2017* both offer such promises. Lloyd's future world is dark and often existentially threatening, and much of what teenagers in the industrialized West may take for granted today is irretrievably lost. However, there are trade-offs for these losses. Losing our habitual lifestyle may be painful, Lloyd suggests, but it may also lead to new solidarities, new value systems, and new modes of agency, all propelled by the hope that a different and in some regards ecotopian society will be possible.

In using ecological catastrophe to motivate personal, political, and ecological change, *The Carbon Diaries* qualify as *critical eco-dystopias*. As Raffaella Baccolini explains, critical dystopias are marked by "an opening for utopian elements in . . . dystopian science fiction,"[8] and this blending of the two related genres, combined with a critical focus and seriousness of intent, can have strong effects on readers' understanding of their current life worlds. As Jane Donawerth argues with reference to the work of Tom Moylan, critical dystopian texts articulate a specific political agency not only on the level of the narrative but also in terms of the reader's relationship to the world, because they open up a possibility for what Moylan has termed "radical hope."[9] Lloyd's Laura Brown learns to transform her anger into something productive, as she begins to understand that life in the world risk society can only get better if

Hope in Dark Times • 71

she and others around the world take the challenges seriously without falling into despair. Social and ecological change, her "carbon diaries" demonstrate, depends upon personal engagement and hard work, and bringing about a better world is a political process driven by hope and desire—a process that never really ends. The transformative potential of these novels makes them successful examples of critical eco-dystopian texts, as they warn young adult readers about the future while mobilizing them into action.

Ecological Crisis and the Hopeful Dystopian Young Adult Novel: A Contradiction?

In their introduction to *Utopian and Dystopian Writing for Children and Young Adults* (2003), Carrie Hintz and Elaine Ostry state that "a startling number of works in the dystopian mode for young adults deal with post-disaster and environmentally challenged scenarios."[10] They anticipate that this genre will become increasingly popular because it offers a productive place to address the fears and questions that interest young adult readers. Hintz and Ostry name novels like Adrien Stoutenburg's *Out There* (1971), Robert C. O'Brien's *Z for Zachariah* (1975), and Robert Swindell's *Brother in the Land* (1984) as typical examples of eco-dystopian young adult fiction. To these we could add a host of more recent North American publications such as Susan Beth Pfeffer's Last Survivors series (2008–2010), Jacob Sackin's *Islands* (2008), Suzanne Weyn's *Empty* (2009), Paolo Bacigalupi's *Ship Breaker* (2010), and Cameron Stracher's *The Water Wars* (2011). Recent publications in the UK, including Lloyd's novels but also Kate Thompson's *The White Horse Trick* (2010) and Julie Bertagna's Exodus trilogy (2002–2011), further underline that Hintz and Ostry's prediction was correct: environmental and ecological topics are becoming increasingly popular in dystopian young adult fiction, and their treatment more critical, complex, and provocative.

Bleak as the future scenarios portrayed in these novels are—dealing with critical issues such as climate change, resource depletion, and species extinction—none of them ever leaves its young readers without hope at the end of the story. This preserving of a glimmer of hope even in the darkest future scenario is in fact prevalent in most dystopian texts—even in those written for an adult audience—but, as I mentioned earlier, it is much more pronounced in young adult fiction. Jack Zipes even argues that it is one of its central features. Young readers, he writes, "need utopian and dystopian literature" because it can "provide hope for a different and more humane world."[11] To many writers of young adult novels, failing to provide that hope would be deeply unethical. Monica Hughes, author of the Isis trilogy (1980–1983), reminds us of the dictum that "you may lead a child into the darkness, but you must never turn out the light," and argues that even the most dystopian young adult text must retain hope in order to be attractive to young readers and socially responsible. "Dystopian

72 • Alexa Weik Von Mossner

worlds are exciting," she writes, "but the end result must never be nihilism and despair."[12] Lois Lowry, author of *The Giver* (1993), similarly states that young readers "need to see some hope for [a better] world. I can't imagine writing a book that doesn't have a hopeful ending." Given that many young adults today are forced to "handle dystopia every day . . . in their lives, their dysfunctional families, their violence-ridden schools," Lowry argues, the fiction they read should not be even more depressing than their real-world lives.[13] This is a fine line to tread, however, because it is difficult to take seriously the "dystopian" real-world experiences of teenagers in literary fiction and not end up with a depressing narrative. In fact, even depressing narratives can play an important role in the development of teenage minds and identities.[14] In the case of young adult dystopias, which by definition imagine future worlds gone wrong, the genre itself demands that the topic be depressing. The crucial question is whether in such a case the author can risk to "turn out the light" by extinguishing all hope at the end of the novel. And the fact remains that only very few, if any, writers of teenage novels have been willing to do that, not least because the death of hope precludes all personal and political action.

However, there remains a creative dilemma created by the chasm between the topical interests of YA dystopias and their need to provide a hopeful ending. Kay Sambell sees a problematic tension between this literature's intention to caution "young readers about the probable dire consequences of current human behaviors" and their impulse "to counsel hope and present the case for urgent social change." She attests that "whereas the 'adult' dystopia's didactic impact relies on the absolute, unswerving nature of its dire warning, the expression of moral meaning in the children's dystopia is often characterized by degrees of hesitation, oscillation, and ambiguity."[15] Unlike the writers of "adult" dystopia, Sambell argues, the authors of novels for children and young adults do not dare have their morally appealing heroes fail in the end, and have things get worse. The catastrophic scenario must be devastating enough to create a fully realized dystopia, yet salvageable enough for the protagonist to survive and even thrive in these altered conditions, requiring a balancing act that may threaten the very plausibility of the initial dystopian world. By attaching a hopeful ending to an otherwise dystopian story, she suggests, these writers undermine the imaginative and ideological coherence of their fictional worlds and thus the strength of their creative vision.

While I agree with Sambell that the need for an element of hope can lead to creative tension if the fictional world depicted does not, in fact, allow for such hope, I disagree that this is a problem specific to young adult dystopian writing. By way of example, think of the complaints we read in otherwise enthusiastic readings of Cormac McCarthy's Pulitzer Prize-winning novel *The Road* (2005), about the ambiguous or even disingenuous ending of the narrative, which seems to offer some hope for the boy's survival in a completely devastated and inhumane world (this is even more pronounced in John Hillcoat's film adaptation of the novel). Secondly, not all dystopian scenarios are as bleak as the one we encounter in *The Road*, and offering a pessimistic outlook on future developments does not necessarily mean excluding all possibilities for improvement and amelioration. What makes *The Road* so radical in its vision is that it presents us with a *natural* world that is destroyed beyond repair or recovery. In McCarthy's fictional future, the trees are as dead as the soil, the rivers, and the oceans. Nothing is left of "nature" but a few humans who have taken to eating each other. It is very difficult to create believable moments of hope in such a world because a thoroughly dead planet is unlikely to sustain any life form above the level of bacteria for the next few thousands of years. A similar critique could be leveled against the happy ending in Andrew Stanton's animated blockbuster film *WALL-E* (2008). Because it imagines a world in which only a roach and a robot can survive, it is hard to believe that a few returning plants signal that the trash-covered planet has recovered enough to sustain human life again. In other words, the radically postapocalyptic scenarios of these narratives stand in the way of authentically hopeful endings.

However, not all of the recent young adult novels I have mentioned go as far in their imagination of ecological risk and crisis. While they need to make their fictional scenarios radical enough to be exciting, there is no obligatory need to push them all the way to the apocalypse. Lloyd's *The Carbon Diaries 2015* and *2017* imagine climatic, ecological, and social changes that are often more drastic and rapid than the scenarios laid out by scientists today. But even as Lloyd "pumps up the volume" for dramatic effect, the changes she imagines mostly remain within the realm of the possible, and she leaves open whether or not the natural world in her novels is beyond mitigation or not, thus creating a space for hope. No one in the novels knows what the future will hold, a fact that brings the characters on a par with us and our own knowledge about our current situation: we, too, do not know whether we have already heated the planet to the point where even the most ambitious efforts will fail to prevent large-scale change and disaster. Like Lloyd's characters in *2015*, teenagers today are forced to live and act within this realm of ecological uncertainty and risk, and *The Carbon Diaries* suggest that the responsibility for dealing with these risks and for shaping society in the twenty-first century ultimately rests in the hands of their generation.

Living with Ecological Risk: *The Carbon Diaries 2015*

The Carbon Diaries 2015 opens a few days before the UK introduces nationwide carbon rationing. We learn from Laura Brown's diary that her family is in "deep denial."[16] Her mother is "Being Very Positive" and insists that she will be able to keep her Saab hydro-hybrid convertible, her father admonishes his children—"We shouldn't just focus on it being difficult"—and her older sister Kim has locked herself into her room and refuses to engage with her family or the world (1). Laura is the only one who watches the news in order

74 · Alexa Weik Von Mossner

to "check out the countdown to rationing" (2–3), even as she has to sneak out to a friend's house to do so because her parents will not move away from the family TV, seeking diversion in watching back-to-back shows like *Dumbo*, *Mary Poppins*, and *Judy Garland: A Tribute in Song* while they still can.

Being the best-informed member of her family, Laura is in a position to explain to her readers how the country got to this point: after the "Great Storm" devastated the country, the British Government decided that the internationally agreed-on 60% carbon reduction by 2030 was not going to be enough and that it would be the first country to introduce carbon rationing, hoping Europe and the rest of the world would follow suit. From January 8, 2015 on, all British citizens will have to live with a carbon allowance of 200 Carbon Points per month, regardless of whether they spend it on heat, food, or travel. In addition, all consumer products will have Carbon Points built into the price to account for carbon dioxide produced in manufacture and shipping. Every bit of energy the family consumes will now be deducted from the value of their Carbon Cards, and, as Laura dryly remarks, when they get "down to the last red . . . [they will be] all alone, sobbing in the dark" (7).

It is clear to Laura that these new regulations will turn her life upside down, but she also admits to not really understanding what they will mean for her future. Although she points out—not without a hint of irony—that everyone will have a *choice* of what to spend their Carbon Points on, she realizes her freedom to choose will be noticeably curtailed from now on. What she cannot know, however, is how drastically it will be limited. It doesn't take long for her family to realize that 200 Carbon Points will not only be not nearly enough to keep the Saab running, but also not enough to keep the TV or the fridge going or the house well heated. Laura begins to understand that, because of carbon rationing, life as she knew it has ended, and that her dearest wish—to live a normal teenage life—is rapidly becoming a thing of the past. When heavy snowstorms kill dozens of people in Europe, she finds it unbelievable that "a bloody *plant*"—a tree falling on a live cable on the Swiss border—is able to lead to a devastating power cut in all of Italy and thinks about how she "never knew that cold could kill people like that" (15–16, italics original). Slowly it begins to dawn on her what it means to live in a world risk society: there is no safe place in a world of global insecurity because there is no being outside this world.

Although Laura starts to recognize the large-scale impact of the world risk society, she nevertheless remains absorbed by the micro-level personal and family concerns more typical of adolescent life. At the same time, she is highly critical of her parents who are "*so* desperate for everything to be normal" (16, italics original). Although this exactly mirrors her own yearnings and desires, she has nothing but contempt when she sees the same in her mother and father. She feels that, as a teenager, she should have a right to a certain (carbon-saturated) normalcy and that her parents, as grown-ups, should somehow be on top of the situation instead of oscillating between false

Hope in Dark Times • 75

cheerfulness, anger, and denial. After only two weeks of carbon rationing she notes in her diary that the biggest drawback of the new situation is that it forces her family to share the same house and indeed the same room much of the time, and she does not "know if our family can survive being *together*" (16, italics original). Never an ideal or even well-functioning family to begin with, the Browns go through multiple moments of crisis that eventually threaten to rip the family apart. Both parents lose their jobs as a result of the rationing— Laura's father worked in the now doomed tourism industry—and they are all put on a carbon offenders program after Kim secretly takes two return flights to Ibiza, using up her family's carbon ration for the whole year. The increasingly extreme weather does its part to exacerbate the situation. Heavy blizzards in the winter are followed by a severe drought in the summer, which leads to water and food shortages and eventually to social unrest. The fall of 2015 brings storm floods so high that they top the Thames Barrier and flood the city of London, killing thousands of people and very nearly Laura's parents and her sister. In short, it is a year of environmental and social disaster on the micro as well as on the macro level. This is all on top of Laura's love life— another disaster area—and the multiple troubles she experiences at school and with the capricious members of her band.

Laura relates all of these troubles in the candid, witty, and spontaneous way one might choose when telling one's diary the truth about things as one sees it. Most of the time she believes that her parents are idiots, her sister is evil, her band members radicals, and that the world has gone mad. She goes through moments of intense anger and gripping fear, as for example during one of the frequent power cuts when she gets stuck in a subway train, "trapped underground, pressed tight, heat rising, pitch-black" (29). She also experiences moments of exhilaration and boundless joy, as when the rain sets in after a period of drought, or when the rain finally stops after having submerged her world for weeks on end. And she somehow deals with the fact that her unemployed and depressed father starts keeping pigs and growing crops in their urban backyard; that her mother subsequently moves into a commune; and that her boyfriend leaves her because he can no longer bear his life in London. What really worries her, however, is that her friends are becoming increasingly politicized and radical. "I don't want everything to be political," she writes emphatically into her diary. "I want everything to be normal" (37).

The young adult reader will likely understand that desire. It is the desire for a "better world" that is characterized not so much by an ideal society that lives in harmony with nature, but by total freedom and security, unlimited resources, a complete lack of responsibilities and obligations, happy but invisible parents, emotional stability, and a rewarding but undemanding love life. Something along these lines is what Laura calls "normal"—probably the most frequent word in her diary next to "carbon." But the more the reader gets involved in her story, the more she understands that Laura's "normalcy" is an

76 · Alexa Weik Von Mossner

ambiguous signifier at best, as it stands for different things at different times and never for the "normal life" she used to have before rationing. Ecological risk and environmental crisis have a profound effect on the way Laura lives, but they do not disrupt a previously perfect life because her life never was perfect. And, as her parents and friends keep telling her at various points in the novel, her yearning for a "normal" world is marked by egotism and denial— something Laura hates to see in others. It will take Laura the better part of the next two years to find out what world she really finds desirable and which means to bring about political, social, and ecological change she is willing to accept. While she is not yet an activist in *The Carbon Diaries 2015*, she will start to grow into one in the sequel novel as she learns to move beyond her preoccupation with the desire for a "normal" life and begins to recognize not only the larger global impact of climate change but also the complex dynamic of the world risk society.

Fighting Global Environmental Injustice: *The Carbon Diaries 2017*

Lloyd places a gap between her two novels, letting a whole year pass before her readers meet Laura again on January 2, 2017. When they do, she is still the same passionate, witty, and notoriously stubborn girl they left behind when closing the cover of the first novel. However, her life circumstances are quite different. Laura's parents have moved to a small farm in the countryside and are often concerned about the safety of their daughter, who has remained in the city to pursue her studies. London has by now become an even scarier place, and a number of things have changed in the larger world, too. We learn early on that in a historic agreement 160 countries have signed up for global carbon rationing in response to drastically high greenhouse gas levels in the atmosphere and steadily rising average global temperatures. The environmental crisis around Laura continues to worsen in *The Carbon Diaries 2017*, and is shown to have ever more profound effects on societies around the world. The first pages of the book show a map of the world that marks water-related conflicts in various countries and Laura will soon physically take her diary to France and Italy, and imaginatively even further, to the Middle East, North America, Africa, and Asia. Her ex-boyfriend now lives in Germany, her sister in Indonesia, and her friend Kieran in New York, and she frequently receives text messages and images (shown as illustrations in the book) that tell her about manifestations of ecological and social crisis in other locales. Lloyd thus turns the attention of her protagonist—and her readers—towards transnational and global concerns, putting local problems into their larger ecological, economic, and political context.

Much more than the first novel, which concentrates on Laura's family, the second book revolves around her band and the topic of political radicalization. Her friend Claire, "who's gone all hard-line political since she started

Hope in Dark Times • 77

journalism at UEL," and her (new) boyfriend Adi have all along criticized Laura's strict refusal to become politically active and her almost desperate desire for normalcy.[17] This conflict becomes increasingly more pronounced when Laura gets evicted from her London apartment. She ends up at the Docks, a place that is now mostly underwater and a refuge for the Dox, a group of politically radical—and vegan—squatters. While this is an agreeably cheap solution to her problem, it brings her in close contact with the Dox people, whom the police suspect of supporting a mysterious new terrorist organization called the 2, which targets the remaining symbols of global capitalism.

However, it is only after Adi walks out on her to work in a refugee camp in Sudan and her band goes on a low-budget concert tour through France that things really start to change for Laura. While in France, she witnesses the rise of the right-wing *Front National*, which galvanizes the population's fears and growing anger about power cuts and supply shortages to the point where all foreigners are considered dangerous and unwanted intruders. Laura realizes that the movement's toxic mixture of nationalism and xenophobia is fuelled by changing environmental and material conditions, but she is not yet able to see the larger picture. When Adi catches malaria and gets transported to a hospital in Palermo, she and a friend make their way down to Sicily, which is overflowing with African refugees whose homes have been made uninhabitable by climate change. The state of the European world as described in Laura's diary confirms Ulrich Beck's prediction that the poorest people in the world "will be the least able to adapt themselves to the changes in the environment" and that "an exodus of eco-refugees and climatic asylum seekers will flood across the wealthy North." The novel also confirms Beck's assumption that "crises in the so-called Third and Fourth Worlds could escalate into war."[18] In fact, we do not even need to look that far as the first of multiple water wars breaks out between Israel and Palestine, and soon in countries all across Europe.

Laura is shocked by her up-close-and-personal encounter with the victims of the world risk society and outraged at the way the Italian government treats them. The tone of her diary entries expresses her disturbance, temporarily losing its playfulness as well as its sassiness when she ponders that "Palermo's like nowhere I've ever been; it's like Europe in collision with Africa" (184). And while she still experiences a moment of "pure, pure *happiness*" when she learns that Adi is going to survive (186, italics original), she also realizes that he now has truly become a political radical like Claire and some of her other friends. She wonders how "it's all gotten so heavy so quick. It's like I'm being dragged in against my will. I don't even believe in politics, all that left and right . . . it's all crap . . . But then I look across the road at the detention center [for the African refugees] and what's happening there is so wrong. Maybe Adi's right, there is no choice now" (194–195). Perhaps, Laura realizes, the amount of choice she has in her life is even more limited than she had thought, because, as Adi keeps telling her, the decision to stay out of politics

78 • Alexa Weik Von Mossner

is a political decision, too, and one that he at least finds deeply unethical. The social repercussions of climate change constitute moral dilemmas for Lloyd's characters that become more and more uncomfortable as the world spirals out of control, leading some of them even to join the terrorist organization the 2 in order to put "an end to this disgusting, messed-up, futile, hypocritical system that is screwing the planet" (214).

Laura finally reaches the point where she, too, can no longer stand back and watch. On their way back home to the UK, she and her friends witness a conflict over water between a group of poor farmers and the Italian military. Laura remembers how "we had a moment, a tiny gap in time in which to pull back off the road, sneak away" and how they then instead "walked forward and fell in line with the people" because *there just wasn't anything else to do*" (223, italics original). For the first time, Laura decides to protest against environmental injustice and step up for the rights of others. As a result, she gets tear-gassed, arrested, and thrown into a detention camp, and when she finally gets deported to the UK, her understanding of herself has changed. She now cannot believe that some people in London just keep living their normal lives, seemingly uncaring about what is going on in the rest of the world. With her new-found activist impulse, Laura becomes part of a broad-based civil disobedience movement that, supported by "global all-out strikes in Norway, Germany, Sweden, Spain, Brazil, Mexico, Venezuela and China," forces the increasingly authoritarian British Government to step down after it has killed dozens of its own citizens and injured thousands more (314). This instance of cosmopolitan solidarity in the face of social and environmental injustice is the most openly utopian moment in the novel. Interestingly enough, it once again mirrors Beck's understanding of the world risk society, which, he hopes, "sets free a 'cosmopolitan moment'" because "global risks force us to confront the apparently excluded other."[19] Beck has been criticized for being unduly idealistic and hopeful in his prognostications.[20] However, as Ernst Bloch and other utopian thinkers have argued, hope is an essential element in any visionary political project that tries to make the world a better place, and it is needed in even the darkest times.

All is not well, however, at the end of *The Carbon Diaries 2017*. The novel leaves its readers with an open ending and a global environment that continues its downward slope. The nature of the problem precludes a neat and happy ending. However, we are also left with a Laura who no longer desires to be "normal" but instead desires a better world with "no bombs, no guns, no escape" and is determined to help bring it about (321). The narrative told over the two novels thus is a typical coming-of-age story that comes to us in the guise of a critical eco-dystopia. In this sense, they echo Tom Moylan's description of the critical dystopia as a genre that, at its best, reaches "toward Utopia not by delineation of fully detailed better places but by dropping in on decidedly worse places and tracking the moves of a dystopian citizen as she or he becomes aware of the social hell and—in one way or another, and not always

Hope in Dark Times • 79

successfully—contends with that diabolical place while moving toward a better alternative."[21] This is exactly what Lloyd portrays in *The Carbon Diaries*.

However, what gives her eco-dystopian novels their particular critical edge is that they do *not* actually depict a diabolical place but a social and ecological world as outlined in the prognoses of some of the leading scientists of our time. This makes them different from the postapocalyptic young adult novels discussed by Claire Curtis as well as from the ecological utopias explored by Elaine Ostry in their respective contributions to this volume. Not only is the break with the present not as radical as it is in the texts discussed in those chapters, among them Pfeffer's Last Survivors series and Bertagna's Exodus trilogy, there is also no strict division between the city and nature, reminding readers that such a division never actually existed. The uncomfortable realism and proximity of Lloyd's future world is further underlined by the fact that she has chosen to set them in the *very* near future: 2015 is really just around the corner. It is difficult to read these novels and not wonder just how realistic these fictional scenarios may be and how much they indeed give you a glimpse into what awaits you in your own future—especially if you are sixteen years old.

Conclusions

At the end of her critique of the dystopian mode in novels for young readers, Kay Sambell calls for "a new, more fluid style of didacticism in dystopian writing for children" which would mean "that authors must find ways of progressively resisting the pessimistic thesis of the dystopian scenarios they have invoked."[22] I find helpful Sambell's suggestion that writers should scrutinize whether their dystopian scenarios actually *allow* for an at least partially hopeful ending. In the case of eco-dystopian novels dealing with climate change, this is a particular challenge because, as is well known, the effects of climate change will only be visible when it is way too late for mitigation. Lloyd has dealt with this representational problem by dramatizing the future effects of climate change while remaining realistic about mitigation options. Her characters at some point learn to accept that they will never go back to the world they used to know, that from now on they are going to "dwell," as Frederick Buell has put it, in perpetual environmental crisis,[23] and that their future lives will be marked by continuous adaptation to changing environmental conditions. No one knows how radical or dangerous these changes will be—this is the nature of the world risk society. However, living in the world risk society, the two novels also make clear, does not preclude utopian hope or political action; on the contrary, if we believe Ulrich Beck, it actually in the long run produces a cosmopolitan and cooperative world order simply because the surviving humans realize that they will have to collaborate if they do not want to collapse. The same is true for the critical eco-dystopia; because of its mixing of dystopian and utopian elements and its emphasis on

80 · Alexa Weik Von Mossner

political agency, it in fact necessitates the presence of hope in an otherwise perhaps dreary fictional future.

Another way in which Lloyd resists the "pessimistic thesis of the dystopian scenario" is to tell her story with a good dose of humor and lightness. Even when, as Laura puts it, "the shit's really hit the fan" (*2017*, 218), she is able to keep up her self-deprecating attitude and to put things in a way that makes us smile or laugh out loud. Her lighthearted and often mocking tone not only provides comic relief in the face of disaster but also effectively mitigates the didactic strain of the narrative. And so it is hardly surprising that Lloyd admits in her preface to the second book that, as a teenager, she "loved funny books, with lead characters who never wanted to teach you a thing: Holden Caulfield, Adrian Mole, Huckleberry Finn" (*2017*, n.p.). Like the first-person narrators of Salinger, Townsend, and Twain, Lloyd's Laura Brown is both critical and comic, and her narrative often tells us more about herself and her world than she realizes. She prefers to give us the impression that what made her become political, in the end, was the simple fact that "*there just wasn't anything else to do*" (*2017*, 223, italics original). However, it is clearly not only circumstances that make her change her mind, but also the influence and support of her friends, lovers, and parents. While Lloyd is careful not to romanticize the parent-child relationship, she portrays a family—built both on biology and friendship—that provides the support to help Laura grow. While there is disappointment as well as betrayal, the bottom line is that the family sticks together when things get tough.

Even if Laura doesn't, Lloyd certainly *does* want to teach her readers a thing or two, but she cleverly keeps away from the overdetermined didacticism that Sambell finds so problematic. By making her heroine a girl who for the longest time insists on staying out of politics even as everybody around her wants to drag her into them, Lloyd avoids having her narrator become too didactic and preachy. It is the other people around Laura who passionately voice different possible positions in the face of environmental crisis, and Laura tends to relate them with some skepticism. Lloyd thus leaves it to her young readers to figure out which of the multiple voices Laura relates to them they want to believe, although the narrative clearly invites them to align themselves with Laura and thus come, at least for the duration of the reading experience, to the conclusion that something must—and can—be done about the current state of the world.

Notes

1   United Nations, "Global Issues: Climate Change," http://www.un.org/en/globalissues/climatechange/index.shtml.
2   James Hansen, *Storms of My Grandchildren: The Truth about the Coming Climate Catastrophe and Our Last Chance to Save Humanity* (London: Bloomsbury 2011), ix.

Hope in Dark Times · **81**

3   Bill McKibben, *Eaarth: Making Life on a Tough New Planet* (New York: St. Martins Griffin, 2011), 1. The scenario McKibben describes in fact sounds so much like a terrifying dystopian setting that we are forced to remind ourselves that it is meant to be non-fiction, however speculative.

4   Vanessa Thorpe, "Forget Harry Potter: Saci Lloyd Thrills Teenagers with a Heroine Who Battles Climate Change and Extremism," *The Observer*, January 17, 2010, http://www.guardian.co.uk/books/2010/jan/17/carbon-diaries-saci-lloyd-television.

5   Ulrich Beck, *World at Risk* (London: Polity Press, 2009), 37.

6   See Ernst Bloch, *The Principle of Hope*, trans. Neville Plaice, Stephen Plaice, and Paul Knight (Cambridge, MA: MIT Press, 1986).

7   Ruth Levitas, *The Concept of Utopia* (Bern and New York: Peter Lang, 2010), 221.

8   Raffaella Baccolini, "Gender and Genre in the Feminist Critical Dystopias of Katharine Burdekin, Margaret Atwood, and Octavia Butler," in *Future Females, the Next Generation: New Voices and Velocities in Feminist Science Fiction Criticism*, ed. Marleen S. Barr (Lanham: Rowman, 2000), 13.

9   Jane Donawerth, "Genre Blending and the Critical Dystopia," in *Dark Horizons: Science Fiction and the Dystopian Imagination*, ed. Raffaella Baccolini and Tom Moylan (New York and London: Routledge, 2003), 30; and Tom Moylan, *Scraps of the Untainted Sky: Science Fiction, Utopia, Dystopia* (Boulder, CO: Westview Press, 2000), 157.

10 Carrie Hintz and Elaine Ostry, introduction to *Utopian and Dystopian Writing for Children and Young Adults*, ed. Carrie Hintz and Elaine Ostry (New York and London: Routledge, 2003), 12.

11 Jack Zipes, "Foreword: Utopia, Dystopia, and the Quest for Hope," in *Utopian and Dystopian Writing for Children and Young Adults*, ix.

12 Monica Hughes, "The Struggle between Utopia and Dystopia in Writing for Children and Young Adults," in *Utopian and Dystopian Writing for Children and Young Adults*, 156.

13 Carrie Hintz and Elaine Ostry, "Interview with Lois Lowry, Author of *The Giver*," in *Utopian and Dystopian Writing for Children and Young Adults*, 199.

14 When, in a recent article in the *Wall Street Journal*, Meghan Cox Gurdon complained about the inappropriate and potentially damaging "darkness" of much recent young adult fiction, her piece received hundreds of mostly outraged responses, some of them by well-known authors of award-winning books, such as Sherman Alexie and Laurie Halse Anderson. Their point was not only that Gurdon failed to do justice to the complexity and wide range of the young adult genre, but also that she refused to acknowledge the potentially important function of "dark" novels in the lives of teenagers. Gurdon's second article, published as a response a few days later, created a similar stir. Meghan Cox Gurdon, "Darkness Too Visible," *The Wall Street Journal*, June 4, 2011, http://online.wsj.com/article/SB10001424052702303365740457 6357622592697038.html, and "My

82 • Alexa Weik Von Mossner

'Reprehensible' Take on Teen Literature," *The Wall Street Journal*, June 28, 2011, http://online.wsj.com/article/SB100014240527023043144045764115 81 289319732.html.

Interestingly, an online poll on the *Wall Street Journal* website reveals that 89.4% of the 7,804 people who voted believe that dark themes in youth fiction are helpful to teenagers because they help them navigate adolescence. Only 10.6% of voters think that such fiction is harmful for young adult readers. http://online.wsj.com/community/groups/wsj-reading-group/topics/dark-themes-youth-fiction-helpful.

15 Kay Sambell, "Presenting the Case for Social Change: The Creative Dilemma of Dystopian Writing for Children," in *Utopian and Dystopian Writing for Children and Young Adults*, 163, 164.

16 Saci Lloyd, *The Carbon Diaries 2015* (New York: Holiday House, 2008), 2. Subsequent references will be cited parenthetically in the text.

17 Saci Lloyd, *The Carbon Diaries 2017* (New York: Holiday House, 2009), 8. Subsequent references will be cited parenthetically in the text.

18 Beck, *World*, 37.

19 Ibid., 15.

20 For critical debates around Beck's thought on the world risk society and its cosmopolitizing effects, see the special issue of the *British Journal of Sociology* on *Varieties of Second Modernity* 61.3 (2010), edited by Beck and Edgar Grande; for a critique of Beck's use of the concept of cosmopolitanism see also Luke Martell, "Global Inequality, Human Rights and Power: A Critique of Ulrich Beck's Cosmopolitanism," *Critical Sociology* 35.2 (2009): 253–272.

21 Moylan, *Scraps*, 106.

22 Sambell, "Presenting the Case," 173.

23 Frederick Buell, *From Apocalypse to Way of Life: Environmental Crisis in the American Century* (New York and London: Routledge, 2003), xiv.

Works Cited

Baccolini, Raffaella. "Gender and Genre in the Feminist Critical Dystopias of Katharine Burdekin, Margaret Atwood, and Octavia Butler." In *Future Females, the Next Generation: New Voices and Velocities in Feminist Science Fiction Criticism*, edited by Marleen S. Barr, 13–34. Lanham: Rowman, 2000.

Beck, Ulrich. *World at Risk*. London: Polity Press, 2009.

Beck, Ulrich and Edgar Grande, eds. *Varieties of Second Modernity*. Special issue, *British Journal of Sociology* 61.3 (2010).

Bloch, Ernst. *The Principle of Hope*. Translated by Neville Plaice, Stephen Plaice, and Paul Knight. Cambridge, MA: MIT Press, 1986.

Buell, Frederick. *From Apocalypse to Way of Life: Environmental Crisis in the American Century*. New York and London: Routledge, 2004.

Donawerth, Jane, "Genre Blending and the Critical Dystopia." In *Dark Horizons: Science Fiction and the Dystopian Imagination*, edited by Raffaella Baccolini and Tom Moylan, 29–46. New York and London: Routledge, 2003.

Gurdon, Meghan Cox. "Darkness Too Visible." *The Wall Street Journal*, June 4, 2011. http://online.wsj.com/article/SB10001424052702303657404576357622592697038.html.

Hope in Dark Times • 83

———— "My 'Reprehensible' Take on Teen Literature." *The Wall Street Journal*, June 28, 2011. http://online.wsj.com/article/SB10001424052702304314404576411581 289319732.html.

Hansen, James. *Storms of My Grandchildren: The Truth about the Coming Climate Catastrophe and Our Last Chance to Save Humanity*. London: Bloomsbury, 2011.

Hintz, Carrie and Elaine Ostry. "Interview with Lois Lowry, Author of *The Giver*." In *Utopian and Dystopian Writing for Children and Young Adults*, edited by Carrie Hintz and Elaine Ostry, 196–199. New York and London: Routledge, 2003.

————. "Introduction." In *Utopian and Dystopian Writing for Children and Young Adults*, edited by Carrie Hintz and Elaine Ostry, 1–22. New York and London: Routledge, 2003.

Hughes, Monica. "The Struggle between Utopia and Dystopia in Writing for Children and Young Adults." In *Utopian and Dystopian Writing for Children and Young Adults*, edited by Carrie Hintz and Elaine Ostry, 156–162. New York and London: Routledge, 2003.

Levitas, Ruth. *The Concept of Utopia*. Bern and New York: Peter Lang, 2010.

Lloyd, Saci. *The Carbon Diaries 2015*. New York: Holiday House, 2008.

————. *The Carbon Diaries 2017*. New York: Holiday House, 2009.

Martell, Luke. "Global Inequality, Human Rights and Power: A Critique of Ulrich Beck's Cosmopolitanism." *Critical Sociology* 35.2 (2009): 253–272.

McKibben, Bill. *Eaarth: Making Life on a Tough New Planet*. New York: St. Martins Griffin, 2011.

Moylan, Tom. *Scraps of the Untainted Sky: Science Fiction, Utopia, Dystopia*. Boulder, CO: Westview Press, 2000.

Sambell, Kay. "Presenting the Case for Social Change: The Creative Dilemma of Dystopian Writing for Children." In *Utopian and Dystopian Writing for Children and Young Adults*, edited by Carrie Hintz and Elaine Ostry, 163–178. New York and London: Routledge, 2003.

Thorpe, Vanessa. "Forget Harry Potter: Saci Lloyd Thrills Teenagers with a Heroine Who Battles Climate Change and Extremism." *The Observer*, January 17, 2010. http://www.guardian.co.uk/books/2010/jan/17/carbon-diaries-saci-lloyd-television.

United Nations. "Global Issues: Climate Change." http://www.un.org/en/globalissues/climatechange/index.shtml.

Zipes, Jack. "Foreword: Utopia, Dystopia, and the Quest for Hope." In *Utopian and Dystopian Writing for Children and Young Adults*, edited by Carrie Hintz and Elaine Ostry, ix–xi. New York and London: Routledge, 2003.

Chapter Five

Educating Desire, Choosing Justice?

Susan Beth Pfeffer's Last Survivors Series and Julie Bertagna's *Exodus*

Claire P. Curtis

I come to this project as a political theorist interested in the ways that fiction enables us to experience the force of theoretical ideas. Postapocalyptic fiction, with its focus on life "after the end," brings to life the possibility of a new community: out of the ashes of the old, we create structure. Legitimate structure is built on consent, and because we can imagine (or in postapocalyptic fiction experience) life without government, *we* are responsible for creating that order anew. We are familiar with this story: rational and free adults exchange the right to do whatever they desire for some modicum of protection by a governmental power created by the consent of the people. But not all inhabitants of a potential community are adult, rational, or even potentially free.[1] Some members of the community are debilitated by age, accident, or disability; some are rejected as members based on race or gender. Given the focus on young and vulnerable protagonists, young adult postapocalyptic fiction provides a potential space for those without power to play a part in the creation of a new community. And yet how willing are young adult postapocalyptic texts to take up this revolutionary potential?

In this essay I focus on two postapocalyptic texts that take up life immediately after a disaster.[2] These texts present readers with young protagonists who are dealing with world-ending events and sustained attention is paid to life after the end. Each text has the opportunity to engage the reader in the process of community building. But only one text follows through on this opportunity. Susan Beth Pfeffer's *Life as We Knew It* (2006) is a conservative repackaging of society that encourages passivity in the reader, while Julie

86 • Claire P. Curtis

Bertagna's *Exodus* (2008) is a transformative text always struggling with its new beginning. The protagonists in both are young women without extraordinary power or skills, who must face up to the end of the world as they know it. Each woman struggles for daily survival and discovers on whom she can rely, learning about herself and about strengths she never knew she had. But these similarities are superficial. If Bradford et al. are right that utopian/dystopian fiction for young adults is meant to "offer shape to children's anxieties and aspirations,"[3] then the shapes these novels give to those "anxieties and aspirations" are radically different. Pfeffer's book, starting with a world-ending event over which we have no control, an asteroid strike, emphasizes anxiety about the unknown and the uncontrollable, and recommends adherence to a familiar, unjust order. Bertagna starts with a world-ending event over which we have more control, global sea rise, but sees the problem to be solved not as the *fact* of anxiety, but the responses of others to that anxiety. This text urges the reader to desire to keep trying to find ways to live together.

Traditionally the dystopian text begins in the midst of the dystopian world. The reader's work is to learn about that world and slowly come to understand its dystopian status. As Raffaella Baccolini and Tom Moylan note, "Since the text opens *in media res* within the nightmarish society, cognitive estrangement is at first forestalled by the immediacy and normality of the location . . . However a counter-narrative develops as the dystopian citizen moves from apparent contentment into an experience of alienation and resistance."[4] The postapocalyptic text engages dystopia in a different way. It typically opens with normalcy, in the world in which the reader lives. Before this world is destroyed, the characters are living lives that the reader sees as her own. And so the dystopian postapocalyptic text wrestles with both the dystopian event and with a dystopian aftermath. The reader must be warned against both nuclear proliferation, for example, and authoritarian overreaction, while being taught to desire not simply a world where the cataclysmic event will not happen (a world that we may have no control in creating) but also to desire a world absent authoritarian overreach. The dystopia comes from the cataclysmic event and its subsequent effects. Resistance, in a postapocalyptic account, is resistance both to the apocalyptic event and to a narrative of human motivation that sees dictatorial power as inevitable.

For example, in Robert Swindells's *Brother in the Land* (1984), the novel opens, "It was a hot day in the summer holidays. People kept coming in the shop for ice-cream and candy and coke. We lived in Skipley, behind the shop, open seven days a week and the bell drove you daft. I'd have gone off on the bike but Mum said I had to play with Ben."[5] This is a fully recognizable world for the reader—a boy, responsible for a younger brother during the summer holidays, complaining about the shop bell. A boy whose world, like ours, includes summer holidays, a heat that produces a desire (easily sated) for ice cream and soda. A boy whose bike is his escape from the drudgery of his daily life. Two pages later, after crawling into an abandoned WWII pillbox on the

Educating Desire, Choosing Justice? • 87

side of the road to avoid a summer thunderstorm, "I saw the flash. It was terrifically bright. I screwed up my eyes and jerked my head away" (7). In three pages the reader transitions from a familiar world to a world recognizable only through her postnuclear fears. *Brother in the Land* does not shy from exploring those fears: the cloud "an obscene mushroom on its crooked stem," the dying burn victims, the black rain, "my first corpse: the first of many," a nameless man in a facemask and protective suit who threatens to shoot, and "the town laid waste below" (8, 15, 17).

Once the protagonist's (and the reader's) world is dismantled, the primary narrative of the postapocalyptic text develops as the heavy-handed response to the apocalyptic event. The nameless man in the protective suit above will soon be revealed as a member of a militaristic group that demands all food supplies and kills injured survivors all in the interest of consolidating power for their own gain. This is a common adult response to cataclysmic events in young adult postapocalyptic fiction. Usually such accounts then include a counter-narrative where the protagonist resists that authoritarian turn, teaching the reader to fear both the event and the response adults brings to the event.

The text "educates" the reader's desire. The reader ends her reading experience thinking differently about the world in which she wants to live: "To educate desire, to stimulate it, to awaken it . . . Desire must be taught to desire, to desire better, to desire more, and above all to desire otherwise."[6] The reader's experience of reading shapes the way she sees the world and the way she wants the world to be. There is a normative content to this education; critics should be aware of a shift in that content from the emancipatory to the constrained. Susan Beth Pfeffer's novels contrast well with Julie Bertagna's precisely on this point: what do we want young readers to desire? I argue that we should fear the shape of the utopian impulse present in Pfeffer's text and instead encourage (and encourage the reading of) the utopian impulse of Bertagna's. Through an examination of the protagonists' actions in the face of a dystopian postapocalypse, I contend that the reader of Bertagna's text is being persuaded to "desire otherwise" while the reader of Pfeffer's text is being persuaded to limit her desires. Bertagna offers an expansive, often frightening world of possibilities and uncertainty; but it is a world where the young protagonist will always strive to move forward toward something better. Pfeffer's counter-narrative offers a narrow world of stingy pseudo-safety in which the young protagonist is continually encouraged to side with the adults who are intent on producing an unjust order.

Apathy and the Last Survivors

The Last Survivors series by Susan Beth Pfeffer (*Life as We Knew It* [2006], *The Dead and Gone* [2008], *This World We Live In* [2010]) follows two teenage protagonists through the same event—a cataclysmic asteroid strike on the moon that alters the moon's orbit and moves it closer to earth. The subsequent

88 · Claire P. Curtis

tsunamis, earthquakes, volcanic eruptions, and nuclear winter-like landscape produce the kind of social upheaval familiar to readers of postapocalyptic fiction: everything has changed, every expectation of life must be rethought. The very titles highlight Pfeffer's immersion in the postapocalyptic genre. *Life as We Knew It* signals the initial shock of dealing with a world so radically changed that nothing seems certain. In *The Dead and Gone*, it is not simply that the material conditions of life have changed. Families have also been destroyed, and the death of those family members reasserts the distance between the living and the dead: the dead have no idea what the world has become. The third book, *This World We Live In*, offers a kind of resolution, shifting to the *post* of the postapocalyptic text.

I focus on Miranda, the protagonist of books one and three. (Alex, the protagonist of book two, shows up in Miranda's world in book three.) The first novel presents Miranda, a high school student with typical interests, living with her mother and younger brother and with an older brother away at college. Her parents are divorced, her father has remarried, and his second wife is expecting a child. Miranda's life is that of a fully recognizable middle-class teenager in small-town America. As she notes in the text, which is written as her journal:

> Got a 92 on the history test. I should have done better.
>
> Mom took Horton to the vet. He's fine. I worry a little bit about him now that he's ten. How long do cats live?
>
> Sammi told me she is going to the prom with Bob Patterson. I know I shouldn't be jealous but I am, not because I like Bob (actually I think he is kind of creepy), but because nobody asked me. Sometimes I think no one ever will.[7]

As with *Brother in the Land*, this is an easily recognizable beginning to which readers can relate. Miranda is worried about school, friends, dances, and her cat. She fights with her mom and is uncertain about her place in the high school hierarchy.

After the event her world narrows to the sunroom of her home. Her family experiences dwindling food supplies, loss of electricity, flu, diminished sunlight, and increasing cold. Miranda's diary reactions to the apocalyptic ending of her world are familiar and, for a reader of postapocalyptic fiction, often pleasantly discordant. She both fears her family's situation and responds to it in refreshingly non-heroic ways. She is not out to save her world:

> I'm the one not caring. I'm the one pretending the earth isn't shattering all around me because I don't want it to be. I don't want to know that there was an earthquake in Missouri. I don't want to know that the Midwest can die, also, that what's going on isn't just tides and tsunamis. I don't want to have anything more to be afraid of.
>
> I didn't start this diary for it to be a record of death (71).

Expressed fairly early in the journal, this desire to not know is understandable. The reader can see Miranda's desire to close off her ears and pretend that her life is as it was. The reader also wants to know more, but the text will not succumb to those prurient desires. There is little violence—no mobs, no cannibals, no pyrotechnics. The text insists on not delivering the usual fare of the postapocalyptic genre. Instead you get a fairly quiet story about the survival of one family living on the outskirts of a small, rural Pennsylvania town. Unlike *Brother in the Land*, the fears here are somehow smaller: starvation, pandemic flu, exposure.

Lacking the typical violence of postapocalyptic texts, the book also lacks any overt heroics. In fact there is a kind of anti-heroism in play. Miranda tries on a mini-heroic role when she shares information about food distribution with a friend a few days after the event. Miranda's mother rejects out of hand any such concern for others: "I will not have Jonny or Matt or you starve because you want to include a friend. This isn't the time for friendships, Miranda. We have to watch out only for ourselves" (101). The mother fears that the time taken to alert the friend might have lost Miranda's chance for the food distribution. While the postapocalyptic genre is rife with examples of how the selfish are punished, here the text affirms Miranda's mother's response.[8] Since postapocalyptic fiction often plays with how we save ourselves both as individuals and as members of a community, there is something off about Miranda's mother's warning here. But since Pfeffer never really presents the mother as unsympathetic, the reader begins to find herself in a dystopian text with no capacity for resistance. It initially seems as if there is no need for such resistance, but by the end of the first book the response by others to the apocalyptic event is revealed, and with it the absence of any resistance by Miranda.

With a ten-day supply of food left for the four members of her family, Miranda walks the snowy miles into town hoping to find a letter from her absent father who is heading west with his young, pregnant second wife. Miranda believably presents this journey to town as potentially her last act. She is the only one in the family strong enough for the five-mile walk; her younger brother Jon is the family's best hope for long-term survival if Miranda removes herself from the diminishing food supplies. Miranda is potentially sacrificing herself and she does so in a typically low-key fashion. However, Miranda survives the journey, and at City Hall she learns that for the last month food has been distributed to town residents. Mr. Danworth, a town clerk, says to Miranda: "Program's been going on for four weeks now ... So this young lady is entitled to at least four bags ... then next Monday we'll send someone out to your home with food for the rest of your folk. Monday's delivery day. How does that sound?" (333).

Here is the first sign to the adult reader knowledgeable in the ways of postapocalyptic fiction that something is not quite right. How can there be governmental food distribution when there is no government? Miranda and her family are cut off from most other people; they are wholly dependent on their

90 • Claire P. Curtis

own ability to collect water, remove snow, treat their accidents and illnesses. This sudden reference to government services raises important questions. Why was her family ignored until now? How did her town get food deliveries? The answer, revealed in the third book, is access to those with power: "It's all connections, and we're lucky that Mayor Ford has some. His wife's cousin is married to the governor. We got our share, maybe even more."[9] The apocalyptic asteroid strike has not taken out the government (which runs counter to most postapocalyptic texts), and furthermore that government now serves only those with power or connections.

What emerges from the destroyed world is a familiar narrative: the rich, the powerful, the connected will organize to help themselves. At the beginning of the third book, *This World We Live In*, Danworth informs Miranda and her brother that food will no longer be delivered; it will be available only to those strong enough to come and get it. "You're going to let people die," Miranda retorts. To which Danworth says, after noting his own disappointment, "But it's the government. It makes the rules, and we have to follow them" (17–18). Miranda is unhappy, but reports this matter-of-factly. She will not author the dystopian counter-narrative of resistance, but instead favors a more conservative acquiescence to this dystopian reality of might makes right. She aligns herself with those who not only refuse help to those not connected, but will actively destroy others in order to create a space of safety. This turn to the clearly dystopian calls out for a counter-narrative of resistance. Instead Miranda offers a tepid shoulder shrug.

As *This World We Live In* opens, a few months after the end of the first book, there is familiar talk of a return to normal. "Someday schools will be open again," Mom said. "Things will be more normal. You need to do your work now for when that happens" (7). It is never clear how far the mother understands the world in which she and her children currently live. The moon's orbit will not go back to where it was, and the sun has not shone since the volcanic eruptions and earthquakes produced clouds of haze. The text offers no reason to believe that food can be grown. And yet the idea of the "normal" happening elsewhere persists. This suggests a kind of persistent cluelessness in the face of destruction that is typical of characters who do not survive apocalyptic events. Yet since the text is written as a journal, the continuous entries reveal that Miranda does in fact survive.

But the theme of normalcy is more than a departure from the typical postapocalyptic text. It also provides a cover for Miranda's ultimate choice to seek out an unjust living situation. Miranda will find "normal" by refusing to think about the consequences of living normally in a world gone wholly awry.[10] Miranda notes, "The president had kids. The vice president had grandkids. Millionaires and senators and movie stars had families. Those kind of people don't subsist on two cans of vegetables a day" (*This World*, 9). Miranda asserts this as a fact about her world: she is surviving (barely) on cans of vegetables. Others (the rich, the powerful, the famous) must be living better lives elsewhere: "Somewhere there must be a place where people are eating eggs and drinking milk. I don't know where, or how they get the food, but I bet somewhere in what's left of America, there are places with food and electricity and lots of books to read" (*This World*, 9). Miranda is experiencing life after a natural disaster that knew no geographic boundaries, yet she has no sense that such a disaster would destroy social boundaries. Nor does she reveal any desire to change those social structures.

If there are people who are living on more than two cans of vegetables a day, and if it is the case that those people are the rich, the powerful, and the connected, then the text should offer space to resist that reality. Postapocalyptic texts usually do (and should) offer resistance first by breaking down the impact of wealth, power, and connections in a world destroyed. Money is not useful for bartering cans of food; wealth and fame are irrelevant for staying warm and finding food and water. The text is not taking advantage of a familiar postapocalyptic realization that disaster impacts the rich and the poor alike and is avoiding the emancipatory power of such a claim of basic equality. Somehow these connected people emerged unscathed from the impact of the event.

Those who are now at the top of the social and political structure, preapocalypse, will maintain that status. No argument is offered for how and why they do so, and so the reader is left to supply an answer. Are such people just naturally superior? Stronger? Better able to withstand starvation? Surely not. Here the powerful and connected will buy their way into safety.[11] Miranda wants access to that safety. But she only sees that access as a possibility when she discovers that Alex has tickets for entry. She is not going to challenge the script of who gets in and who is left out; she will dream of entrance until someone with access makes it available to her.

The reader learns that Miranda is not deluded in her musings about the reach of fame and fortune. Adults confirm for her that she will not get access to places of organized safety: "It doesn't matter where any of the safe towns are . . . None of us could get in. We're not important enough. They're for politicians, people like that" (*This World*, 193). These "safe towns" are where people with access and connections are living and being cared for, protected from the consequences of this catastrophic world. The safe towns were emptied of their regular inhabitants in order to make room for those who could purchase entrance. Miranda learns this from a young woman named Syl, who recounts the story of two men whose job included cleaning out these towns:

> We were all a little bit drunk that night, and they started bragging about how many people they'd killed. Then they started talking about the first time they'd killed someone. And one of the guys said the first time he'd killed people was when he'd been assigned to clear out a college to make it a safe town. It was funny, he said, because it was Sexton University and he'd applied there and been rejected, and there he was, shooting

92 · Claire P. Curtis

> professors who were resisting. I said I hope he got the dean of admissions, and he laughed (*This World*, 194–195).

This is where Miranda wants to go: to a town emptied of its original inhabitants through state-organized murder. Miranda's desire is not being questioned. In her diary she does not think through the consequences of going to a town set up in this way. Perhaps Pfeffer thinks the reader understands that this is a mistake and can resist Miranda's choice. But the reader has been given no tools to resist. If Miranda does not question the circumstances of this town, then why should the reader?

Surely we can expect a dystopian text to ask its young readers to think beyond their own potential dependency and desire for personal safety. Imagine a version of *The Hunger Games* (2008) where Katniss simply lets her sister Prim go off to the games. This version would not be written because we do not expect our books to simply confirm what we understand to be injustices in the world. Our expectation is that these characters will both recognize *and* resist these injustices. These books are set up so that the reader can see how someone "just like them" can play an active role in making the world more just. Pfeffer's safe towns are tyrannical fiefdoms, and most postapocalyptic texts would illustrate the overthrowing of such tyranny. Instead the reader is encouraged to root for Miranda's plan to go and live among the unjust.

This is a problematic ending. Miranda's mother might claim of the safe town, "There's a world to live in, a world that needs us" (*This World*, 237), but again the text has given no indication of what Miranda and her family can do for this new world. It is a new world built on a model of an old, feudal world: a model of hierarchies and unequal distribution of hard work and benefits that the reader's world has seemingly rejected. The text gives no indication that this world is either justifiable or that it can be resisted.[12] This is a text that presents injustice as a fact to be accepted and adaptation to injustice as the best-case scenario for moving forward. Miranda is not a young protagonist who sees herself as having a role to play in shaping how we can live together peacefully. Pfeffer's text then offers no opportunity for the reader to desire such an active role.

Agency and Exodus

There are resistant young adult, postapocalyptic texts that give readers an opportunity to confront their anxieties and aspirations and play a role in creating a world where one's own desires are not the only ones at stake. Unlike *Life as We Knew It*, which starts in the world of the reader, Julie Bertagna's *Exodus* opens in the year 2099 on an island, Wing, in the North Atlantic Ocean. Mara Bell has lived her whole life on Wing, one of the few islands remaining after global sea rise. But the oceans are still rising and Mara's world is changing.

Educating Desire, Choosing Justice? • 93

From the reader's perspective *Exodus* is doubly apocalyptic. The novel opens in a world postapocalyptic to our world, and the continuing sea rise means that the world will quickly become postapocalyptic for Mara. This doubled cataclysm multiplies the warnings to the reader. We don't want to end up in Mara's situation, but while Mara and her people have no control over the rise of the sea, the reader, who is prior to both cataclysmic sea rises, does have some control. Candleriggs, one of the Treenesters who escaped from the sky city long ago, recounts to Mara:

> But in the scorching hot summers of the '30s and '40s the oceans rose faster than anyone ever expected. All the predictions had been wrong. And all the political agreements that were supposed to prevent global warming had long fallen through. The world's governments couldn't seem to agree on anything—or stick to the treaties that they did manage to agree on. Suddenly it was all too late.[13]

A contemporary young reader is thus given a time line: twenty to thirty years from *Exodus*'s publication (when today's reader is an adult) political agreements will break down, and the seas will rise faster than expected. That time line gives the reader motivation, time, and an idea of what has failed. The reader is given tools to resist in her own world, modeled by Mara in her world. That *Exodus* includes a cataclysmic event over which the reader has some modicum of control signals a text where the protagonists, who have no control over the sea rise, will seek control over their living situation. The text provides a nuanced argument about how Mara's people both respond to disaster and regroup for starting over. *Life as We Knew It* presents an event that is out of our control and a group of characters who see themselves as having no control. But here the reader is given double control: to change the direction of our own society, and to respond to apocalyptic events. *Exodus* encourages action with an eye to group survival; the characters in *Exodus* are motivated by the fact of injustice, and understand the idea of risk in a different way.[14]

Exodus opens with the people on Wing celebrating the winter solstice and the return of sunshine after a dark winter of near-constant storms. At that celebration, Tain, the oldest member of the community, reminds people that the sea continues to rise and that it is past time for them to act. Mara clearly wants to be convinced that there is nothing to fear: "People say it won't happen . . . They say the ocean will settle again in the summer and we'll be safe" (15). This is a familiar refrain: that safety will simply happen. Mara resists the evidence—a continually rising high tide mark—because accepting that evidence means that everything in her world will change. Tain challenges Mara to draw her own conclusions: "'But you can use your eyes, Mara, even if they can't!' he cries. 'You're not a child anymore and I won't lie to you'" (15). Though Mara is fifteen at the start of the novel, she is expected to act, by helping others in

94 • Claire P. Curtis

her community to recognize that the seas are rising and they must leave their rapidly shrinking island.

Mara is an active player in the debate over what to do. Because she has kept her "cyberwhizz" active, she explores the internet ("the Weave") and has found reference to "New World cities." These are confirmed by Tain's memory of news stories from long ago, depicting cities being built over the water. These cities (like Miranda's safe towns) are places where Mara thinks the people of her community will be safe. Mara does not keep this knowledge to herself (as Miranda does); she takes on the task of convincing others, starting with friends her age. Those friends worry about the rising seas but are understandably stymied about how to respond. Gail asks: "But what can we do? . . . Even if it's true—and it's *not* . . . we couldn't just launch out on the ocean and hope we come across one of those New World cities. I don't believe they exist. It's too incredible . . . We would *know* if there were giant cities out there. Someone would have come and told us" (27, italics original). Gail presumes that if there were people living safe lives out of the way of the rising seas then the people of those cities would come rescue the people of Wing. This too is a common presumption in both books. How is it that in a world falling apart there is not "someone" who will step up and rescue people? Mara will struggle against what she sees as unjust adult reactions to cataclysmic events; Miranda will simply accept the adult response (and will fail to see it as unjust). Mara will create a new political community. Miranda looks out for herself and turns a blind eye to the absolute injustice of the "safe town" she wishes to inhabit.

Gail's brother Rowan ridicules the worldview that assumes help will be available: "Like hell they would! They'd do exactly what we've done and just look after themselves" (27). Rowan doubts both whether these cities exist and, if they do, whether their inhabitants would act to rescue anyone. The best-case scenario here is that the cities do exist and that, for some reason, do not know that Wing or its people exist. Mara returns again and again to her cyberwhizz, hoping to find evidence of and a location for these cities. In "the Weave" she meets a cyberfox from one such city, "New Mungo," also located in the North Atlantic. Mara must now convince her fellow islanders that it is worth the risk of leaving their island for New Mungo. Mara has no magical properties; but she will be listened to, in part because of the support of her parents.[15] Mara initially gains credence because adults around her treat her with respect:

> Then, urged forward by her father, Mara suddenly found herself on the altar, telling everyone who was crammed into the tiny church of the evidence she had found of the existence of the New World (62).

Mara's mother urges people to listen. Mara asks, "You believe in the New World?" Her mother replies, "I believe in *you*" (63, italics original). The text provides a model of substantive maternal support that grounds Mara's later actions. Contrast this with Miranda's mother who is critical of Miranda's capacity to do the

Educating Desire, Choosing Justice? • 95

right thing. Here Mara's mother expresses both faith and trust in Mara: faith that Mara, like her grandmother before her, will be able to convince people to leave the island, and trust that, despite her limited evidence, Mara is right in her beliefs about New Mungo's existence and location.

That people are relying on Mara makes their eventual arrival at New Mungo all the more disconcerting. After weeks of sailing through storms with diminishing supplies and separated from the other boats of Wing, they arrive at the city only to discover (as Mara had feared) that it is surrounded by a high wall. But the wall is not the only sign that all may not be well here in New Mungo: "There is no land or harbor, only a blurred mass that heaves and bobs around the city. A huge, dull-colored live thing. The vile, rotting stench of an open drain hits as the clustering thing sharpens into focus. Mara gasps as she sees it's a heaving mass of humanity. A chaos of refugee boats crams the sea around the city and clings like a fungus to the huge wall that seems to bar all entry to refugees" (72). Inside the walls, people are living lives of privilege. Outside those walls people scrape out an existence, hoping only to be chosen for slave labor within the walls: "Rich and poor, all ages, all kinds of people, are crushed here into a common pulp of human misery" (74). *This* apocalyptic event produced (outside of the city's walls) equality of despair. We learn that most inside the city have no idea what is outside of their city, which has no windows and is riddled with virtual displays. But the leaders of the city know, sending police boats to protect the walls and find slave labor. Mara finds her safe town only to realize that it is neither safe nor just. She acts to challenge the injustice of their barred entry, starting the resistant counter-narrative to the dystopian world this postapocalyptic account presents.

Mara's route to resistance includes saving herself, the survivors from Wing, and those that she finds along the way: the refugees in the boats, the Treenesters (refugees from the sky city), the ratbashers (children with webbed hands and feet, the result of an experiment gone awry, who run wild on the island bases of the sky city's towers), and the slave laborers held in the bowels of the towers. Mara's postapocalyptic world includes a variety of human types, and her eventual plan to seek refuge on Greenland includes rescuing as many of these people as she can. Unlike Miranda, single-mindedly focused on herself and Alex, Mara has a wider gaze, seeing her own family's struggle for survival as impacting others as well. Mara's perspective educates readers away from their own private desires for love and comfort, and toward a desire for a world where all can live together and thrive.

It is not simply that Mara acts more ethically than Miranda does, although that is surely true. Mara's way of thinking is truly political. Mara must gain access to the city, commandeer a supply ship, and find a map to Greenland. After accessing the city she is confronted with a dystopian virtual world whose inhabitants are clueless, not simply about the refugees outside the city's walls, but also about the ocean, the possibility of land, and the very existence of other humans living lives different from their cyberworld. Mara's life in the

96 · Claire P. Curtis

"real world" has hardly prepared her for the visually stunning cyberworld. The sky city is dazzling, but also unreal:

> She looks at the pond with clear eyes. The fish are fake and swim in end-less electronic circles. The tree and its bird, the crystal sky and sunset, all are fake too. Even the bridge is made of mock stone. It's a false enchant-ment. Now Mara is bitter, right to the brim. It gives her the burst of en-ergy she needs (233).

Recognizing the hollow pleasures of the sky city, Mara has the resources to go beyond her immediate comfort and maintain her focus on finding a way to rescue the refugees.

Mara emerges as a political figure who can lead to meaningful change. Along the way, she must negotiate the needs and desires of multiple people with competing interests. She is not their savior, and her plan will not be per-fect, but her reaction to the dystopian and apocalyptic events of her life is inclusive and expansive. She recognizes obvious injustice and sees herself as responsible to help fight against it. She encourages the people of Wing to sail for the sky city, and she knows it is wrong for the sky city to block the refugees from entrance. It is not simply personal responsibility that spurs her to action but a recognition that she must act more broadly:

> She must fight to save what she can of the future that her parents, and her grandparents . . . struggled to give her.
> The only way she can give any meaning to their lost lives is to keep fighting for her own future, and the futures of the urchins, the Treenest-ers, and the refugees (310–311).

Mara knows there is risk: her plan to sail for Greenland is as uncertain as her plan to sail for the sky city. (Books two and three take up this narrative: all is not ideal on Greenland.) Mara accepts that risk, acknowledging that mere safety is not a desirable political outcome. Mara wants a community that will learn from its past and will work toward a future in which these disparate survivors build something new together: "I'm going to tell everyone [their story of escape] so that one day, when we find land, the story will live on in the world and the people who come after us will know how they came to be free. And maybe, somehow, our story will help them to be strong in their lives" (340).

The postapocalyptic genre is inherently political. Ending the world is only the beginning of the text. What happens when we start over takes up the cen-tral question of political philosophy: how can a group of people with dispa-rate aims and interests live together peacefully? Some novels intentionally choose to reject political community (Jean Hegland's *Into the Forest* [1997]), and some refuse to provide conditions for the possibility of political com-munity (Cormac McCarthy's *The Road* [2006]). However, when young adult

Educating Desire, Choosing Justice? • 97

postapocalyptic novels such as Pfeffer's Last Survivors series ignore the work of creating a political community, as if that work is not done by all of us, then young readers are done a disservice. Creating community is messy work, and more voices serve the needs of more people. Young adults deserve to have a voice in the process. How can readers learn about becoming full members of a community if the newly imagined worlds written for them also silence them? Mara of *Exodus* is not perfect: she must strive "to hold on to a sure sense of what is fair and right" (342). But she recognizes in herself a capacity to speak, to be heard, and to act. Her voice, and the story that she will tell of the many survivors of this postapocalyptic world, can awaken a desire in readers to think about the role they can play as young adults and the responsibilities they might have in creating a new world.

Notes

1   One can read these texts as writing social contract scripts: bring a group of people from a state of nature to civil society through the social contract. Critics of the social contract highlight the ways in which the traditional script is not fully inclusive: Carole Pateman, *The Sexual Contract* (1988), Charles Mills, *The Racial Contract* (1997), and recent work by Martha Nussbaum such as *Frontiers of Justice* (2006). I do not emphasize the moment of the contract in this paper, but rather the ways in which the protagonists of these books approach their own role in a community.

2   Other texts (what Elizabeth Braithwaite labels the "social order" and quest/adventure text) focus on life in an already existing society that emerged from the crisis, potentially generations before the protagonist's birth. These texts use postapocalyptic imaginings as the route to dystopia (e.g. Anderson, *Feed* [2002]; Cave, *Sharp North* [2004]; Westerfeld, *Uglies* [2005]; Collins, *The Hunger Games* [2008]; Goodman, *The Other Side of the Island* [2008]; Bacigalupi, *Ship Breaker* [2010]). See Elizabeth Braithwaite, "Post Disaster Fiction for Young Adults, Some Trends and Variations," *Papers: Explorations into Children's Literature* 20.1 (2010): 8.

3   Clare Bradford, Kerry Mallan, John Stephens, and Robyn McCallum, *New World Orders in Contemporary Children's Literature: Utopian Transformations* (New York: Palgrave Macmillan, 2008), 11.

4   Raffaella Baccolini and Tom Moylan, eds., *Dark Horizons: Science Fiction and the Utopian Imagination* (New York: Routledge, 2003), 5, italics original.

5   Robert E. Swindells, *Brother in the Land* (New York: Holiday House, 1984), 5. Subsequent references will be cited parenthetically in the text. Other postnuclear young adult novels of the 1980s include Louise Lawrence, *Children of the Dust* (1985), and Hugh Scott, *Why Weeps the Brogan* (1989). These postnuclear texts clearly capture the fears of growing up in the Cold War under a nuclear threat. This is a less immediate dystopia for

98 • Claire P. Curtis

the 2011 reader. But for those of us who were young in the Cold War it is the ur-postapocalyptic fear.

6 Miguel Abensour, qtd. in Christine Nadir, "Utopian Studies, Environmental Literature, and the Legacy of an Idea: Educating Desire in Miguel Abensour and Ursula K. Le Guin," *Utopian Studies* 21.1 (2010): 29.

7 Susan Beth Pfeffer, *Life as We Knew It* (Boston: Houghton Mifflin Harcourt, 2008), 5. Subsequent references will be cited parenthetically in the text.

8 In Pat Frank's *Alas, Babylon* (1959), the greedy who steal gold from irradiated Miami themselves die of radiation poisoning; in Larry Niven's *Lucifer's Hammer* (1977), those who steal from others are required to either join up with or be served up to the ritualistic cannibalistic group; in Cormac McCarthy's *The Road* (2006), the reader admires the son's willingness to share with others.

9 Pfeffer, *This World We Live In* (Boston: Houghton Mifflin Harcourt, 2010), 17. Subsequent references will be cited parenthetically in the text.

10 Weik von Mossner's "Hope in Dark Times" (this volume) explores further the ways in which the "normal" enforces a status quo and limits protagonists' agency.

11 The film *2012* (2009) also includes the wealthy and connected gaining access to safety and some ordinary people trying to break through. But at least there the question of whether or not it is right to limit survival to those people is raised. And their wealth is only helpful because the events were prepared for ahead of time.

12 Some postapocalyptic texts in a more reactionary strain do offer this justification, such as William Forstchen's *One Second After* (2009).

13 Julie Bertagna, *Exodus* (New York: Walker and Co., 2009), 199. Subsequent references will be cited parenthetically in the text.

14 Elaine Ostry also uses *Exodus* as an example of a text with young characters struggling with the realities of adult responsibilities in her contribution to this volume, "On the Brink: The Role of Young Adult Culture in Environmental Degradation."

15 The Treenesters insist that Mara is foreordained to be their savior, based on a rhyme and a carving in the remains of the Glasgow cathedral. But Mara does not act to change the conditions under which they all live because of their belief that she is "the one." She does so because she feels, internally, that she can and must act.

Works Cited

Baccolini, Raffaella and Tom Moylan, eds. *Dark Horizons: Science Fiction and the Utopian Imagination*. New York: Routledge, 2003.

Bertagna, Julie. *Exodus*. New York: Walker and Co., 2009.

Bradford, Clare, Kerry Mallan, John Stephens, and Robyn McCallum, eds. *New World Orders in Contemporary Children's Literature: Utopian Transformations*. New York: Palgrave Macmillan, 2008.

Braithwaite, Elizabeth. "Post Disaster Fiction for Young Adults, Some Trends and Variations." *Papers: Explorations into Children's Literature* 20.1 (2010): 5–19.

Nadir, Christine. "Utopian Studies, Environmental Literature, and the Legacy of an Idea: Educating Desire in Miguel Abensour and Ursula K. Le Guin." *Utopian Studies* 21.1 (2010): 24–56.

Pfeffer, Susan Beth. *The Dead and Gone.* Boston: Houghton Mifflin Harcourt, 2008.

———. *Life as We Knew It.* Boston: Houghton Mifflin Harcourt, 2008.

———. *This World We Live In.* Boston: Houghton Mifflin Harcourt, 2010.

Swindells, Robert E. *Brother in the Land.* New York: Holiday House, 1984.

Chapter Six
On the Brink
The Role of Young Adult Culture in Environmental Degradation

Elaine Ostry

Young adult dystopias usually pit the teenager against the adult world. However, M.T. Anderson's *Feed* (2002), Julie Bertagna's Exodus trilogy (2002–2011), and Scott Westerfeld's Uglies trilogy (2005–2007) implicate teenagers in environmental doom.[1] These authors define young adult culture in terms of two of the culprits of our ecological problems: technology and consumerism. To challenge adolescent readers, they present them with two kinds of utopia. The technological utopia echoes youth culture with its love for technology, consumption, and distraction, whereas the ecological utopia promotes maturity with its emphasis on self-reliance, self-restraint, hard work, decision-making, and community. The technological utopia favors mediated experience—even replacing nature in the process—whereas the ecological utopia promotes unmediated experience with real consequences.

In presenting these competing visions of utopia, Anderson, Bertagna, and Westerfeld hope to foster personal growth and social change through environmental awareness. In *Feed*, an advanced form of the internet has been transplanted into people's minds, and nature is largely destroyed. Global warming has drowned most of the world in the Exodus trilogy, and sky cities like New Mungo have been built to withstand the storms. In the Uglies trilogy, everyone is made pretty at age sixteen, and although nature exists, contact with it is not valued. Each of these scenarios complicates the binary between technology and nature by suggesting that nature needs technology to survive. The hope for such cooperation, however, is undercut by ambivalent endings. These complexities invite teenage readers to rethink their approach to both nature

102 • Elaine Ostry

and technology, confront the role of young adult culture in environmental disaster, and through these processes, grow up.

Fostering Adolescent Growth

Technological utopias, or "utopias of abundance," reflect popular youth culture's obsession with consumption, which distinguishes the technological from the ecological utopia.[2] With their huge cities and cyber-worlds geared to the young, technological utopias emphasize plenitude. Their model is the shopping mall. According to Marius de Geus, "These technological utopias are based on a spectacular degree of technological progress . . . which enables a continuous increase in the production of goods and services."[3] As Titus in *Feed* says, "All you have to do is want something and there's a chance it will be yours."[4] Although there is rationing in Bertagna's New Mungo, there is no sense of need or hunger, but rather of technological wonder. In *Uglies*, "practically anything . . . came out of the wall" in the city.[5] Ultimately revealed as dystopian, these cities show the negative aspects of urban teenage life—consumerism, constant entertainment, cyberspace—and the lack of civic engagement and personal growth that result.

The dystopia is a young dystopia, and its faults are the faults present in teenage popular culture. By criticizing the technological utopia, these authors want their teenage readers to think about what popular culture does not encourage them to think about, such as environmental degradation. Violet's father confronts Titus: "Why don't you go along and play your games? We're the land of youth . . . Go out and take what's yours" (*Feed*, 290). He equates being young with being superficial and greedy. In an interview, M.T. Anderson states that in our world, "Everything's young, everything's short-term."[6] This shortsightedness leads to disaster because no one plans ahead or thinks beyond his or her sphere. As Violet says, "Do you know the earth is dead? . . . No. No, no, no . . . We go sledding. We enjoy being young" (*Feed*, 273). The city is like a coddling, controlling parent that encourages this behavior. Like parents, the cities offer security as well as stuff. "*All shall be well*," the feed tells Titus (*Feed*, 148, italics original) and, as Dr. Cable says in *Uglies*, "This city is a paradise, Tally. It feeds you, educates you, keeps you safe" (*Uglies*, 106). Tally's friend Shay remarks that "the problem with cities" is that "everyone's a kid, pampered and dependent and pretty" (*Uglies*, 226). The city will not allow children to grow up but keeps them in a state of dependence: it "program[s]" them (*Uglies*, 278). Much as parents shield children from ugly facts, the city keeps them ignorant of the social ills that make their shining environments dystopian.

In ecological utopias, or "utopias of sufficiency," however, protagonists can at last escape the infantilizing control of the city and grow up.[7] Geus states, "The basic difference between these utopias lies in the notion of whether an ideal society should enjoy material abundance and luxury or be based on satisfaction and sufficiency."[8] Each book, aside from *Feed*, presents, as a challenge to the technological utopia, an ecological utopia whose inhabitants live in nature harmoniously despite limited resources, and deeply respect nature as valuable in itself. In *Uglies*, Tally visits the Smoke, the community of runaways living in the wild. An ecological utopia of treed islands, the netherworld, lies underneath New Mungo, and despite scarcity and danger, the inhabitants—the Treenesters—survive in harmony with their limited environment, later establishing a second ecological utopia called Candlewood in Greenland. Ecological utopias are characterized by scarcity rather than abundance; in them, "a perfect situation is not compatible with excess: abundance does not make people happy ... the perfect society is not sought via prosperity, but individual and social happiness is instead found in a conscious relinquishment of material pleasures and the *restraining* of human wants."[9] In the ecological utopias of the Exodus trilogy, being without material luxuries is not a choice but a necessity, yet the superiority of a simple life in tune with nature is made clear. Ecological utopias require protagonists to use "naturalist intelligence," learning based on the natural world, to develop critical thinking and physical strength, creating a world where one has a purpose beyond buying things. In *The Last Child in the Woods* (2008), Richard Louv argues that only in wild, unsupervised nature, as found in these communities, can children develop such resourcefulness.[10] (Treenesters eat with bird beak spoons.) Young adults also develop leadership skills when in nature (except in *Feed*); in the netherworld and the Smoke, they take charge in order to contribute to their communities' survival and live in harmony with nature. Unlike the technological dystopia, the ecological utopia encourages young adults to be active, not passive, and to consider the needs of the community above their own desires, all part of growing up.

Tally in *Uglies* exemplifies how the values of the ecological utopia help characters mature: at first a passive girl who cannot wait to become pretty, she becomes a rebel leader championing nature. She initially thinks that it is "wrong to live in nature, unless you want to live like an animal," but must take a two-week journey alone to the Smoke (92). She sees how vast nature is compared to the city—"Tally had always thought of the city as huge, a whole world in itself, but the scale of everything out here was so much grander"—and learns to appreciate it (152). She drops what D.H. Lawrence called the "know it all state of mind" (arguably common in the young) that nature challenges.[11] Just as Louv would have it, she cannot depend on anyone else. Consequences in nature are much graver than in the city, as when Tally nearly crashes down a cliff. When faced with difficult decisions, alone, Tally *Youngblood* starts to grow up. The wild is "dangerous," and she has to use her head to survive, feeling "stronger than ever before" (151, 230). With scarcity and hard work, she realizes, things take on greater value than in the city, where they are "disposable and replaceable" (232). In the city, during their operations, people are given lesions on their brains that take away independent thought,

104 • Elaine Ostry

but those with professions that involve risk and decision-making lose their lesions. Likewise, life in nature has taught her to take risks, make decisions, and resist being controlled. Tally learns that she is part of nature, and that just as nature does not "need an operation to be beautiful," neither does she (230). By the end of the third book, Tally makes herself the guardian of nature. She and David vow to protect it from human activity, and she identifies with it completely: "*The wild still has teeth. Special teeth, ugly teeth. Us. . . . Be careful with the world, or the next time we meet, it might get ugly.*"[12] Her mental and physical powers—and her agency—have all developed exponentially. It is as her friend Shay implied, that going to the Smoke and leaving the infantilizing city would make them "grow up" (*Uglies*, 226).

Approaches to Nature and the Mediation of Experience

In the technological utopia, "people attempt to dominate the natural environment: nature is viewed as an *instrument* to satisfy the incessantly increasing desires of humankind," rather than as intrinsically valuable.[13] As a result of this attitude, in all of the books except the Uglies trilogy, nature has been ravaged. However, instead of taking responsibility for this destruction, the technological utopia covers it up in two ways: substituting technology for nature, and co-opting nature for consumerism. New Mungo does not have anything natural in it: the Leaving Bridge and Looking Pond are lovely, but "the fish are fake and swim in endless electronic circles."[14] They eat "noofood"—"no-food"—that is brightly colored and tasty but unsatisfying. Similarly, nature in *Uglies* is replaced: inhabitants' bodies are substituted with pretty bodies complete with plastic cheekbones. When out in nature, Tally starts to see how "being in the city all the time made everything fake" (*Uglies*, 74). In *Feed*, technology thoroughly takes the place of nature. The feed itself supplants the natural brain and becomes entangled with all natural functions so that the body cannot live without it. Like *Exodus*'s noofood, *Feed*'s meat farm with "huge hedges" of tissue parodies real food (*Feed*, 142). Fake environments completely replace natural ones: the weather is manufactured in domes, with artificial suns, and Clouds™ are sucked out of vents. In *Feed*, nature is the tool of consumerism: the feed uses romantic images of nature to sell Titus an upcar, and even the bottom of a lake shows an advertisement. The lesions that *Feed*'s inhabitants suffer as a result of their toxic environment are reframed as fashion statements touted by celebrities. Image trumps reality, preventing characters from approaching environmental calamity with maturity and reason.

The ecological utopia, by contrast, "insists that humans should treat and use the natural surroundings with care: contact with nature is considered to be of great importance."[15] The goal is to live in harmony with nature. Trees, a common symbol of this relationship, are treated "with respect" in the netherworld; the Treenesters "knock on them politely before [they] go to nest,"

On the Brink · 105

and killing them is a crime (*Exodus*, 178). In *Uglies*, Tally is shocked at how the Smokies cut down trees, but she realizes that they re-establish balance by planting them as well. She is also initially repulsed by hunting, but the Smokies kill "only species that didn't belong in this part of the world or that had gotten out of control" (*Uglies*, 230). Tally adopts a more nuanced view of how people can interact with nature than the city's propaganda admits. In *Feed*, only Violet criticizes the reckless consumerism that leads to environmental degradation, such as the destruction of trees (for an air factory!). While championing nature, both Tally and Violet develop critical thinking skills, which are necessary for figuring out ways to live harmoniously with nature, rather than thoughtlessly destroying it.

Even though citizens debase and devalue nature, protagonists long for it. This longing can be referred to as "biophilia," Edward O. Wilson's term for "the urge to affiliate with other forms of life."[16] According to this theory, "humans have an innate affinity for the natural world, probably a biologically based need integral to our development as individuals," so lack of contact with nature stunts our personal growth.[17] Whether they realize it or not, characters in these books suffer from nature deficit disorder, the "human costs of alienation from nature," which include "diminished use of the senses [and] attention difficulties."[18] In New Mungo, Mara "yearns for natural light," and only the fake pond offers inhabitants the space for reflection that nature used to provide (*Exodus*, 246). *Feed* provides us with the most damaged environment, and yet Titus notices nature whenever it appears, even the wood door of Violet's house, and enjoys sunsets and breezes. Violet's last wishes mostly pertain to nature, such as "*watch[ing] the last fishes*" (*Feed*, 229, italics original). They are drawn to what they lack—and need.

Ignoring this longing, the technological utopia favors mediated over direct experience. In *Exodus* and *Feed*, cyberworlds distract people most effectively, just as modern teenagers are caught in the worldwide web. In *Exodus*, the cyberworld is called Noospace, or Noos, from the Greek for "mind" or "intellect" (*Exodus*, 219). The pun of Noos/noose shows its destructive nature: "the beautiful Noos has wrapped itself invisibly, powerfully, around the Earth. And holds its world spellbound" (*Exodus*, 245). The term Noospace—"no-space"—connotes the utopian pun of "no-place." In *Feed*, people cannot escape the feed's constant stimulation—and advertisements. Like Noospace, the word "feed" has a double implication. It feeds the people, giving them what they want, but it also feeds on them, controlling them. These alternate realities are run by corporations interested in profit rather than people, and they distract citizens from reality and social responsibility. As Titus falls asleep, the feed murmurs to him: "*All shall be well . . . and all shall be well . . . and all manner of things shall be well*" (*Feed*, 148, italics original). Julian of Norwich claimed that these were the words of Jesus; Anderson twists them ironically to show not faith in God but faith in the feed and what it provides. This lullaby lulls Titus into complacency, and alludes to the "trumpet" in *Brave New World* that murmurs propaganda to the children as they sleep.[19] The cyberworlds keep characters from developing into questioning, informed, and empowered citizens.

The spell that cyberworlds cast also removes citizens from fellow human beings. Dol in *Exodus* shows a "stunning lack of interest" in the stranger Mara (*Exodus*, 238). "Real life bores Dol," Mara realizes; only cyberspace can interest her (*Exodus*, 243). However, Mara also sees its appeal: "It would be so . . . tempting to slip inside this magic spell and ignore what lies outside" (*Exodus*, 232). Most New Mungo residents are ignorant of the existence of the refugees, who are never shown in Noospace; likewise, those with the feed do not think about people in less fortunate countries, and Titus does not realize that a quarter of Americans lack the feed. Similarly, the constant parties in *Uglies* help distract the pretties from their real plight—the loss of their independent minds along with their ugly bodies—and separate them from the rest of society. David's mother in *Uglies* says that people in a city "spend their whole lives in a bubble" (*Uglies*, 260), and in *Feed*, each house or neighborhood really is in a bubble. This retreat, or denial, comes at social costs. Citizens are insular and self-interested; the fractured society that results is certainly immature. In a bubble, citizens cannot gain perspective, take responsibility, or develop agency.

Just as in our popular culture, young city dwellers in *Exodus* and *Feed* are urged to consume entertainment and buy things. As both the targets and representatives of consumerist society, teenagers are particularly susceptible to this spell. Their childish dependence on technology serves a consumerism that is dangerously mind-altering, appealing to the senses in a way that mimics direct experience. New Mungo has an Arcadia full of "bright shops and strange entertainments" like "cybervizits and safaris, realsports and feel-movies, blisspools, solhols, zoominlums, colorjetting, sensawave clubbing, fear circuses, and a hundred other[s]" (*Exodus*, 231, 254). The Looking Pond is a "false enchantment," and young people go to a club called En*trance* (*Exodus*, 233). The teenagers in these books seem to want to feel something directly and powerfully, perhaps in unconscious response to their fake environments, but ironically, their behaviors detract from true, direct experience. The pretties in *Uglies* are encouraged to party and drink, and that is all, it seems, that the teenagers in *Feed* do, unless they are at a mall. Titus and his friends also ride uninsulated wires and go into "mal," meaning deliberate malfunction, which has the disorienting effect of drugs. Even though these experiences are intense, they divert the teenagers from direct experience and worldly responsibilities, assuring their continued childish state.

Ecological utopias, however, bring teenagers the unmediated experience that helps them face reality and take responsibility—and grow up. In nature, teenagers find the unmediated, raw experience that cities cannot give them. They reject what Robin Moore calls the "secondary, vicarious, often distorted, dual sensory (vision and sound only), one-way experience of television and other electronic media"[20] in favor of direct experience marked by "fully activated senses" and paying attention to one's surroundings.[21] Tally relishes the life of the senses in nature, even if it is unpleasant. In the Smoke, "life was much more intense than in the city," with cuts that cannot be medsprayed away (*Uglies*, 229). Titus and Violet only seem to ignore the feed when they are in nature. Mara, having previously lived close to nature, is not intrigued by the "*real, extreme* fear" promised by War Games (*Exodus*, 305, italics original). The values of the ecological utopia so necessary for developing agency—independence, responsibility, self-reliance, resourcefulness—can only be transmitted through direct experience.

Even in *Feed*, where everything is unremittingly mediated by the feed, there is some attempt at direct experience. Violet occasionally insists on talking "in the air" rather than through the telepathic m-chat of the feed, and, by the end, Titus tries to resist the feed in order to have a direct—and natural—conversation with her: "I tried to talk just to her. I tried not to listen to the noise on the feed, the girls in wet shirts offering me shampoo" (*Feed*, 196, 296). Although he is still using the feed to talk to her, finding stories on it she would like, at least he is looking for news and not childish entertainment. At last he tries to focus his attention on what he can actively find on the feed rather than passively succumb to its "noise"—the first time he has used a pejorative term for the feed. Elevating the unmediated life means elevating agency, as an unmediated life is one without constant guidance. In the unmediated natural environment, young adults can gain a greater sense of control. No doubt this can be alluring to the young reader who lives in an infantilizing media bubble with limited contact with nature. However, this process demands that protagonists and readers "unplug" themselves from their popular culture and embrace nature.

While at first the texts seem to introduce a strong binary between nature and technology, the books complicate this binary, and this blurring of boundaries teaches the reader an important lesson of maturation: the need to accommodate and create a balance between opposite views. The cities in the Exodus and Uglies trilogies are technological utopias that are actually sustainable. New Mungo uses solar, wind, and wave power. In *Uglies*, "We exist in equilibrium with our environment . . . purifying the water that we put back in the river, recycling the biomass, and using only power drawn from our own solar footprint" (106–107). Its inhabitants view past citizens as immoral and ignorant in their wastefulness. However, this "utopian technology"[22] does not mean that nature is respected. The lack of contact with nature is key. Although the cities collapse the binary of nature and technology in a practical way, psychologically the divide remains, and the values of nature are lost to their citizens. The biophilia shown in technological utopias is one way in which the boundaries between the technological and ecological utopias become permeable, and the sustainability of these cities emphasizes biophilia by suggesting that rather than merely preserving nature, people should embrace it and the values it encourages.

Ironically, elements of the technological utopia are necessary to the ecological utopia. In *Pretties*, the sequel to *Uglies*, Tally discovers a kind of anthropological reservation of people living a Stone Age life; however, this natural enclave is hardly a utopia to her as it is marked by filth, entrapment, lack of privacy, and constant blood feuds. In *Uglies*, the latrines in the Smoke stank, but in *Pretties*, their sewage is treated with "nanos" and becomes inoffensive.

108 · Elaine Ostry

After all, "the Smokies had almost all been born in cities, however much they loved nature. They were products of a technological civilization, and didn't like bad smells."[23] These examples from *Pretties* suggest that Westerfeld has tried to give a more nuanced view of technology as his series progresses.

The binary is complicated further by the heroines themselves. They are all symbols of nature—but of technology, too, suggesting the value of technology. Tally and Violet are both advocates for nature with technologically modified bodies. An amalgamation of nature and technology in her Specials body with "monofilament-sheathed muscles," Tally scoffs at how David is "random: a creature put together by nature" (*Specials*, 1, 24–25). This would seem to put her completely in the camp of the technological utopia; however, she is created in part to protect the environment, a role she embraces. Technology, then, can and must be used for nature's ends—and nature needs technology, ironically, to survive the worst effects of technology. Violet's technological body, crumbling apart because of her feed's malfunction, shows the need for a balance between nature and technology.

Unlike the above heroines, Mara does not have a technological body; however, this leader of ecological utopias owns a cyberwhizz that ties her to the Weave, the broken worldwide web of the past. Through the Weave, she meets Fox, who inspires her to leave for his city of New Mungo. Fox, plotting revolution, uses the Noos to connect with fellow rebels and the general public, incite revolt, and engineer economic collapse. After the revolution seems assured, Mara decides to use the Weave's "crucial knowledge of the drowned world" to prevent past mistakes from recurring.[24] Like Tally, she aims to use technology to preserve nature as her society reinvents itself.

The collapse of the binary in these central characters points the reader to a more complex—and more mature—way of viewing technology. Technology in itself is not evil; rather, the authors suggest removing technology from the negative values of the technological utopia. This requires letting go of the self-absorption, mediated experience, and passivity previously associated with technology, and embracing the critical thinking and direct experience of the ecological utopia. It means seeing how technology can benefit a community rather than entertain an individual, and how it can preserve nature rather than destroy it. Adolescent readers can understand the binary of technological and ecological utopias not in terms of black and white, but more usefully in shades of grey. This sense of nuance corresponds to adolescents' growing understanding of the complexities of the world and the responsibilities they inherit with it.

The Ambivalent Ending: Elegy or Call to Action?

The authors present the lesson that technology can be used judiciously to help nature, but the endings of the books, particularly that of *Feed*, imply that the future of their worlds remains uncertain. Lisa Garforth suggests that Kim

Stanley Robinson and Ursula K. LeGuin figure the apocalypse as a "fresh start" with the "possibility of a better way of being," "hint[ing] at eco-apocalypse in order to foreground choice and agency."[25] In these young adult books, the same development occurs, but the hope that young protagonists show through their maturation is overshadowed by the doom of environmental destruction. This shows the central conflict in young adult dystopias: the despair of the dystopian genre runs counter to the trope of hope in young adult fiction. Kay Sambell writes that authors of young adult dystopias "often . . . suggest the future possibility, however slim, of a safe space that child protagonists may inhabit," although that may go against the "terms of the preceding narrative logic."[26] Natalie Babbitt suggests that children's literature contains "something which turns a story ultimately toward hope rather than resignation and contains within it a difference not only between the two literatures but also between youth and age."[27] But young adult literature—like teenagers themselves—occupies an uneasy space between childhood and adulthood, resting on a spectrum that has children's literature on one end and literature for adults on the other. The amount of despair that books decide to end with depends on where writers place adolescents on the maturity spectrum. How much gloom can they handle? Alexander Welsh writes, "Unless we study endings, we cannot understand how our own assumptions about human life and social change differ from those of the past."[28] The endings of these books for teenagers reflect a change in how we look at adolescents and their social role. By following through on the narrative logic that Sambell champions, these writers suggest that adolescent readers can handle the despair, but without the assurance of a happy ending, the importance of characters developing with the help of nature's values seems as limited—and undermined—as their agency.

The Uglies and Exodus trilogies do not end on highly triumphant notes. Yes, the New System will be established in the world of *Uglies*, but future environmental damage—return to twentieth-century Rusty ways—is hinted at by the city Diego's clearcutting, previously outlawed. Tally's manifesto at the end makes it clear that she feels her skills for environmental protection will be needed in further conflicts, and that the cities have not internalized the necessary lesson about balancing technology and nature. The Exodus trilogy similarly ends on a note of ambiguity: although Fox's revolution appears to be succeeding, "there's a battle ahead yet" (*Aurora*, 298). Mara sees the possibility for technology to open up the interior of Greenland, including Candlewood, thereby criticizing the isolation of this ecological utopia. Although she sees the past knowledge contained in the cyberwhizz as a means of avoiding former mistakes, she then nearly destroys it, still ambivalent about its value. The trilogy ends without a reunion of Mara and Fox and without the establishment of a new world, only its possibility.

The ending of *Feed* is far gloomier, as damaged nature takes its revenge on the technological utopia. By the end of *Feed*, swarms of bees come out of the walls as nature rebels. People are clearly going to die soon, but nature,

110 · Elaine Ostry

"so adaptable," will likely rule once more, with "new kinds of fungus . . . that were making jungles where the cables ran. There were slugs so big a toddler could ride them sidesaddle" (*Feed*, 191). The possibility of nature repairing itself is cheering news for the giant slugs but does not bode well for humans. Anderson's ending—"everything must go" (300)—can be viewed in two different ways. As Michael Levy suggests, "It may be a sign that Titus has finally seen the light and will stop at nothing to destroy the malignant, consumption-based society within which he has heretofore been trapped. Alternatively, we may simply be watching society spiraling down into its own self-made black hole."[29] Even if Titus does manage to destroy his corrupt society through a newfound maturity and agency, though, he is still faced with an environment so poisoned that people are losing their skin. With the death of nature comes our death because we *are* nature, and its possible regeneration need not include us. No amount of personal growth can change that.

Feed in particular delivers mixed messages about adolescent agency, as it is both an elegy and a call to action. Characters are helpless to save their natural world, setting an elegiac tone as the readers are asked to mourn the loss of the fictional world; it also implies readers' own lack of agency in the face of environmental catastrophe. Adding to the elegiac tone are ironic allusions to one of the first ecological utopias: Eden. In *Feed*, the use of "Eden" and "Utopia" as unit headers is clearly ironic because the garden on the moon is dead, the society dystopian. Overall, Edenic images highlight "fallen man," rather than what Eden denotes, "luxury,"[30] or implies, a new beginning.

At the same time, however, the books are meant to be calls to action. Hope primarily resides not in the books themselves, but in how profoundly young readers learn their environmental lessons. Writers call upon young adults to prevent the fictional futures from becoming reality. One of Jane Goodall's "three principles of hope" is that "energetic, committed young people are learning about the environment at an earlier age."[31] In "Our Future as a Species: A View from Biological Anthropology" (2003), Melvin Konner says that young people are "the key to the tipping point process" because they "have vision and energy, they are open-minded, and they are neither committed to the status quo nor complacent about its dangers." They must "imagine a new world"; these young adult dystopias intend to aid this process.[32] Anderson says in an interview that he "turn[s] to kids for answers. They haven't yet been fully inducted into the values and pieties of the adult political and financial world. They still feel outrage . . . It is from them that the solutions must come."[33] Bertagna addresses her readers in her preface to *Exodus*: "*Stand at the fragile moment before the devastation begins, and wonder: is this where we stand now, right here on the brink?*" (*Exodus*, 1, italics original).

This is a "tough love" or "scared straight" approach to environmental activism, in which, as Carrie Hintz and I have noted, "dystopias function as cautionary tales for a young audience, warning them to take care of the Earth and each other."[34] Whether it works is questionable. The lack of hope in *Feed*

On the Brink · **111**

and the lack of strong hopeful closure in the Uglies and Exodus trilogies may lead readers to despair as often as encourage them to join Greenpeace. It does seem contradictory to expect more from teenage readers than what their fictional counterparts can deliver. The criticism of adolescent popular culture in all the books points the finger at adolescents themselves, and this accusation may inhibit the desire to change as well. Ironically, the writers present popular culture as destructive and dominating but give much responsibility to their young readers as well as their protagonists, as if adolescents could easily separate from the popular culture that overwhelms them. Indeed, if adolescent culture itself is criticized in these novels as blinded by technology, entertainment, and consumer goods, then the idea that young people are not "committed to the status quo" fails to convince. It is ironic how Anderson states that teenagers "haven't yet been fully inducted into the values and pieties of the adult political and financial world" when Titus and his friends are entirely indoctrinated in the values of consumer capitalism, of the technological utopia. Even Violet is not completely immune. Where is the pure example for readers to follow?

Yet there is another way to view this conundrum. Being "scared straight" does work for some, and perhaps, in a noisy world, writers must exaggerate to get their readers' attention. Perhaps the more complex, even if contradictory, approach of these writers honors the ability of readers to realize that there are no easy answers to the problems we face, particularly those of the environment. The hopeful ending can be seen as somewhat forced and infantilizing, a bone thrown to the young reader. Instead, despair and inconclusiveness may encourage adolescents to face inconvenient truths, and, rather than curl up in a fetal position, be inspired to make sure environmental doom like that of the novels never comes to pass. Maybe young people, through these ecological utopias, can see the appeal of living within narrower means, and of developing the individual and communal values associated in these texts with the natural world. The call to action that would force them to change their culture may be an alluring one despite the despair of the narrative. It may help them see themselves and their culture more clearly, discerning the real from the fake, the direct from the mediated. Because the world is becoming increasingly urban, and technology is not going away, adolescents do not have the luxury of thinking of nature as a utopian escape. They will have to reassess their attitudes towards nature, technology, and their own techno-infused culture. This process may lead eventually to a more sustainable society as well as greater individual maturation.

Notes

1　The publication of *Extras* (2007) makes *Uglies* a series, not a trilogy. However, the first three books have a narrative arc centered on Tally, the city,

112 · Elaine Ostry

and the Smoke that makes them function as a trilogy. *Specials* is advertised on the cover as "the final volume in the highly acclaimed UGLIES trilogy."

2 Marius de Geus, *Ecological Utopias: Envisioning the Sustainable Society* (Utrecht, The Netherlands: International Books, 1999), 21. For a critique of Geus, see Lisa Garforth, "Green Utopias: Beyond Apocalypse, Progress, and Pastoral," *Utopian Studies* 16.3 (2005).

3 Geus, *Ecological Utopias*, 22.

4 M.T. Anderson, *Feed* (Cambridge, MA: Candlewick Press, 2002), 48. Subsequent references will be cited parenthetically in the text.

5 Scott Westerfeld, *Uglies* (New York: Simon Pulse, 2005), 232. Subsequent references will be cited parenthetically in the text.

6 James Blasingame, "An Interview with M.T. (Tobin) Anderson," *Journal of Adolescent and Adult Literacy* 47.1 (2003): 99.

7 Geus, *Ecological Utopias*, 20.

8 Ibid., 21.

9 Ibid., italics original.

10 Richard Louv, *Last Child in the Woods: Saving Our Children from Nature-Deficit Disorder* (Chapel Hill, NC: Algonquin Books of Chapel Hill, 2008).

11 D.H. Lawrence, *Phoenix: The Posthumous Papers of D.H. Laurence*, ed. Edward D. McDonald (New York: Viking, 1936), 141, qtd. in Louv, *Last Child*, 59.

12 Scott Westerfeld, *Specials* (New York: Simon Pulse, 2006), 372, italics original. Subsequent references will be cited parenthetically in the text.

13 Geus, *Ecological Utopias*, 22, italics original.

14 Julie Bertagna, *Exodus* (New York: Walker and Co., 2002), 233. Subsequent references will be cited parenthetically in the text.

15 Geus, *Ecological Utopias*, 22.

16 Edward O. Wilson, *Biophilia* (Cambridge, MA: Harvard University Press, 1984), 85, qtd. in Louv, *Last Child*, 43.

17 Louv, *Last Child*, 43.

18 Ibid., 36.

19 Aldous Huxley, *Brave New World and Brave New World Revisited* (1932; New York: HarperPerennial, 2005), 35–36.

20 Robin C. Moore, "The Need for Nature: A Childhood Right," *Social Justice* 24.3 (1997): 209, qtd. in Louv, *Last Child*, 66.

21 Louv, *Last Child*, 58.

22 David Dickson, *Alternative Technology and the Politics of Technical Change* (London: Fantana, 1974), 101, qtd. in Krishan Kumar, *Utopia and Anti-Utopia* (Oxford: Basil Blackwell, 1987), 406.

23 Scott Westerfeld, *Pretties* (New York: Simon Pulse, 2005), 274.

24 Julie Bertagna, *Aurora* (London: Macmillan, 2001), 280. Subsequent references will be cited parenthetically in the text.

On the Brink · **113**

25 Garforth, "Green Utopias," 398, 403, 399.
26 Kay Sambell, "Presenting the Case for Social Change: The Creative Dilemma of Dystopian Writing for Children," in *Utopian and Dystopian Writing for Children and Young Adults*, ed. Carrie Hintz and Elaine Ostry (New York: Routledge, 2003), 172–173.
27 Natalie Babbitt, "Happy Endings? Of Course, and Also Joy," in *Children's Literature: Views and Reviews*, ed. Virginia Haviland (London: Bodley Head, 1973), 158, qtd. in Sambell, "Presenting,"165.
28 Alexander Welsh, "Foreword," *Nineteenth-Century Fiction*, special issue: *Narrative Endings* 33.1 (1978): 1, qtd. in Walter Pape, "Happy Endings in a World of Misery: A Literary Convention between Social Constraints and Utopia in Children's and Young Adult Literature," *Poetics Today* 13.1 (1992): 180.
29 Michael Levy, "'The Sublimation of Real Life': Malls, Shopping, and Advertising in Recent Young Adult SF," *The New York Review of Science Fiction* 18.7 (2006): 12.
30 Danielle Lecoq and Roland Schaer, "Ancient, Biblical and Medieval Traditions," in *Utopia: The Search for the Ideal Society in the Western World*, ed. Roland Schaer, Gregory Claeys, and Lyman Tower Sargent (New York: Oxford University Press, 2000), 38.
31 Kathryn Graham, "Exodus from the City: Peter Dickinson's *Eva*," *The Lion and the Unicorn* 23.1 (1999): 84.
32 Melvin Konner, "Our Future as a Species: A View from Biological Anthropology," in *Viable Utopian Ideas: Shaping a Better World*, ed. Arthur B. Shostak (Armonk, NY: M.E. Sharpe, 2003), 240.
33 Blasingame, "Interview," 98.
34 Carrie Hintz and Elaine Ostry, introduction to *Utopian and Dystopian Writing for Children and Young Adults*, ed. Carrie Hintz and Elaine Ostry (New York: Routledge, 2003), 12.

Works Cited

Anderson, M.T. *Feed*. Cambridge, MA: Candlewick Press, 2002.
Babbitt, Natalie. "Happy Endings? Of Course, and Also Joy." *Children's Literature: Views and Reviews*, edited by Virginia Haviland, 155–159. London: Bodley Head, 1978.
Bertagna, Julie. *Aurora*. London: Macmillan, 2011.
———. *Exodus*. New York: Walker and Co., 2002.
———. *Zenith*. London: Young Picador, 2007.
Blasingame, James. "An Interview with M.T. (Tobin) Anderson." *Journal of Adolescent and Adult Literacy* 47.1 (2003): 98–99.
Dickson, David. *Alternative Technology and the Politics of Technical Change*. London: Fantana, 1974.
Garforth, Lisa. "Green Utopias: Beyond Apocalypse, Progress, and Pastoral." *Utopian Studies* 16.3 (2005): 393–427.
Geus, Marius de. *Ecological Utopias: Envisioning the Sustainable Society*. Utrecht, The Netherlands: International Books, 1999.
Graham, Kathryn. "Exodus from the City: Peter Dickinson's *Eva*." *The Lion and the Unicorn* 23.1 (1999): 79–85.
Hintz, Carrie and Elaine Ostry. Introduction to *Utopian and Dystopian Writing for Children and Young Adults*, edited by Carrie Hintz and Elaine Ostry, 1–20. New York: Routledge, 2003.

114 • Elaine Ostry

Huxley, Aldous. 1932. *Brave New World and Brave New World Revisited*. New York: HarperPerennial, 2005.

Konner, Melvin. "Our Future as a Species: A View from Biological Anthropology." In *Viable Utopian Ideas: Shaping a Better World*, edited by Arthur B. Shostak, 237–244. Armonk, NY: M.E. Sharpe, 2003.

Kumar, Krishan. *Utopia and Anti-Utopia*. Oxford: Basil Blackwell, 1987.

Lawrence, D.H. *Phoenix: The Posthumous Papers of D.H. Laurence*. Edited by Edward D. McDonald. New York: Viking, 1936.

Lecoq, Danielle and Roland Schaer. "Ancient, Biblical and Medieval Traditions." In *Utopia: The Search for the Ideal Society in the Western World*, edited by Roland Schaer, Gregory Claeys, and Lyman Tower Sargent, 35–82. New York: Oxford University Press, 2000.

Levy, Michael. "'The Sublimation of Real Life': Malls, Shopping, and Advertising in Recent Young Adult SF." *The New York Review of Science Fiction* 18.7 (2006): 10–12.

Louv, Richard. *Last Child in the Woods: Saving Our Children from Nature-Deficit Disorder*. Chapel Hill, NC: Algonquin Books of Chapel Hill, 2008.

Moore, Robin C. "The Need for Nature: A Childhood Right." *Social Justice* 24.3 (1997): 203–220.

Pape, Walter. "Happy Endings in a World of Misery: A Literary Convention between Social Constraints and Utopia in Children's and Adult Literature." *Poetics Today* 13.1 (1992): 179–196.

Sambell, Kay. "Presenting the Case for Social Change: The Creative Dilemma of Dystopian Writing for Children." In *Utopian and Dystopian Writing for Children and Young Adults*, edited by Carrie Hintz and Elaine Ostry, 163–178. New York: Routledge, 2003.

Welsh, Alexander. "Foreword." *Nineteenth-Century Fiction*, special issue: *Narrative Endings* 33.1 (1978): 1–2.

Westerfeld, Scott. *Extras*. New York: Simon Pulse, 2007.

———. *Pretties*. New York: Simon Pulse, 2005.

———. *Specials*. New York: Simon Pulse, 2006.

———. *Uglies*. New York: Simon Pulse, 2005.

Wilson, Edward O. *Biophilia*. Cambridge, MA: Harvard University Press, 1984.

Part Three

Radical or Conservative?

Polemics of the Future

Chapter Seven
"The Dandelion in the Spring"
Utopia as Romance in Suzanne Collins's *The Hunger Games* Trilogy

Katherine R. Broad

The New Heroines of YA Dystopian Fiction

Suzanne Collins's The Hunger Games trilogy (2008–2010) has been widely celebrated for its portrayal of a tough-minded young woman who, through a mix of gumption and luck, challenges authority to become a central figure in a larger revolution against a violent dystopian regime. Collins boldly flouts literary stereotypes that keep female protagonists waiting at home, and proclaims that girls can do anything boys can do, including strategize, make demands, and even hunt and kill. Readers across the blogosphere have written extensively about their excitement over Katniss and her fight. "I would encourage my daughter to read this series," writes one fashion blogger. A former political science professor glows, "I am thrilled that a popular book series features a strong, kick-ass-and-take-names female character."[1] Feminist pop culture authority *Bitch Magazine* extols "Katniss Everdeen's value as a feminist heroine" and includes *The Hunger Games* on its list of "100 Young Adult Books for the Feminist Reader."[2] It is hardly an exaggeration when Meghan Lewitt declares this "tough-as-nails" protagonist "the most important female character in recent pop culture history." "Katniss Everdeen is more than just a teen idol of the moment," Lewitt insists. "She is a heroine for the ages."[3]

But even as readers are raving about the ways Katniss can inspire young female readers by modeling a strong and competent heroine, a closer reading suggests that her character also imparts a very different message, one that tells girls the importance of growing up to find satisfaction in heterosexual

118 • Katherine R. Broad

love and the nuclear family. For all its attention to Katniss's rebellion, The Hunger Games trilogy is, significantly, a love story, tracing Katniss's fluctuating desires for two boys who fight alongside her. As one teen reviewer describes the second book in the series, "This is about Katniss and her love and how they manage to get called back to the Hunger Games and how they manage to outsmart the Capitol."[4] This reader is only thirteen and uses four exclamation points to underscore how "amazing" the books are, but her enthusiasm highlights the centrality of romance to the novel. Readers are as much on the edge of their seats asking "Peeta or Gale?" as they are wondering how the trio will outrun, outsmart, and outlast the enemy at their heels. Most adult critics tend to read the romance as a secondary concern, and those who do see it as more central to the novels tend to wish it wasn't.[5] Yet if there are "a bunch of big ideas driving the book, from the injustice of a few people living in comfort while the rest of the world goes hungry to the priority placed on entertainment in a society where many do without necessities,"[6] another driving force is undoubtedly romance. The love triangle plays a significant role in fueling the narrative progression toward a better world: each boy represents a different path out of dystopia, making the outcome of the romantic choice nothing less than what the future society will be. The courtship narrative therefore says a great deal about Katniss's revolutionary potential and, in turn, raises significant questions about her revered status as a feminist icon for readers of all ages.

The Love Triangle

The Hunger Games (2008), *Catching Fire* (2009), and *Mockingjay* (2010) describe a future U.S. known as Panem, comprised of a wealthy Capitol surrounded by twelve impoverished districts. As retribution for a long-ago rebellion, the Capitol makes each district select a boy and girl by lottery to compete in the annual Hunger Games. The twenty-four tributes are dressed up, paraded around, forced to perform for judges, and then placed in an arena where they fight to the death in a televised bloodbath. The last child remaining is crowned victor and his or her district given enough food to survive for the year. Katniss becomes a tribute when she volunteers to take the place of her younger sister, Prim. In the arena with her is Peeta Mellark, the baker's son, who once risked a beating from his mother to give Katniss a loaf of bread when she was starving. Katniss and Peeta manage to survive the games in the first book, only to be thrust into another game in book two, this time with the tributes chosen from among the victors of past years. At the end of *Catching Fire*, Katniss escapes the arena and joins a rebel group, but the Capitol captures Peeta. In *Mockingjay*, she tries to save him while becoming the leading figure of a revolution bent on overthrowing the Capitol and establishing a new democratic republic in Panem.

"The Dandelion in the Spring" • 119

Readers might protest that Katniss is surely not preoccupied with having a boyfriend, given that she repeatedly proclaims she's not interested in boys or dating. When we first meet her best friend and childhood confidant, Gale, she maintains, "There's never been anything romantic between Gale and me," and even though she thinks he'll marry one of the girls who ogle him at school, she insists, "It makes me jealous but not for the reason people would think. Good hunting partners are hard to find."[7] Yet as Laura Miller points out, Katniss can be unreliable as a narrator, especially in instances when her internal desires contradict her alleged wants. For example, while she turns up her nose at the Capitol's opulence, "her professed claim to hate it all is undermined by the loving detail with which she describes every last goody."[8] This does not mean readers should not trust when a female protagonist says "no," but in traditional romance literature, a professed disinterest in love is easily remedied over time: "The hero makes the heroine accept what she craves while she gets to deny how much she craves it."[9] Based on the conventions of romance and Katniss's own capriciousness, her insistence that she has no romantic interest in Gale instead draws attention to what Stephen King calls the "sorta-crush" she is developing.[10]

The contradiction between Katniss's professed disinterest and her nascent desires becomes a productive source of tension throughout all three novels. In continuing her posturing against romance, Katniss is initially furious when Peeta works with mentor Haymitch Abernathy, who won the games years before, to present themselves as star-crossed lovers rather than adversaries when they enter the games. She complains that Peeta's public declaration of love has turned her "into some kind of fool in front of the entire country" and fears "he made me look weak!" (*Hunger*, 135). But while Katniss associates romance with vulnerability, their love story turns out to be an immeasurable aid. As expected, the crowd goes wild over their tale, increasing their appeal to sponsors who send them aid like food, water, and medicine in the arena. Their appeal to the audience is also an appeal to the reader—romance makes a good story. The citizens of Panem are glued to their TV screens watching Katniss's romance unfold just as the reader eagerly turns the pages of the book wondering how the budding triangle will resolve.

Initially, then, the performance of Katniss's fake romance with Peeta draws the reader into the drama at the same time that it reiterates the spectacle of the games themselves, typifying all that is wrong with the dystopian regime. The romance plot self-consciously calls attention to itself as a way of manipulating an audience's emotions to ensure its continued engagement: Collins takes pains to depict the pettiness of the makeup, camera crews, and reality-TV nature of the games, and of the publicized courtship itself. But as the drama progresses, Katniss starts believing the story of her love for Peeta. She reminds herself to act wild about Peeta when she knows the cameras are on her but also finds herself longing for private moments with him—for real kisses, not televised ones. When Peeta tells her he's been in love with her since they were five,

120 • Katherine R. Broad

she thinks, "For a moment I'm almost foolishly happy and then confusion sweeps over me. Because we're supposed to be making up this stuff, playing at being in love, not actually being in love. But Peeta's story has a ring of truth in it . . . could it all be true?" (*Hunger*, 301). At the same time, she wonders how all this kissing is going to play to her best friend back home. With Katniss's feelings for Peeta growing increasingly muddled, the novels transform romance from a strategy and ploy into a central and pressing concern. Even as Katniss is forced to keep acting out her love for Peeta in *Catching Fire*, the idea that she is utilizing the conventions of romance for political leverage against the Capitol is complicated, if not downright undercut, by how much her act becomes real to her.

In considering the ways romance is figured as strategic and then as sincere, I confess that throughout much of my first reading of the trilogy, I hoped Katniss would refuse the fictionalization of her life and the narrative of her love for Peeta that had been created without her consent. I thought she would wind up with Gale, not only because I agreed with *People* magazine's assertion that the "boy back home" was "Katniss's real soulmate,"[11] but because I thought choosing Gale meant choosing her own path and rejecting the stories constructed about her. My surprise and disappointment that Katniss (spoiler alert) winds up with Peeta forced me to confront the ways I had willfully misread the novels. Gale is the revolutionary figure, the one who rails against the Capitol, seeks to initiate change, and actually does things besides get injured and pine for Katniss. But subsequent readings revealed to me the myriad ways in which the novels set up Peeta to be the "right" choice for Katniss. In working through the logic that informs the resolution of the courtship drama, I came to better understand the novels' conception of change. What I missed in my first, hopeful reading is the extent to which the novels present Gale as the necessary but ultimately undesirable underside of revolutionary politics. Instead, Collins supports Peeta, loyal lover who dreams of a quiet and private home life as the end goal of utopia and the reason for social change.

Saving the Baker's Son

Katniss initially avoids courtship not because she dislikes either suitor, but because she feels she must avoid marriage and reproduction at all costs. The dystopian society is overwhelmingly against the nuclear family, the social unit the novels will come to idealize as the antithesis to all the dystopia represents. Katniss's childhood was brutally cut short after her father was killed in a mining accident, and her "beaten-down" mother never recovered from her despair (*Hunger*, 3). She recalls how, "at eleven years old, with Prim just seven, I took over as head of the family" because "my mother could no longer care for us" (*Hunger*, 27).[12] But even if Katniss could one day give her own children the safety and care she lacked in her upbringing, she could never protect them

"The Dandelion in the Spring" • 121

from being eligible for the games. This is why Katniss announces in the first few pages of *The Hunger Games*, "I never want to have kids" and later reiterates, "I know I'll never marry, never risk bringing a child into the world" (9, 311). Nor can she picture an alternative; when Gale responds that he might want kids if he didn't live in District 12, Katniss retorts, "But you do" (*Hunger*, 9).

Katniss's inability to picture a world in which it would be safe to have kids sets the stage for her utopian transformation, as the narrative expands her horizon of possibility to include child-bearing as an option. In *Catching Fire*, after Katniss has survived the first games, her sense of the possible starts to shift. In the arena one night in the second games, Peeta announces he will sacrifice himself so she can survive. Katniss wonders if what Peeta says is "a reminder to me that I could still one day have kids with Gale." She is quick to reject this option, because "that's never been part of my plan," but then considers another scenario in which Peeta survives to have kids. "If only one of us can be a parent," she thinks, "anyone can see it should be Peeta." This notion of parenting leads Katniss to voice a new, utopian possibility predicated on reproduction: "As I drift off, I try to imagine that world, somewhere in the future, with no Games, no Capitol ... Where Peeta's child could be safe."[13] This is the first time we hear Katniss "imagine that world" where children are not threatened by the Capitol's violence.

Longing for this possible future, Katniss's rebellion is largely fueled by her desire for a stable family and home. She looks forward to being "able to afford the kind of love that leads to a family, to children" (*Hunger*, 373). Later on, she also yearns for a time back when "I knew what my place was in the tightly interwoven fabric that was our life," a time that "seems so secure" (*Catching*, 7). Carrie Hintz suggests that YA utopian fiction and speculative writing provides "almost an exaggerated way for the young adult to find his or her voice, and this voice is seen having a deep effect on a wider society." But rather than giving "young people the impression that they have the capacity to remake or revision society anew," Collins's trilogy exhorts Katniss to use this voice for a more modest and conservative purpose: creating the family she never had.[14] It's possible to read such a message positively; Melissa Gross seems quite optimistic when she determines that the "wish for tomorrow presented" in YA dystopias like Lois Lowry's *The Giver* (1993) is not "power, recognition, or fame ... what these adolescents want is family love."[15] But to what extent does this wish for the safe and the stable risk eclipsing the transformative potential of both adolescent rebellion and dystopian literature to imagine other worlds?

That Katniss's revolutionary status is fueled by her wish to realize the normative family life embodied by Peeta's future children effectively circumscribes the impact of her rebellion, making his safety her primary concern. This is not to say that saving others is an unworthy goal, or that revolutionary justice is somehow legitimate only when enacted for ones we don't know rather than ones we do. My point is rather that since Katniss is so focused on Peeta, she goes out on a limb only to save him; her heroism is

122 • Katherine R. Broad

highly limited and determined by their romance and by her idealized vision of family life. Hence at the end of the first games, actions that are interpreted as revolutionary are anything but. When Peeta and Katniss are the last tributes standing, Katniss picks poisonous berries so they can commit suicide together, sparing her the responsibility of murdering him (only one tribute can win). Before the berries pass their lips, a broadcaster announces the rules have changed and both may live, lest the Capitol wind up with no winners at all. The gesture is interpreted across Panem as a rejection of the games and defiance against the Capitol, but it was never calculated to inspire revolution.

With Peeta's survival, the desire to protect him as a future parent then comes to shape Katniss's revolutionary potential as an ostensible figure for social change. In *Mockingjay*, Katniss has been rescued from the arena by a group of rebel forces from District 13, an area once thought destroyed by the Capitol. The rebels see Katniss as "the face of the hoped-for rebellion" and want her to become the "Mockingjay," a "symbol of resistance" (*Catching*, 150). Katniss is reluctant to assume this role, in part because she does not trust the rebels and in part because she is loath to take on tasks that go beyond ensuring her personal survival. Only when Gale asks Katniss what she is going to do to save Peeta, who has been captured by the Capitol, does she finally announce what she has been resisting: "I'm going to be the Mockingjay."[16] Laura Miller reads this as "a free, affirmative choice,"[17] but it's still one Katniss has been manipulated into, and it is only to protect Peeta. Romance cements Katniss's cause to the revolution at the same time that it renders her a docile subject manipulated by both sides of the war.

As the Mockingjay, Katniss's involvement in the revolution is contingent upon Peeta's safety. The rebels stage a risky operation to rescue Peeta from the Capitol because Katniss is too distraught to function while he is endangered. As they explain, "We can't lose the Mockingjay now. And you can't perform unless you know Snow can't take it out on Peeta" (*Mockingjay*, 164). The rescue goes a little too easily, though, because it turns out the Capitol wants Katniss to have Peeta back after they "hijack" his memories and brainwash him into thinking Katniss is evil. Katniss is devastated less by the loss of Peeta than by the loss of his love for her: "All those months of taking it for granted that Peeta thought I was wonderful are over" (*Mockingjay*, 232). Although she tries to run into Gale's arms, the substitute is inadequate and she finds she cannot perform her heroics while Peeta is still in pain. Katniss's rebellious acts are motivated by Peeta, not by politics; she realizes "my fixation with assassinating Snow has allowed me to ignore a much more difficult problem. Trying to rescue Peeta from the shadowy world the hijacking has stranded him in" (*Mockingjay*, 269). To the extent that Katniss's fight is with the Capitol, it is over its treatment of Peeta and whether it will be possible to create a world in which he—and their future children—will be safe.

"The Dandelion in the Spring" • 123

While Katniss is the symbol of the revolution and Peeta her muse, it is unclear what either of them actually do besides provide a face for the rebels. The one who engages directly in revolutionary activities is Gale. An expert hunter with uncanny ability in "thinking like our enemy" (*Mockingjay*, 98), Gale's ruthlessness becomes apparent when he devises a plan to attack District 2, the last district to fall to rebel forces. Gale treats the district's stronghold as a wild dog den, deciding they can either trap the "dogs" inside or "flush them out" (*Mockingjay*, 202). Instead of securing the den, the rebels bomb it out of commission, along with the victims trapped inside. Gale defends the costs of victory because "by taking them out, we prevented further attacks," but he worries Katniss will think him "heartless" (*Mockingjay*, 222, 221). And she does: Katniss acknowledges the point of war is to kill, yet she fears Gale's rationalizations could justify "killing anyone at any time" (*Mockingjay*, 222). She struggles to explain the problem with Gale's approach, all the while knowing Peeta "would be able to articulate why it is so wrong" (*Mockingjay*, 211). It is Gale's final act of war that finally clarifies for Katniss the full costs of revolution: as silver parachutes drop over a horde of fleeing children, the kids rush to them, thinking they are aid. The parachutes then detonate in a fiery explosion that leaves Katniss's sister Prim among the countless dead.

Even though the parachutes are essential for toppling the Capitol and winning the war, their use reproduces the same destructive logic the rebels are ostensibly oriented against. Gale justifies his violence with the incisive statement, "I have been following the same rule book President Snow used," locking the perpetrators into an endless cycle of violence (*Mockingjay*, 186). Katniss rejects Gale's methods as a viable means of achieving a better future, yet that future remains predicated on the actions she condemns. Katniss herself is unable to escape this spiral; in the moment in which she is about to kill Snow, she raises her bow and kills the new president Coin instead, toppling the rebel regime. It is unclear how Katniss's individual feat of heroic violence enacted against the concept of heroic violence initiates some kind of alternate world order, but somehow this instance leads to the installation of a replacement government and the triumph of a new society.

This kind of straight talking and merciless action leads readers like John Green and Yvonne Zipp to read Katniss as entirely unsentimental,[18] but Katniss's insights into the nature of violence lead to a surprisingly mawkish reverie. Deciding that love must help to moderate her destructive sensibilities, Katniss concludes that she and Gale are simply too much alike. Her claims that he knows her better than anyone else, and that around him she can be herself, are in fact strikes against him. Eventually she decides:

> What I need to survive is not Gale's fire, kindled with rage and hatred. I have plenty of fire myself. What I need is the dandelion in the spring. The bright yellow that means rebirth instead of destruction. The promise that

124 • Katherine R. Broad

life can go on, no matter how bad our losses. That it can be good again. And only Peeta can give me that (*Mockingjay*, 388).

Never mind that it is Gale who helps Katniss survive when they are starving children in District 12—Katniss is more interested in the symbols of survival: springtime, yellow, flowers, Peeta. What Katniss suggests through this flight into lyricism is that proper heterosexual relationships cannot be between people who are too similar. She must balance the temperaments of the sexes to form a union suitable for fertility and growth.

It is therefore Peeta who offers a new future counter to the violent dystopian realm. Katniss repeatedly insists Peeta is "truly, deep-down better than the rest of us" (*Catching*, 277) because he never kills anyone in the arena (although the fact that others call him "a victor by chance" [*Catching*, 277] downplays the central role Katniss plays in keeping him alive). Uncorrupted by the harsh adult world (Katniss repeatedly calls him "boy" and "the boy with the bread"), Peeta is an ideal balance for Katniss's ruthless spirit. When President Coin proposes "a final, symbolic Hunger Games" using the children of those who had been in power in the Capitol, Katniss says, "I vote yes . . . for Prim" (*Mockingjay*, 370). But while she votes for the renewed games because "Nothing has changed. Nothing will ever change now," Peeta holds out hope for another world: "'No!' bursts out Peeta. 'I vote no, of course! We can't have another Hunger Games!'" (*Mockingjay*, 370, 369). Peeta's vote is a vote for another kind of future. And while it is a vote against Katniss, the novel is clear that his path is the right one. We are supposed to feel Katniss has made the wrong decision in this moment; the point is that Peeta countermands her. As Haymitch tells Katniss, "You could live a hundred lifetimes and not deserve him, you know" (*Catching*, 178). Peeta exists to remind Katniss of the better way.

A "Cop-Out" Conclusion

But although Peeta is meant to represent the better option, the choice of a suitor is one that Katniss is never allowed to make; she simply winds up with the one who pursues her back to the bombed out District 12 at the end of the war. There is no moment of decision, no expression of desire, and no evidence of Katniss exhibiting agency or control over her life. Instead, the resolution to the triangle built up through all three volumes is entirely passive. After Prim's death, we learn only that Gale has "some fancy job" in District 2, presumably working for the new government. Katniss feels "relief" and gives no more mention of her former friend (*Mockingjay*, 384). When Peeta shows up on her doorstep to plant flowers—that symbol again—Katniss suddenly overcomes her despair. Even as the novels drag out the question of which one she will choose, in the end, the men make the choice for her. Just as she does as a

"The Dandelion in the Spring" • 125

revolutionary figure, Katniss yields to others to make decisions for her, making the correct choice only when there is no choice left to be made.

The series' conclusion in an epic heroine defaulting to a safe, stable, and highly insular heterosexual reproductive union—a union so much like the social and sexual status quo of our own world—raises questions about just what has been transformed by Katniss's harrowing fight. For the epilogue, much like the ending to the Harry Potter series, concludes with a vision of the next generation safe and smiling, as Katniss and Peeta's children run around on their "chubby toddler legs" (*Mockingjay*, 389). With no knowledge of the games, these children are secure in their childhood and protected from the world in a way Katniss never was. This picture of childhood innocence thus becomes the end result of all Katniss has fought for. If the upshot of overthrowing a dystopian regime is being able to settle down and have kids, then whatever happens in the rest of the country will not involve Katniss. We get no vision of what this new society looks like, how it is structured, or how Katniss spends her time with the few hundred others left in the district. But this end vision is utopian for the way it fulfills her dream of a seemingly impossible world without the Capitol, offers an obvious improvement over the previous dystopian regime, and highlights the possibility of enacting social change, however limited. This utopia is less a political arrangement than a conception of home as a stable, loving home and nuclear family, insular and protected from the outside world.

In showing us this tough fighter watching her children play, Collins follows what Deborah O'Keefe terms the "cop-out pattern" in which "heroines ultimately [give] up their independent vision and [subside] . . . into traditional behavior."[19] Annis Pratt calls this depiction of female growing up a kind of "growing down." Lorna Ellis elaborates, "The protagonists begin as self-assured young women who question their subordinate place in society, but the endings find them less active, less assertive, and reintegrated into society through marriage."[20] That Katniss's cop-out comes across in a short epilogue does not diminish the importance of this concluding vision to the overall narrative. It reframes the way we read the rest of the novels as it redirects the energies of the narrative from social upheaval to the maintenance of a reproductive status quo and ensures that Katniss's rebellion serves to keep her an appropriately gendered, reproductive, and ultimately docile subject.

Thus even with the trilogy's seeming gender equality—girls can do anything, like beat the boys in the arena and assassinate the president—Katniss is hardly a feminist figurehead. As Elaine O'Quinn explains, "Traditional fiction for girls encourages them to be suffering, passive, bystanders of life."[21] Katniss certainly suffers, and despite all her heroics with a bow and arrow, she is a passive heroine, manipulated into outfits, relationships, arenas, and TV shoots, trying to figure out what everyone wants from her while asserting little of her own needs and goals. When she does make demands, it is to ensure the safety of her beloved—as when she makes Peeta's immunity a condition of her assumption

126 • Katherine R. Broad

of the Mockingjay role. It is also hard to see Katniss standing up tall on her own when we contend with how duty-bound and wracked with guilt she remains. Despite her brief moments of rebellion, she is deeply preoccupied with obedience (and her rebelliousness is always rewarded as the right thing to have done). In being uncertain about whom to trust, she feels helpless and confused, oscillating between which men—Peeta, Gale, or Haymitch—might best help her.

That Peeta is associated with utopian gentleness and Katniss with dystopian violence, upsetting stereotypical gender associations, should not lead us to think that their gender roles are truly reversed or that the text offers more open examples of gender possibilities. The potential disruption of traditional gender roles in making Katniss the savior and Peeta the one who needs saving is superficial rather than substantive; after all, the good girl is supposed to help others, not be helped herself. Although Katniss wins the games, her mission to rescue Peeta reinforces the stereotype that "boys must win, so they need somebody to beat" while "girls must create harmony, so they need somebody to help."[22] At one point, Gale says he knows Katniss will kiss him "because I'm in pain . . . that's that only way I get your attention," but later he compares himself to Peeta, concluding, "I'll never compete with that. No matter how much pain I'm in" (*Mockingjay*, 130, 197). The fact that Katniss winds up with the boy who suffers the most, rather than reversing gender roles and showing a male character as helpless, affirms that despite her tough exterior, Katniss is still associated with caretaking.

Katniss's passivity ensures that she isn't too forward, too desiring, or too brash. Her reluctance to take the spotlight, rather than heightening any later heroism, assures readers she is not overly assertive. As Susan Fraiman explains, in "nineteenth-century views of proper development," girls were taught that "to be exceptional is to be morally suspect."[23] Katniss gets around her unbecoming behavior by insisting she never wanted to stand out. Laura Miller's reading here is informative:

> If Katniss sought to be the center of attention, if she chose to string along two handsome young men more than willing to give their lives for hers, if she wanted to have her every moment photographed and admired, if she dreamed of leading the revolution, if she longed to compete and to win—if she had any ambition at all—she would be a bad girl by such a standard.[24]

Katniss is a hero to the extent that a symbol, rather than a decisive actor, can be heroic, and to the extent that she convinces us she never wanted to be a hero in the first place. Perhaps it is a step forward for YA dystopias to allow female characters moments of success. But it is a small step if that success is only allowed to happen *to* female characters, rather than come from their agency and action, and if it primarily serves to uphold rather than transform the status quo.

Ultimately, the final image of complacent adulthood with husband and children suggests that Katniss's instances of rebellion are permissible for girls, not women. Writers traditionally give children greater leeway with gender; it is only when girls grow up that they must lose their independent agency and adopt properly gendered behavior. For instance, Jane M. Agee argues that in Newbery Award-winning children's books *Caddie Woodlawn* (1935) and *Jacob Have I Loved* (1980), female characters are allowed to spend their youths as tomboys, but authors "bring their characters back into conventional gender roles rather abruptly when the characters become young women."[25] Girls like Caddie and Louise skin their knees and dream about their futures, but their wayward adventures must eventually come to a close.[26] Katniss takes to the woods in her father's hunting coat because of her youth; although she is smart, resourceful, and a superior markswoman, her growing up involves removing herself from political involvement and retreating to the domestic sphere in order to raise children.

Angela Hubler suggests that such a condemnation of latent oppression is inadequate because it presumes a liberal feminist paradigm, which imagines individuals as free agents able to make their own decisions while disregarding how larger social, political, and economic structures can limit personal choice. Hubler makes the important point that "replacing stereotypical depictions of women and girls with liberated ones is insufficient to overcome women's subordination," because "no matter how strong and independent blacks and women might be, they cannot eradicate these systems of inequality simply by proving themselves or educating those in power."[27] I agree, but I don't see how that leads Hubler to determine that "it is not crucial . . . whether the conclusion to *Caddie Woodlawn* or *Jacob Have I Loved* is feminist or a capitulation to gender stereotypes."[28] Nor do we have to choose between these two forms of feminist activism. It is vital that we push back against popular interpretations of characters like Katniss as feminist agents and icons for young women and call out YA dystopian novels that hinge on gender stereotypes that flatten female characters into passive roles as mothers and wives. There are forces at work that shape opportunity, yet literary representations of female characters participate in shaping these choices by reproducing and so further normalizing standards for female behavior and expectations for romance. As Joanne Brown and Nancy St. Clair assert, "Because girls' stories have conventionally ended with a marriage or mating in which the female protagonist assumes a subordinate role, fiction about empowered girls must find ways to subvert that ending."[29] One important way for YA dystopias to imagine social transformation that does more than reinsert female characters into conservative gender roles is therefore perhaps to start by complicating, subverting, or even downright rejecting the conventions of the romance plot that place women in such positions.

Notes

1 Alison Gary, "Not Fashion Related: *The Hunger Games*," *Wardrobe Oxygen*, October 20, 2011, http://www.wardrobeoxygen.com/2011/10/not-fashion-related-hunger-games.html#.TsU_lk-W5m0; Laura McKenna,

128 · Katherine R. Broad

"Feminism and *The Hunger Games*," *Apt. 11D*, November 15, 2011, http://www.apt11d.com/2011/11/feminism-and-the-hunger-games.html.

2 Sarah Seltzer, "Hunger Pangs: Hunting for the Perfect Heroine," *Bitch Magazine* 51 (2011): 40; Ashley McAllister, "100 Young Adult Books for the Feminist Reader," *Bitch Magazine*, January 28, 2011, http://bitchmagazine.org/100-young-adult-books-for-the-feminist-reader.

3 Meghan Lewitt, "Casting 'The Hunger Games': In Praise of Katniss Everdeen," *The Atlantic*, March 9, 2011, http://www.theatlantic.com/entertainment/archive/2011/03/ casting-the-hunger-games-in-praise-of-katniss-everdeen/72164/.

4 Shelby, "Catching Fire," *Genrefluent*'s *Bistro Book Club*, July 1, 2009, http://genrefluentteentalk.blogspot.com/2009/07/catching-fire-by-suzanne-collins.html.

5 See Lewitt, "Casting"; Stephen King, "The Hunger Games," *Entertainment Weekly*, September 12, 2008, 139; and Carol Stabile, "Review Essay: 'First He'll Kill Her Then I'll Save Her': Vampires, Feminism, and the *Twilight* Franchise," *Journal of Communication* 61 (2011): E7.

6 Yvonne Zipp, "Classic Review: *The Hunger Games*," *Christian Science Monitor*, December 27, 2008, http://www.csmonitor.com/Books/Book-Reviews/2010/0829/Classic-review-The-Hunger-Games.

7 Suzanne Collins, *The Hunger Games* (New York: Scholastic Press, 2008), 10. Subsequent references will be cited parenthetically in the text.

8 Laura Miller, "Fresh Hell: What's Behind the Boom in Dystopian Fiction for Young Adults?," *The New Yorker*, June 14, 2010, http://www.newyorker.com/arts/critics/atlarge. /2010/06/14/100614crat_atlarge_miller.

9 Laura Miller, "'The Hunger Games' vs. 'Twilight,'" *Salon.com*, September 5, 2010, http://www.salon.com/books/laura_miller/2010/09/05/hunger_games_twilight.

10 King, "The Hunger Games," 139.

11 Sue Corbett, "Mockingjay," *People* 74.8, September 13, 2010, http://www.people.com/people/archive/article/0,,20418879,00.html.

12 The parental abandonment that marks Katniss's life as dystopic is a common theme in YA literature; the absent parent allows the protagonist to embark on adventures that would be impossible with an adult checking in. See Carrie Hintz, "Monica Hughes, Lois Lowry, and Young Adult Dystopias," *The Lion and the Unicorn* 26.2 (2002): 254; and Melinda Gross, "*The Giver* and *Shade's Children*: Future Views of Child Abandonment and Murder," *Children's Literature in Education* 30.2 (1999): 105–106.

13 Suzanne Collins, *Catching Fire* (New York: Scholastic Press, 2009), 354. Subsequent references will be cited parenthetically in the text.

14 Hintz, "Monica Hughes," 255, 263.

15 Gross, "Future Views," 115.

16 Suzanne Collins, *Mockingjay* (New York: Scholastic Press, 2010), 31. Subsequent references will be cited parenthetically in the text.

"The Dandelion in the Spring" • **129**

17 Miller, "Games vs. Twilight."

18 Zipp, "Classic Review"; and John Green, "Scary New World," *The New York Times*, November 7, 2008, http://www.nytimes.com/2008/11/09/books/review/Green-t.html.

19 Deborah O'Keefe, *Good Girl Messages: How Young Women Were Misled by Their Favorite Books* (New York: Continuum, 2001), 22.

20 Annis Pratt, *Archetypal Patterns in Women's Fiction* (Bloomington: Indiana University Press, 1981), 30; Lorna Ellis, *Appearing to Diminish: Female Development and the British* Bildungsroman, *1750–1850* (Lewisburg: Bucknell University Press, 1999), 16.

21 Elaine J. O'Quinn, review of *Good Girl Messages: How Young Women Were Misled by Their Favorite Books*, by Deborah O'Keefe, and of *Declarations of Independence: Empowered Girls in Young Adult Literature, 1990–2001*, by Joanne Brown and Nancy St. Clair, *NWSA Journal* 15.1 (Spring 2003): 169.

22 O'Keefe, *Good Girl*, 43. O'Keefe elaborates, "The books our elders urged us to read showed girls who wanted to help; any girl characters who wanted to *be* helped and supported were scorned in these books . . . The good girl's goal was usefulness not happiness—though she was taught that usefulness was the same as happiness" (153, italics original).

23 Susan Fraiman, *Unbecoming Women* (New York: Columbia University Press, 1994), 8.

24 Miller, "Games vs. Twilight."

25 Jane M. Agee, "Mothers and Daughters: Gender-Role Specialization in Two Newbery Award Books," *Children's Literature in Education* 24.3 (1993): 180.

26 On representations of "feminine tomboyism," see Michelle Anne Abate, *Tomboys: A Literary and Cultural History* (Philadelphia: Temple University Press, 2008), 223.

27 Angela E. Hubler, "Beyond the Image: Adolescent Girls, Reading, and Social Reality," *NWSA* 12.1 (2000): 89, 95.

28 Ibid., 93.

29 Joanne Brown and Nancy St. Clair, *Declarations of Independence: Empowered Girls in Young Adult Literature, 1990–2001* (Lanham: The Scarecrow Press, 2002), 27.

Works Cited

Abate, Michelle Ann. *Tomboys: A Literary and Cultural History*. Philadelphia: Temple University Press, 2008.

Agee, Jane M. "Mothers and Daughters: Gender-Role Specialization in Two Newbery Award Books." *Children's Literature in Education* 24.3 (1993): 165–183.

Brown, Joanne and Nancy St. Clair. *Declarations of Independence: Empowered Girls in Young Adult Literature, 1990–2001*. Lanham: The Scarecrow Press, 2002.

Collins, Suzanne. *Catching Fire*. New York: Scholastic Press, 2009.

———. *The Hunger Games*. New York: Scholastic Press, 2008.

130 · Katherine R. Broad

———. *Mockingjay.* New York: Scholastic Press, 2010.

Corbett, Sue. "Mockingjay." *People* 74.8, September 13, 2010. http://www.people.com/people/archive/article/0,,20418879,00.html.

Ellis, Lorna. *Appearing to Diminish: Female Development and the British* Bildungsroman, *1750–1850.* Lewisburg: Bucknell University Press, 1999.

Fraiman, Susan. *Unbecoming Women.* New York: Columbia University Press, 1994.

Gary, Alison. "Not Fashion Related: *The Hunger Games.*" *Wardrobe Oxygen,* October 20, 2011. http://www.wardrobeoxygen.com/2011 /10/not-fashion-related-hunger-games.html#.TsU_lk-W5m0.

Green, John. "Scary New World." *The New York Times,* November 7, 2008. http://www.nytimes.com/2008/11/09/books/review/Green-t.html.

Gross, Melinda. "*The Giver* and *Shade's Children*: Future Views of Child Abandonment and Murder." *Children's Literature in Education* 30.2 (1999): 103–117.

Hintz, Carrie. "Monica Hughes, Lois Lowry, and Young Adult Dystopias." *The Lion and the Unicorn* 26.2 (2002): 254–264.

Hubler, Angela E. "Beyond the Image: Adolescent Girls, Reading, and Social Reality." *NWSA* 12.1 (2000): 84–99.

King, Stephen. "The Hunger Games." *Entertainment Weekly,* September 12, 2008, 139.

Lewitt, Meghan. "Casting 'The Hunger Games': In Praise of Katniss Everdeen." *The Atlantic,* March 9, 2011. http://www.theatlantic.com/entertainment/archive/ 2011/03/casting-the-hunger-games-in-praise-of-katniss-everdeen/72164/.

McAllister, Ashley. "100 Young Adult Books for the Feminist Reader." *Bitch Magazine,* January 28, 2011. http://bitchmagazine.org/100-young-adult-books-for-the-feminist-reader.

McKenna, Laura. "Feminism and *The Hunger Games.*" *Apt. 11D,* November 15, 2011. http://www.apt11d.com/2011/11/feminism-and-the-hunger-games.html.

Miller, Laura. "Fresh Hell: What's Behind the Boom in Dystopian Fiction for Young Adults?" *The New Yorker,* June 14, 2010. http://www.newyorker.com/arts/critics/atlarge/2010/06/14/100614crat_atlarge_miller.

———. "'The Hunger Games' vs. 'Twilight.'" *Salon.com,* September 5, 2010. http://www.salon.com/books/laura_miller/2010/09/05/hunger_games_twilight.

O'Keefe, Deborah. *Good Girl Messages: How Young Women Were Misled by Their Favorite Books.* New York: Continuum, 2001.

O'Quinn, Elaine J. Review of *Good Girl Messages: How Young Women Were Misled by Their Favorite Books,* by Deborah O'Keefe, and of *Declarations of Independence: Empowered Girls in Young Adult Literature, 1990–2001,* by Joanne Brown and Nancy St. Clair. *NWSA Journal* 15.1 (2003): 169–172.

Pratt, Annis. *Archetypal Patterns in Women's Fiction.* Bloomington: Indiana University Press, 1981.

Seltzer, Sarah. "Hunger Pangs: Hunting for the Perfect Heroine." *Bitch Magazine* 51 (2011): 39–42.

Shelby. "Catching Fire." *Genrefluent*'s *Bistro Book Club,* July 1, 2009. http://genrefluentteentalk.blogspot.com/2009/07/catching-fire-by-suzanne-collins.html.

Stabile, Carol. "Review Essay: 'First He'll Kill Her Then I'll Save Her': Vampires, Feminism, and the *Twilight* Franchise." *Journal of Communication* 61 (2011): E4–E8.

Zipp, Yvonne. "Classic Review: *The Hunger Games.*" *Christian Science Monitor,* December 27, 2008. http://www.csmonitor.com/Books/Book-Reviews/2010/0829/Classic-review-The-Hunger-Games.

Chapter Eight
The Future Is Pale
Race in Contemporary Young Adult Dystopian Novels

Mary J. Couzelis

As Jack Zipes mentions in the foreword to *Utopian and Dystopian Writing for Children and Young Adults* (2003), young adult novels need to depict utopias and dystopias because they allow readers to critique their contemporary society in the hope of social change.[1] Surprisingly, racial tensions—a significant and continuing cultural concern that faces our world—are often not addressed in futuristic novels. Authors of science fiction who seek to highlight contemporary fears, especially in young adult dystopian novels, do not always realize that ideologies about race are present in the narratives. Frequently, these novels reinscribe current social and racial hierarchies through their character depictions, and these portrayals often privilege the dominant race. Novels that ignore race or present a monochromatic future imply that other ethnicities do not survive in the future or that their participation in the future is not important. Even narratives where authors pretend racial tensions have been eliminated in the future risk trivializing contemporary encounters teens have with prejudice.

Three contemporary dystopian novels recommended by the American Library Association's list for the best young adult books and that, as Zipes suggests, encourage readers to critique modern society—but notably only certain aspects—are Lois Lowry's *The Giver* (1993), Scott Westerfeld's *Uglies* (2005), and Suzanne Collins's *The Hunger Games* (2008). Lowry's Newbery Award-winning fiction tells the story of twelve-year-old Jonas who lives in a futuristic society which elected to end strife by erasing difference, emotions, and memory, and the novel examines communal control, individual choice,

132 • Mary J. Couzelis

and the power of memories. Westerfeld's novel follows fifteen-year-old Tally Youngblood in a world destroyed by oil dependence and greed, and critiques governmental control and free will. Collins's narrative focuses on sixteen-year-old Katniss Everdeen and similarly explores the role of government and individual agency in a postapocalyptic world created by a combination of wars and natural disasters. Frequently, the lack of attention to racial tensions in popular novels such as Lowry's, Westerfeld's, and Collins's risks maintaining hegemonic cultural relations. Often when novels for general audiences address race effectively, they are almost always read as solely "about race" and become marginalized, thereby avoiding critical engagement by mainstream audiences. By maintaining narrative silence about this contemporary issue, these novels perpetuate the hegemonic status quo of pretending race does not matter, which only privileges the dominant race. If these utopian/dystopian novels are to critique current society, then the ideologies about race and class privilege must be exposed. An examination of whiteness in *The Giver*, *Uglies*, and *The Hunger Games* reveals how contemporary young adult dystopian novels do little to question today's racial hierarchies.

White Privilege as Sameness

As Susan Stewart and Susan Lea note in their respective articles, Lowry's *The Giver* (1993) promotes color-blindness by implying that the future is full of "pale" people with "light" eyes.[2] To put it bluntly: the future is populated only by a white race. In Lowry's imagined future, people elect to invoke "Sameness." An elder called "the Giver" tells the protagonist Jonas that people in their past made the choice to eliminate difference and to not see any colors. When Jonas begins to see color, he can detect the color of red in people's flesh. The Giver explains, "There was a time, actually—you'll see this in the memories later—when flesh was many different colors. That was before we went to Sameness. Today flesh is all the same and what you saw was the red tones."[3] This future lacks any racial differences, but what that really means is that the Anglo race, whiteness, is the race *selected*. *The Giver* depicts the race of the future as implicitly white and states that people voluntarily made this choice, thereby implying that people of color elected to become white. This transformation perpetuates the notion that racial minorities want to be white, thus maintaining the status quo of white privilege in the present day.

As Shannon Sullivan argues in *Revealing Whiteness: The Unconscious Habits of Racial Privilege* (2006), "Even though colorblindness usually is intended as a strategy for the elimination of racism and white domination, it actually tends to fuel and be fueled by white privileged habits."[4] White privilege is a subtle form of racism in that white people receive benefits and power just because of their skin color. Sullivan notes that white privilege "operates as unseen, invisible, even seemingly nonexistent,"[5] thus working to hide and continually perpetuate the habits of privilege throughout institutions, including literature. Valerie Babb's *Whiteness Visible: The Meaning of Whiteness in American Literature and Culture* (1998) explores how the ideology of whiteness enters into literature. She suggests, "The ideology of whiteness encourages attitudes that can only deepen cultural stratification" when left unexposed and unquestioned in literature.[6] Unfortunately, many young adult dystopian narratives fail to embrace the critical aspect in regards to race in their effort to tell a story warning about the future.

The characters in *The Giver* do not question what was sacrificed by other races in their "choice" to become white. The text's lack of reflection upon why whiteness is selected is an example of how the habits of white privilege "actively thwart the process of conscious reflection on them, which allows them to seem nonexistent even as they continue to function."[7] When the narrative does invoke a memory of a racialized person, the text fails to open up for critical reflection by the reader. After the Giver explains to Jonas that skin had been different colors, Jonas receives a memory with racial signifiers: "Two of these men had dark brown skin; the others were light. Going closer, he watched them hack the tusks from a motionless elephant on the ground and haul them away, spattered with blood" (100). The only image in the entire narrative of a different race is one of African poachers killing and hacking tusks from an innocent animal. By selecting such a violent and reprehensible image of another race, the text closes the opportunity to question why people would elect for Sameness. Jonas and the Giver never criticize the elimination of racial difference. The child reader, through identification with Jonas, risks becoming socialized into the institution of white privilege. As Stewart notes, "Ultimately, *The Giver* fails to address alterity, reinforces cultural continuity, and actually diminishes opportunities to think in terms of difference."[8] This closure and lack of opportunity for textual and cultural reflection prevents this young adult dystopian novel from being critical of contemporary society's racial hierarchies.

Carrie Hintz and Elaine Ostry believe that "utopian literature encourages young people to view their society with a critical eye, sensitizing or predisposing them to political action."[9] However, this is not always the case. Not all utopian and dystopian fiction creates worlds where readers reflect on their contemporary society, and especially not to the point of considering action. Some narratives risk making the future look so bad that young readers are grateful for their contemporary society as is. This may be the case for *The Giver*, a novel in which Jonas and the reader become horrified over a future where infants and the elderly are murdered. Other dystopian narratives, while focusing on one theme, reinscribe other ideologies that maintain the status quo. Although *The Giver* warns of forgetting history and is critical of Sameness, Lowry diverts attention away from the complexity of racial identity. As Stewart points out, in moments in the text where Lowry could potentially question or criticize the impact of Sameness on people of color, she fails to do

134 • Mary J. Couzelis

so. Stewart argues that while the novel tackles the issue of choice, the author actually sidesteps the notion of "choice" in regards to race by having the characters focus on trivial choices such as clothes.[10] By diverting attention onto something relatively simple, Lowry normalizes the selection of whiteness as the race of the future. As bell hooks warns, a "social framework of sameness, a homogeneity of experience . . . deflect[s] attention away from [white] accountability . . . seek[ing] to erase a vision of accountability and responsibility which could truly empower."[11] In order for young adult dystopian narratives to have the potential desired by scholars like Hintz and Ostry, the narratives need to avoid assumptions that promote contemporary racial hierarchies.

The Beauty of White Privilege

Scott Westerfeld's *Uglies* contains ideologies about race that operate in a similar fashion as Lowry's narrative. Westerfeld portrays a government-controlled future created after the "Rusties," an analog for contemporary America, ruined the planet due to their dependence on oil and continual fighting. A large portion of the conflict is blamed on people having different skin colors and "fighting over who had more stuff."[12] This future indoctrinates everyone into the notion that all children are ugly until they have the mandated "pretty surgery" at the age of sixteen. The protagonist, Tally, begins by believing this ideology and looks forward to becoming pretty as a result of the surgery. This pretty surgery includes having "bones ground down" or "stretched or padded," "nose cartilage and cheekbones stripped out and replaced with programmable plastic," and "skin sanded off and reseeded" (97). Westerfeld's dystopian novel warns about the desire to be pretty like everyone else, the potential dangers of technology when used for something like beauty, and the role the government has in people's lives. The novel's ideology about the government does expose the important lesson that people are indoctrinated by their culture to certain notions of beauty. Early on in the novel, a secondary character, Shay, tells Tally, "But it's a trick, Tally. You've only seen pretty faces your whole life. Your parents, your teachers, everyone over sixteen. But you weren't *born* expecting that kind of beauty in everyone, all the time. You just got programmed into thinking anything else is ugly" (82, italics original). The construction of this dialogue allows young readers the opportunity to reflect on their understood notions of beauty and how they acquire those ideals. Unfortunately, while the text does interrogate ideologies surrounding beauty, it does little to unsettle contemporary racial hierarchies.

In this futuristic novel, the surgery functions to produce the same kind of Sameness that defines Jonas's world. Shay has olive skin, and most people in this novel are either noted as having pale or olive skin. Similar to *The Giver*, the future is constructed of predominantly light-skinned people. But when Tally plays with a computer program to see what she and Shay will potentially look like after their pretty surgery, she gives Shay lighter hair. Remarking that the combination of white-blonde hair and olive skin does not look attractive, Tally suggests she lighten Shay's skin by taking "the shade of the skin closer to the baseline" (43). So Tally lightens the olive skin tone, implying the baseline is white. In order for everyone to be pretty and appealing to all members of society, appearances, including skin tones, are adjusted to be the same: Shay remarks less than enthusiastically that after Tally modifies her image, she looks just like everyone else in New Pretty Town, the side of town where people live after their surgery. The text assumes that whiteness is a part of Sameness in a similar manner as *The Giver* and again this notion of Sameness is racialized by the privileging of whiteness.

Tally also manipulates her own image in the computer program and gives herself ultrahigh cheekbones, catlike eyes, and high arching eyebrows. She states that those parameters are not legal and adjusts to a more conservative look. She does give herself almond-shaped eyes and full lips. She calls some of the options that veer away from the baseline "exotic" and notes that the authorities in her city do not allow such improvements. There is even a "Morphological Congress," a global institution that governs all the cities and "[makes] sure pretties were all more or less the same" (262). The text implies that stereotypical racial markers are only used as an add-on, and not encouraged. Shay points out that even if someone requests certain "morphs" the doctors will do what they want during the pretty surgery, thereby reinforcing the physical traits often associated with whiteness (41). While the text interrogates notions of beauty and characters question the definition of beauty, white privilege masks itself by having the characters never question how race is involved in those definitions.

The government justifies this surgery by stating, "It's the only way to make people equal" (45). Similar to *The Giver*, the rationale to end all conflict is to make people racially similar. This devalues contemporary readers' racial differences, and this whitewashing is an example of the insidious effects of an often unacknowledged ideology of white privilege.[13] Westerfeld even makes the surgical procedure sound like an easy solution to social problems like racism. The doctors' description of the pretty surgery uses metaphors related to recreation, such as the skin being reseeded "like a soccer field in spring," and notes that it "felt like a killer sunburn for a couple of weeks" (97). The novel imagines changing one's race to be as simple as reseeding grass and tolerating a sunburn. By creating a simple, relatively painless solution to the entire problem of racial tensions—erase difference by all becoming pale skinned—the text conveys the ideology that a racialized future does not matter, and that science can easily fix complex social issues.

To further justify racial sameness as an end to racial strife, the novel also calls upon evolution as a justification for the surgery. Many readers may be unaware that even the field of science is prejudiced and founded on a tradition of racism that privileges the white race. Edward James explains, "The 'science'

136 • Mary J. Couzelis

of race has been written almost entirely by Anglo-Saxons, who used all kinds of measurements—particularly of skulls and of intelligence—to demonstrate the fact (which was obvious to them before they began) that Anglo-Saxons were superior in almost every way."[14] For many years, white supremacy and privilege ideology utilized "scientific facts" related to biology, such as finding some races inferior by measuring heads, noses, and jaw lines.[15] While *Uglies* is not necessarily promoting the idea that other races are inferior, the text does not problematize the science of certain Anglo features being purportedly superior and most attractive. The notion of superiority through facial features appears at Tally's school, where she is taught: "There was a certain kind of beauty, a prettiness that everyone could see. Big eyes and full lips like a kid's; smoother, clear skin; symmetrical features; and a thousand other little clues. Somewhere in the backs of their minds, people were always looking for these markers. No one could help seeing them, no matter how they were brought up. A million years of evolution had made it part of the human brain" (16). By relying on science as a rationale for beauty, the text closes off the potential questioning of how scientific practices relate to the history of racism.

Uglies not only fails to critique the racialized history of science, it falters in its invocation of history as a critical tool to interrogate white privilege. In Westerfeld's imagined future, as with many young adult dystopian novels, information about history is controlled by an institution. Raffaella Baccolini argues that when narratives show history as secretive and control information about the past, "history, its knowledge, and memory are therefore dangerous elements that can give the dystopian citizen a potential instrument of resistance . . . the recovery of history is an important element for the survival of hope."[16] History (the reader's present) can be interrogated by having the characters discuss how the schools and other forms of propaganda always portray the Rusties as stupid. The authority figures teach the characters to ridicule the Rusties and to not ask a lot of questions about them since they were so irresponsible. If the reader is to learn to question history and the controlled release of information about history, Tally must learn to question the past in order to change her society. For Tally to grow in regards to racial complexities, she needs to learn that the Rusties did not fight simply because of ugliness and/or difference, and she should question the establishment of whiteness as the standard.

Tom Moylan contends that regaining memory or understanding history allows the protagonist to deconstruct the hegemonic story of history and reaffirm "alternative ways of knowing and living in the world."[17] When dystopian narratives whitewash history, there is a danger that readers will also ignore the questioning of their own past and present in regards to racial events. Baccolini warns, "By leaving out 'embarrassing' memories of an unjust past, official commemorations offer a sanitized version of history and thus extend injustice into the future and foreclose the possibility for change."[18] One of the few times *Uglies* confronts an uncomfortable fact about the past, history is trivialized.

The Future Is Pale • 137

Tally states that the reason for making people look alike was that it was the only way to make them all equal, because "people killed one another over stuff like having different skin color." Tally brushes off this moment of historical racial recognition when she states, "No matter how many times they repeated it at school, she'd never really quite believed that one" (44). Mark Bould believes that "by presenting racism as an insanity that burned itself out, or as the obvious folly of the ignorant and impoverished who would be left behind by the genre's brave new futures, sf [science fiction] avoids confronting the structures of racism and its own complicity in them."[19] Tally's attitude towards complex racial conflict exemplifies Bould's concern over science fiction's role in maintaining forms of racism, such as white privilege.

Uglies frequently veers away from any interrogation with a racialized history that would generate questions about a pale future. After Shay runs away to live with the Smoke, a group of people who have escaped the city in an effort to rebel against the government's control and mandated pretty surgery, Tally joins her. The reunion begins with deception though, as Tally only agrees to go to the Smoke as a spy because the government threatens to refuse her pretty surgery otherwise. Tally is so indoctrinated into the government's definition of beautiful that she is stunned to see adults "ugly" by choice. She is further horrified at how Rusties looked when Shay shows her an old magazine. She calls them "wildly different" looking, characterizing them as "grotesquely fat, or weirdly over-muscled, or uncomfortably thin," and adds that "almost all of them had wrong, ugly proportions" (198). She makes no mention of their skin color differing from her own. This could imply one of three things: one, the magazine contains no people of color, which seems impossible given that the magazine is supposed to be from our own time and contains images of sports stars, actors, artists, musicians, politicians, and comedians; two, she does not think racial differences are significant because she has not been taught that those differences matter in relation to contemporary hierarchies, which also seems doubtful given that the school teaches the students that Rusties killed each other because of different skin color; or three, this is an instance where white privilege again controls the images conveyed by ignoring a confrontation with racial differences in the past. Sullivan argues that white privilege often thwarts moments where the biases of racialized privilege are revealed "because such transformation would risk bringing the traumatic event or shameful values to conscious attention."[20] To have Tally notice different skin colors in the past would highlight that the text promotes a monochromatic future and ignores the complexity of racial differences. Tally's focus on attributes related to beauty closes off the potential for the reader to interrogate racial hierarchies. Tally does not have to confront any history related to racial strife or feel any guilt over the desire to change appearance and select lighter skin tones. *Uglies* becomes yet another text in the long history of science fiction that imagines a color-blind future that "exclude[s] people of color as full subjects."[21]

138 • Mary J. Couzelis

A Segregated Future

Inclusion of multiple races in a futuristic setting could potentially acknowledge minority contributions to culture, prevent ongoing marginalization, and unsettle white privilege ideology. Suzanne Collins's *The Hunger Games* does include multiple races, although her future is as disheartening as Lowry's and Westerfeld's. *The Hunger Games'* future takes place in what was once the U.S., now divided into thirteen districts ruled by the Capitol. Katniss lives in District 12, the mining district, which was once called Appalachia. She notes that everyone who works in the mines looks alike, with black hair, olive skin, and gray eyes, while the merchant class of this district mostly has light hair (blonde) and blue eyes. Later in the book Collins describes other members of the merchant class as having "porcelain white skin," "pale skin," and being "pasty-faced."[22] Immediately this future links class and skin tones in a way that echoes contemporary racial and economic hierarchies. Baccolini states that dystopia "shows how our present may negatively evolve, while by showing a regression of our present it also suggests that history may not be progressive. Paradoxically, then, dystopia depends on and denies history."[23] *The Hunger Games* is problematic in its presentation of a future that denies its reliance on critical aspects of racial history. The text often contrasts districts implying racial hierarchies. Frequently in the text a young reader may recognize District 11 as a reinstatement of slavery, but this depends on the reader knowing American history and also denies that history is repeating itself by not naming the institution that is invoking slavery: white ideology.

Economic and racial segregation become obvious as the Hunger Games begin. During the annual Hunger Games each district is required to send two "tributes," one boy and one girl, ranging in ages from twelve to eighteen years who will fight to the death. Katniss and Peeta, a boy from the merchant class, are the tributes for District 12. As Katniss watches the introduction of other districts' tributes, she describes what strikes her the most about them: "A monstrous boy who lunges forward to volunteer from District 2. A fox-faced girl with sleek red hair from District 5. A boy with a crippled foot from District 10. And most hauntingly, a twelve-year-old girl from District 11. She has dark brown skin and eyes" (45). All the other tributes Katniss describes in terms that do not indicate race; only Rue, the young girl from District 11, gets racialized. Sullivan notes that white privilege operates to set up "the oppositional relationship between white and non-white people that helps guarantee [a person's] whiteness."[24] While observing the other tributes, Katniss does not note anyone's skin tone, except for the two District 11 tributes, Rue and Thresh, thereby highlighting their difference from the others.

Although the two tributes from District 11, the agricultural district, are not explicitly stated to be African American, the textual references to the district's labor, their methods of controlling the workers, and the workers' use of song all make a compelling case for why readers understand Rue to be black.

Rue works with everyone else in her district's orchards. She tells Katniss how they do not go to school during harvest, are not allowed to eat the crops, and are fed just a bit more during harvest "so that people can keep going longer" (202–203). Sullivan contends that when overt white supremacy, as exemplified in slavery, ended, it did not truly end slavery because denial of full human rights continued through "the covert habits of white privilege."[25] Collins's future reinstates slavery even though the institution is not named as such. Rue explains to Katniss that if the workers in District 11 eat any of the crops, "They whip you and make everyone else watch" (202). Katniss is shocked by this, and thinks, "I can tell by her expression that it's not that uncommon an occurrence. A public whipping's a rare thing in District 12" (202). Katniss's life seems privileged in comparison to the slavery Rue endures.

Rue gives a second example of violence by the Peacekeepers to further establish the differences between their districts, telling the story of a "simpleminded child" who was shot for stealing night goggles. Unlike in Katniss's district, this boy was expected to work in the orchards despite having the mental capacities of a three-year-old. Katniss states that none of the Peacekeepers in her district would kill a simpleminded child. In a somewhat patronizing and unintentionally derogatory manner, she even thinks back to how they have a similar girl whom everyone treats as a pet and feeds (204–205). By comparing the two districts, a dichotomy is established that reaffirms white privilege. Katniss's district becomes the preferred realm where people take care of each other, while District 11 is painted as having Peacekeepers that are really futuristic slave bosses that do not value their workers' lives.

Song also links Rue to the American slave tradition. As Isiah Lavender states, "Music is surely a key element in a culture based on slavery because it records an oral history through song."[26] While Rue does not sing songs that tell the history of her people, her song does contain a double meaning that permits a challenge to power. During American slavery, many slaves' songs had a message or special meaning to them, and that same song would simply sound "happy" to the master. The songs contained a level of meaning that could not be understood by an outsider to the community. In the future of *The Hunger Games*, hybrid birds, called mockingjays, mimic human voices. Rue creates a special four-note song that the mockingjays carry to the other workers. She explains, "They carry messages for me . . . I'm usually up highest, so I'm the first to see the flag that signals quitting time. There's a special little song I do . . . And the mockingjays spread it around the orchard. That's how everyone knows to knock off" (212). Rue utilizes music to transmit messages that tell the other workers to stop working. The Peacekeepers hear the song and think the notes are just another bird song, not recognizing the tune as the workers' way of subverting the system. Katniss reveals her status as she thinks, "In our world, I rank music somewhere between hair ribbons and rainbows in terms of usefulness" (211). There is no reason for music to be a means of rebellion in her life. The people in District 12 do not like the way things are, but in

140 • Mary J. Couzelis

no way are they treated as badly as the people in District 11; therefore, they do not need to rely on the tradition of music as subversion of power.

Another method of maintaining assumed hegemonic hierarchies is the use of racist imagery such as images that dehumanize African Americans. Donnarae MacCann explains there were "images of Blacks that ranged from Sambo . . . to brute beast images. The latter made a frequent appearance in the propaganda of white supremacist organizations."[27] There may be some racial ideology working within the text in that Rue and Thresh, the other tribute from District 11, are linked to animals or given animal attributes. When Rue dies, Katniss thinks, "Rue, smaller than ever, a baby animal curled up in a nest of netting" (236). Katniss describes Thresh as "built like an ox" (126). Lastly, when Thresh and Katniss come face to face, she hopes, "Maybe if he knows I helped Rue, he won't choose some slow, sadistic end for me" (287). Both African American characters are linked to animals, and there is something about Thresh that is reminiscent of the brute beast language of white supremacy. Katniss was not worried about any of the other tributes killing in a sadistic way. Her descriptions of him plus the use of "sadistic" harkens back to old stereotypes about why white women should fear large black men.[28]

Lavender argues, "The social construction of race in sf seems to demand a dialectic of superior/inferior relationships designed to promote the domination of one group over another."[29] Even the way Collins depicts Thresh speaking is different from the other tributes. Thresh says to Katniss, "Just this one time, I let you go. For the little girl. You and me, we're even then. No more owed. You understand?" (288). None of the other characters speak in such a broken and simplified manner, thereby accentuating his difference. Rue is also presented as different by depicting her as less civilized than Katniss at one point. When Rue provides herbs to help cure Katniss, her method of healing is held in contrast to how Katniss was taught. Katniss notes how Rue simply grinds the herbs into a paste in her mouth, and thinks, "My mother would use other methods" (200). The narrative presents Rue's method of healing as almost primitive, while making Katniss's mother sound like she would have selected other, more civilized means to crush herbs.

In addition to hierarchies and imagery originating from American slavery and Reconstruction-era stereotypes, the novel also contains a more modern construction as seen through Rue's death. In film and literature, African American characters appear briefly to assist in the development of a white protagonist and then either disappear after or are sacrificed as part of the white character's transformation. This notion of African Americans disappearing or being sacrificed for the good of whites is evident in sf as well. Lavender discusses an sf story that makes the racial hierarchy and sacrifice even more obvious. He states that Derrick Bell's "The Space Traders" (1992) illustrates that "blacks would be willingly sacrificed for the greater good of white self-interest as well as material gain."[30] This stereotypical trope appears in *The Hunger Games* as Rue is killed as a vehicle for Katniss's maturation. Rue's death is the moment that Katniss begins rebelling against the Capitol. As Roberta Seelinger Trites points out, many young adult novels contain graphic death scenes because adult writers seem to believe that teens need to confront death in order to mature. She states, "Both acceptance and awareness serve in the power/knowledge dynamic to render the adolescent both powerless in her fear of death and empowered by acknowledging its power."[31] Katniss feels powerless because she cannot stop Rue's death, but she can rebel against the sterility of the Capitol by placing flowers all over Rue, and she uses her anger about death to catapult her through the next few pages. The reader potentially embraces Rue's death as tragic but necessary for Katniss to change into the fighter she needs to be to win. Unfortunately, this also means that the dark-skinned character is sacrificed for the good of the white protagonist. Collins seems to depend on history to help convey meanings, and yet she seems oblivious to the way she utilizes stock images that endorse white privilege in her own depictions of the District 11 tributes.

Whiteness Today, Paleness Tomorrow

Tom Moylan argues, "A substantial body of sf directly feeds the ideological processes that reproduce the very subject positions required by the political and economic structures of the hegemonic order itself."[32] In Lowry's *The Giver*, Westerfeld's *Uglies*, and Collins's *The Hunger Games*, white privilege works throughout the narratives to maintain today's racial hierarchies. These texts do not challenge contemporary ideologies concerning race, and any textual moments that could potentially allow young readers to interrogate contemporary racial biases are closed off or trivialized. Lowry, Westerfeld, and Collins create fanciful narratives that do exactly what Moylan states; they reproduce subject positions that reinforce white privilege. Elisabeth Anne Leonard finds that science fiction often "attempt[s] to deal with racial issues by imagining a world where they are non-issues, where colour-blindness is the norm. This may be a conscious model for a future society, or a gesture to 'political correctness' by an author whose interests in the story lie elsewhere, but either motive avoids wrestling with the difficult questions of how a non-racist society comes into being and how members of minority cultures or ethnic groups preserve their culture."[33] These three young adult dystopian narratives continue a long tradition in science fiction that "has mirrored rather than defied racial stereotypes."[34]

Notes

1   Jack Zipes, "Foreword: Utopia, Dystopia, and the Quest for Hope," in *Utopian and Dystopian Writing for Children and Young Adults*, ed. Carrie Hintz and Elaine Ostry (New York: Routledge, 2003), ix.

142 • Mary J. Couzelis

2 Susan Louise Stewart, "A Return to Normal: Lois Lowry's *The Giver*," *The Lion and the Unicorn* 31.1 (2007): 24; and Susan G. Lea, "Seeing beyond Sameness: Using *The Giver* to Challenge Colorblind Ideology," *Children's Literature in Education* 37.1 (2006): 52.

3 Lois Lowry, *The Giver* (New York: Houghton, 1993), 94. Subsequent references will be cited parenthetically in the text.

4 Shannon Sullivan, *Revealing Whiteness: The Unconscious Habits of Racial Privilege* (Bloomington: Indiana University Press, 2006), 190–191.

5 Ibid., 1.

6 Valerie Babb, *Whiteness Visible: The Meaning of Whiteness in American Literature and Culture* (New York: New York University Press, 1998), 177.

7 Sullivan, *Revealing*, 6.

8 Stewart, "Return," 26.

9 Carrie Hintz and Elaine Ostry, introduction to *Utopian and Dystopian Writing for Children and Young Adults*, ed. Carrie Hintz and Elaine Ostry (New York: Routledge, 2003), 7.

10 Stewart, "Return," 27.

11 bell hooks, *Black Looks: Race and Representation* (Boston: South End Press, 1992), 14.

12 Scott Westerfeld, *Uglies* (New York: Simon Pulse, 2005), 44 and 147. Subsequent references will be cited parenthetically in the text.

13 I recognize that these societies are dystopian, and therefore the society's intent to make white privilege invisible should not be embraced by readers. However, I do not believe the authors (both Lowry and Westerfeld) are aware of how their novels subtly normalize whiteness. The point is that these novels openly critique other aspects of American society, such as memory, government control, environmentalism, and notions of beauty without fully allowing readers to critique the normalization of whiteness. If the protagonist does not recognize and critique white privilege, there is less chance the reader will.

14 Edward James, "Yellow, Black, Metal and Tentacled: The Race Question in American Science Fiction," in *Science Fiction, Social Conflict and War*, ed. Philip John Davies (Manchester: Manchester University Press, 1990), 26.

15 See Stephen Jay Gould's *The Mismeasure of Man* (New York: W.W. Norton, 1981) for further discussion.

16 Raffaella Baccolini, "A Useful Knowledge of the Present Is Rooted in the Past: Memory and Historical Reconciliation in Ursula K. Le Guin's *The Telling*," in *Dark Horizons: Science Fiction and the Dystopian Imagination*, ed. Raffaella Baccolini and Tom Moylan (New York: Routledge, 2003), 115.

17 Tom Moylan, *Scraps of the Untainted Sky: Science Fiction, Utopia, Dystopia* (Boulder, CO: Westview Press, 2000), 150.

18 Baccolini, "Useful," 119.

19 Mark Bould, "The Ships Landed Long Ago: Afrofuturism and Black SF," *Science Fiction Studies* 34.2 (2007): 180.

The Future Is Pale • **143**

20 Sullivan, *Revealing*, 8.

21 Bould, "Ships," 177.

22 Suzanne Collins, *The Hunger Games* (New York: Scholastic, 2008), 8, 77, 95, 78. Subsequent references will be cited parenthetically in the text.

23 Baccolini, "Useful," 115.

24 Sullivan, *Revealing*, 68.

25 Ibid., 27.

26 Isiah Lavender, *Race in American Science Fiction* (Bloomington: Indiana University Press, 2011), 86.

27 Donnarae MacCann, *White Supremacy in Children's Literature: Characterizations of African Americans, 1830–1900* (New York: Garland Publishing, 1998), 98. See also Patricia Hill Collins, *Black Sexual Politics: African Americans, Gender, and the New Racism* (New York: Routledge, 2004).

28 For further discussion on the stereotype of black men portrayed as predators of white women, see Babb, *Whiteness Visible*, especially 81–82. See also Thomas A. Foster, *Sex and the Eighteenth-Century Man: Massachusetts and the History of Sexuality in America* (Boston: Beacon Press, 2006); and Martha Elizabeth Hodes, *White Women, Black Men: Illicit Sex in the Nineteenth-Century South* (New Haven: Yale University Press, 1997).

29 Lavender, *Race*, 91.

30 Ibid., 115.

31 Roberta Seelinger Trites, *Disturbing the Universe: Power and Repression in Adolescent Literature* (Iowa City: University of Iowa Press, 2000), 119.

32 Moylan, *Scraps*, xvii.

33 Elisabeth Anne Leonard, "Race and Ethnicity in Science Fiction," in *The Cambridge Companion to Science Fiction*, ed. Edward James and Farah Mendlesohn (New York: Cambridge University Press, 2003), 254.

34 Lavender, *Race*, 12.

Works Cited

Babb, Valerie. *Whiteness Visible: The Meaning of Whiteness in American Literature and Culture.* New York: New York University Press, 1998.

Baccolini, Raffaella. "A Useful Knowledge of the Present Is Rooted in the Past: Memory and Historical Reconciliation in Ursula K. Le Guin's *The Telling*." In *Dark Horizons: Science Fiction and the Dystopian Imagination*, edited by Raffaella Baccolini and Tom Moylan, 113–134. New York: Routledge, 2003.

Bould, Mark. "The Ships Landed Long Ago: Afrofuturism and Black SF." *Science Fiction Studies* 34.2 (2007): 177–186.

Collins, Patricia Hill. *Black Sexual Politics: African Americans, Gender, and the New Racism.* New York: Routledge, 2004.

Collins, Suzanne. *The Hunger Games.* New York: Scholastic, 2008.

Foster, Thomas A. *Sex and the Eighteenth-Century Man: Massachusetts and the History of Sexuality in America.* Boston: Beacon Press, 2006.

Gould, Stephen Jay. *The Mismeasure of Man.* New York: W.W. Norton, 1981.

Hintz, Carrie and Elaine Ostry. Introduction to *Utopian and Dystopian Writing for Children and Young Adults*, edited by Carrie Hintz and Elaine Ostry, 1–20. New York: Routledge, 2003.

144 · Mary J. Couzelis

Hodes, Martha Elizabeth. *White Women, Black Men: Illicit Sex in the Nineteenth-Century South.* New Haven: Yale University Press, 1997.

hooks, bell. *Black Looks: Race and Representation.* Boston: South End Press, 1992.

James, Edward. "Yellow, Black, Metal and Tentacled: The Race Question in American Science Fiction." In *Science Fiction, Social Conflict and War*, edited by Philip John Davies, 26–49. Manchester: Manchester University Press, 1990.

Lavender, Isiah. *Race in American Science Fiction.* Bloomington: Indiana University Press, 2011.

Lea, Susan G. "Seeing beyond Sameness: Using *The Giver* to Challenge Colorblind Ideology." *Children's Literature in Education* 37.1 (2006): 51–67.

Leonard, Elisabeth Anne. "Race and Ethnicity in Science Fiction." In *The Cambridge Companion to Science Fiction*, edited by Edward James and Farah Mendlesohn, 253–263. New York: Cambridge University Press, 2003.

Lowry, Lois. *The Giver.* New York: Houghton, 1993.

MacCann, Donnarae. *White Supremacy in Children's Literature: Characterizations of African Americans, 1830–1900.* New York: Garland Publishing, 1998.

Moylan, Tom. *Scraps of the Untainted Sky: Science Fiction, Utopia, Dystopia.* Boulder, CO: Westview Press, 2000.

Stewart, Susan. "A Return to Normal: Lois Lowry's *The Giver.*" *The Lion and the Unicorn* 31.1 (2007): 21–35.

Sullivan, Shannon. *Revealing Whiteness: The Unconscious Habits of Racial Privilege.* Bloomington: Indiana University Press, 2006.

Trites, Roberta Seelinger. *Disturbing the Universe: Power and Repression in Adolescent Literature.* Iowa City: University of Iowa Press, 2000.

Westerfeld, Scott. *Uglies.* New York: Simon Pulse, 2005.

Zipes, Jack. "Foreword: Utopia, Dystopia, and the Quest for Hope." In *Utopian and Dystopian Writing for Children and Young Adults*, edited by Carrie Hintz and Elaine Ostry, ix–xi. New York: Routledge, 2003.

Chapter Nine
Technology and Models of Literacy in Young Adult Dystopian Fiction

Kristi McDuffie

Young adult dystopian novels offer different models of literacy, from illiteracy to multiple versions of literate capabilities. A common theme of this genre is that in the future, due to significant technological advances, many people have lost traditional forms of literacy like writing by hand. This fear that technology is causing illiteracy is widespread in contemporary society today, where teachers, parents, popular essayists, and others complain about the current generation's addiction to texting and reluctance to read. It is perhaps unsurprising, then, that these fears should emerge in texts aimed at young adults themselves. Some texts present unfavorable images of illiterate and uncaring teens, such as in M.T. Anderson's *Feed* (2002), where young adults communicate with technology implanted in their brains and have largely lost the ability to speak aloud. Other texts present traditional literacies as a means of personal agency and freedom amidst controlling societies facilitated by technology, as in Ally Condie's *Matched* (2010), where reading illegal poetry and learning to write by hand are means of rebellion, and Scott Westerfeld's *Uglies* (2005), where young adults use both handwriting and technological advances to subvert the authorities. Such texts offer productive presentations of literacy, but texts that demonstrate young adults excelling in multiple kinds of literacies, such as digital literacies, offer even more productive and nuanced representations of young adults exerting agency and autonomy amidst totalitarian societies. Cory Doctorow's *Little Brother* (2008), for instance, shows a young adult empowered by his capable and crafty technological know-how. This chapter analyzes models of literacy in these four young adult

146 · Kristi McDuffie

dystopian novels in order to explore tensions among technology, old forms of literacy, new forms of literacy, and the possibilities those models offer. Texts that present young adults who engage in multiple forms of literacy to enact change offer the most productive ways of exploring technology's effect on literacy with young adults.

Current Concerns about Technology, Literacy, and Young Adults

Fears about the effects of technology proliferate in popular non-fiction, such as John Brockman's edited collection *Is the Internet Changing the Way You Think?: The Net's Impact on Our Minds and Future* (2011). Nicholas Carr is one of the most well-known critics of technology and its influence on human minds. In his most recent text, *The Shallows: What the Internet Is Doing to Our Brains* (2010), Carr claims that the internet impairs cognitive functioning, an argument primarily based on his own dwindling ability to concentrate amidst a Google culture.[1] Although Carr acknowledges that reading and writing are technologies, he nonetheless argues for the prioritization of traditional print literacy over modern-day web-based literacies due to the former's use of deep attention.[2] These fears about technology are often directed explicitly at young adults, as young adults tend to adopt and celebrate technology more than older generations. N. Katherine Hayles, for instance, details generational differences in attention. She claims that older generations are better at deep attention, which entails "concentrating on a single object for long periods," while younger generations demonstrate hyper attention, which entails "switching focus rapidly among different tasks."[3] Hayles claims that this generational difference is caused by the media and she is concerned with the implications for current educational practices, which rely on deep attention.

In *The Dumbest Generation: How the Digital Age Stupefies Young Americans and Jeopardizes Our Future* (2008), Mark Bauerlein goes so far as to call young adults unintelligent and selfish. This incendiary text argues that teenagers exist in an endless web of social media that leaves them without any time to read, think, or be influenced by wise adults.[4] Bauerlein describes how, despite teenagers having access to more information than ever before due to technology, technology makes them self-interested: "Instead of opening young American minds to the stores of civilization and science and politics, technology has contracted their horizon to themselves, to the social scene around them . . . The fonts of knowledge are everywhere, but the rising generation is camped in the desert, passing stories, pictures, tunes, and texts back and forth, living off the thrill of peer attention."[5] Concerns such as Bauerlein's circulate widely in the popular press and in literature directed at young adults themselves through the genre of young adult dystopian fiction. Sometimes, the critiques are as harsh as Bauerlein's.

Technology and Models of Literacy in Young Adult Dystopian Fiction • 147

Illiteracy in *Feed*

Feed's overt criticism of a decline in literacy reflects current fears about technology and our minds. Mental and literate deterioration is extensive in this futuristic world, where environmental ruin is so widespread that other planets are the suburbs and air is manufactured. Communication occurs primarily through feeds implanted in people's brains, which allow people to "chat" through their minds without speaking aloud. The explicit critique of the novel is that corporations, enabled by technology, have ruined literacy and cognitive ability. Young adults are especially implicated in this deterioration. Titus, the narrator, is a sixteen-year-old stereotypically interested in girls, clothes, and cars. Titus and his friends lack cultural and historic knowledge and literacy. When Titus's friends buy "Stonewall Clogs" as a part of the "Watts Riot" gear fashion line, they have no understanding of the historical context.[6] They have a vague understanding of what riots are, but no knowledge of those particular riots; they are only concerned with the fashion statement.

Loss of literacy is visible primarily through the characters' language, which is an exaggerated form of the way teenagers are perceived to speak now. Titus's first-person, stream-of-consciousness narration demonstrates language and cognitive deterioration:

> School™ is not so bad now, not like back when my grandparents were kids, when the schools were run by the government, which sounds completely like, Nazi, to have the government running the schools? Back then, it was big boring, and all the kids were meg null, because they didn't learn anything useful, it was all like, *da da da da, this happened in fourteen ninety-two, da da da da, when you mix like, chalk and water, it makes nitroglycerin,* and that kind of shit? And nothing was useful? (109, italics original).

This paragraph shows low literacy through run-on sentences, four uses of the stigmatized narrative device *like*, and simple vocabulary with empty modifiers like "big" and "meg." The lack of specificity demonstrated by the "*da da da da*" indicates that Titus does not know history or chemistry or cannot be bothered to explain them. In addition, the multiple question marks display a lack of confidence in his thoughts.

Print literacy is almost non-existent. Titus is confounded by the print texts he encounters through Violet's dad, who used to be a professor. When Titus first enters their house, he notes, "The place was a mess. Everything had words on it. There were papers with words on them, and books, and even posters on the wall had words" (135). Violet's father is an awkward recluse who looks and sounds, in Titus's words, "like a crank" (135). In a futile attempt to save language, Violet's father speaks to Titus in archaic phrases such as, "I am filled with astonishment at the regularity of your features and the handsome generosity you have shown my daughter," and Violet demonstrates her

148 · Kristi McDuffie

embarrassment with responses such as, "You can see why I don't take him out in public much" (136). Violet's father is an outsider and an embarrassment because he embodies sophisticated language and antiquated print culture.

Although Violet eventually recognizes the negative effects of the feeds, Titus doesn't seem to, so the novel ends without much hope. Rather than being a rebellious protagonist, Titus is complacent and uninspiring and fully embodies the fears of technology's impact on literacy found in the popular press. The popularity of this novel suggests that this theme has resonated for adults and young adults alike, although young adults might resist their language being ridiculed and their intelligence and agency being reduced in the text. Since this critique is heavy-handed and indicts young adults, the novel delivers a limited means of engaging in issues of technology and literacy with young adults themselves. The novel does not offer any possibilities for young adults to become informed and enact change, the way that other young adult dystopias such as *Uglies* and *Matched* do. It is ironic, of course, that this critique of the deterioration of literacy is found in a successful printed book.

Reading and Writing as Resistance in *Matched*

Matched depicts a utopian society where most people are "matched" with their future spouse based on a "failproof" algorithm, although some people remain single, whether by choice or coercion. The Society controls most aspects of life, including where people live and what jobs they have. Although Cassia, the sixteen-year-old narrator, takes these directives for granted, several things happen in her life that make her question the Society; one of these is exposure to writing. The characters in the novel are well educated and technologically literate, using computers for communication and homework, but Cassia never learned to write by hand as it is illegal in the Society. She first comes into contact with print literacy when her grandfather gives her Dylan Thomas's famous poem "Do Not Go Gentle into That Good Night" before he is put to death at the age of eighty per the Society's rules. The loss of literacy in this novel includes cultural literacy as the Society has limited cultural artifacts such as songs, artwork, and poems to a hundred of each; the rest were destroyed. Thomas's poem becomes a manifesto for Cassia and her love interest, Ky, who begin to question and rebel against the Society's dominance. Poetry continues to be a site of resistance throughout the novel as Cassia and Ky turn to poetry to learn about dominance and rebellion and exert their own agency by reading forbidden literature.

Cassia's rebellion through consumption turns to production when she is exposed to handwriting. Cassia sees Ky making letters in the grass and reflects that he is "writing in an old-fashioned, curved kind of writing, like the script on my compact. I've seen samples of it before but I don't know how to do it. No one does. All we can do is type. We could try to imitate the figures, but with

Technology and Models of Literacy in Young Adult Dystopian Fiction • 149

what? We don't have any of the old tools. But I realize as I watch Ky that you can make your own tools."[7] Over the next few weeks, Ky teaches Cassia how to write, starting with her name, in an act that signifies considerable autonomy in a Society where conformity and submission are the norm. Handwriting is romanticized by the depiction of cursive as beautiful and by its role in furthering Cassia and Ky's relationship (171). But it also becomes a means for Cassia and Ky to rebel against the society. Ky writes Cassia dangerous notes using charcoal on napkins in order to tell her about himself. Overall, technology functions as a mechanism of control in the text, while print literacy, including canonical literature and writing, is a mechanism for knowledge and rebellion. Traditional literacy is presented as desirable and even necessary for personal agency. Like *Feed*, this novel's existence as a successful printed book creates a vested self-interest in depicting traditional literacy in this manner; the valorization of print literacy is an implicit argument for the novel's own value and existence in a contemporary society where print culture is increasingly obsolete.

Writing and Technology in *Uglies*

In *Uglies*, technology seems to have enabled a utopian society. Everyone undergoes extensive surgery at the age of sixteen to go from "ugly" to "pretty," a standardized level of beauty based upon biological science in order to reduce prejudice and, consequently, war. Technology has also allowed for environmental protection. Since biowarfare ruined contemporary civilization, environmental resources are tightly controlled—power comes from wind and sun and clothes from biodegradable materials. Technology also allows for advanced communication, which occurs through the city infrastructure. But as the protagonist Tally comes to find out, these benefits may be outweighed by the fact that all of these technological advances allow the decision-makers to control everyone and monitor all interactions. The "pretty" operation includes lesions to make the population more easily controlled. The population, made docile by the operation, is complicit with this lack of print and cultural literacy, especially when they are bribed with a lifestyle of fashion and partying right after they turn pretty. Like *Matched*, people do not question the society's decisions or their roles within that society.

As is a common theme, technological advances also have a negative effect on traditional literacy. Technology offers environmentally friendly methods of communication so print literacy has become obsolete and most people cannot write by hand. The loss of print literacy also extends to cultural literacy, as the authorities destroyed texts like old popular magazines that contain information and images the general population is not supposed to see.[8] Readers learn about the loss of the ability to handwrite through Tally's surprise at finding out that her new friend Shay learned to write by

150 · Kristi McDuffie

hand in order to avoid being monitored by the city authorities (94). When Tally wants to write a note to herself so that she can "read her own words" after she volunteers to be a "pretty" test subject at the end of the novel, Shay has to write it for her because she "never learned penmanship . . . They don't require it anymore" (420). Handwritten notes, while rare in the novel, become a way for Tally and Shay to resist authoritarian control, such as when Shay handwrites encrypted directions for Tally to follow her out of the city. Print literacy thus enables Tally and Shay to resist the city authorities. Others use literacy to resist as well; the Smokies, a group of people who have left the city and its control, hoard old books and magazines that have been outlawed. These magazines provide learning experiences for Tally and Shay and contribute to their resistance. Traditional literacy, including both consuming cultural artifacts and producing communication, are thus presented not only as something we should be nostalgic for, but as something that enables personal autonomy and agency. The text sends the message that print literacy is at risk of extinction and should be saved, much like the messages found in popular non-fiction texts. However, the city authorities, rather than technology, are the culprits of the authoritarian state. Technological advances can be positive—they have been used to save the environment—if used responsibly. Tally and Shay do not denounce technology in favor of older forms of literacy and materials; rather, they use both the old forms of literacy and new facets of technology in their rebellion. For example, they use hoverboards, which are like surfboards that float in the air using magnetism, to travel far distances. This text thus provides a useful arena for young adults to investigate themes of technology and literacy because of this complicated view. It is certainly the only text that balances the loss of literacy with the environmental implications of daily newspapers and mass-produced books. Yet there are even broader approaches to literacy that present even more productive views.

Moving towards Multiliteracies

These texts illustrate that young adult dystopian fiction can be a place where adult writers investigate and mediate their fears about technology's effect on literacy, and where traditional print texts are valorized. Complaints about technology's effect on literacy, found in popular non-fiction texts and mirrored in these novels, follow a long tradition of complaints about technology. However, as Dennis Baron points out, "traditional" writing tools are technologies that were often lamented when they came into use. Plato critiqued writing in favor of oral recitation, Henry David Thoreau critiqued the telegraph in favor of pencils, and Samuel F.B. Morse doubted the staying power of the telephone.[9] More recently, teachers worried about the effect of calculators on math skills and spell-check on spelling skills, although these

Technology and Models of Literacy in Young Adult Dystopian Fiction • 151

technologies are now required in classrooms.[10] But rather than complaining about change, some scholars consider the value that technology can have for literacy.

Some pedagogies are moving towards multiliteracies, or models of literacy that incorporate technology. In the 1990s, the New London Group argued for the expansion of literacy pedagogy to move beyond traditional reading and writing to a "multiplicity of discourses," including the "burgeoning variety of text forms associated with information and multimedia technologies."[11] These multiple discourses are visual, aural, spatial, and more, speaking to the diverse forms of language, media, and individual subjectivities of diverse populations. The New London Group speaks to the fear that surrounds this kind of approach, and perhaps alludes to dystopias when they comment, "We may have cause to be skeptical about the sci-fi visions of information super-highways and an impending future where we are all virtual shoppers."[12] But rather than fight the impact technology has on our language, these authors acknowledge the multiliteracies that should and already do exist and want to incorporate them into literacy studies and pedagogy.

Stuart Selber's theory and praxis outlined in *Multiliteracies for a Digital Age* (2004) details a constructive approach to incorporating technology in pedagogy, and his concepts are useful for considering young adult dystopian fiction. Selber notes that educational programs often value functional competency in computer-related issues that do not engage students in critical thought about the technologies, and that a more engaged approach is necessary: "Although students will develop some extremely useful skills under an instrumental approach, they will have a much more difficult time thinking critically, contextually, and historically about the ways computer technologies are developed and used within our culture and how such use, in turn, intersects with writing and communication practices in the classroom."[13] Selber ultimately argues that "teachers should emphasize different kinds of computer literacies and help students become skilled at moving among them in strategic ways." His three approaches to computer literacies are functional (skills-based), critical, and rhetorical; these approaches will develop "students as users of technology, students as questioners of technology, and students as producers of technology."[14]

These approaches to multiliteracies illustrate that computer and digital literacies are not simply celebrations of technology or ways to have fun. Rather, recent technology, much like traditional literacy tools, can also serve as a site of resistance and agency. This approach to literacy provides a more productive way to engage in issues of technology and literacy than the unilateral critiques found in popular non-fiction. Furthermore, young adult dystopian novels that display more complicated views of literacy than those that valorize hand-writing and canonical literature can provide more fruitful means of engaging in these questions than texts that are overtly reproachful. In fact, one text already does.

152 · Kristi McDuffie

Digital Literacies in *Little Brother*

In *Little Brother* by Cory Doctorow, San Francisco becomes a police state after a terrorist attack. Marcus, the teenage protagonist, starts off as a smart and precocious techie who uses his knowledge and skills to circumvent his high school's security systems to skip school and participate in a scavenger hunt with his techie friends. While Marcus is out on the scavenger hunt, terrorists blow up the Bay Bridge and pandemonium ensues. In the rush, Marcus and three of his friends are caught and imprisoned by the Department of Homeland Security. Marcus immediately resents being forced to sacrifice his privacy by giving officials his phone and laptop passwords and, due to his initial verbal resistance, becomes a particular target of Homeland's investigation. Eventually, Marcus is released but told to keep quiet. San Franciscans quickly become subject to extreme monitoring with increased security checks and electronic surveillance. Adults, like Marcus's father, are tolerant of the impositions as a cost of increased security. Marcus, however, finds the intrusion unacceptable and begins to fight back. One of his first acts of resistance is to find a way around the monitored internet. He creates an alternate internet, called the Xnet, by running an independent operating system and internet browser on his Xbox. He passes out the software to his friends and a large, private network of young adults is quickly established through Xboxes; furthermore, this private network becomes the site of rebellion against the police state.

Marcus's aggressive use of technology sends a message that young adults can and should be participants and agents, rather than victims, of technology. To support this idea, after Marcus sets up the independent network, he comments, "The best part of all of this is how it made me *feel:* in control. My technology was working for me, serving me, protecting me. It wasn't spying on me. This is why I loved technology: if you used it right, it could give you power and privacy."[15] In addition to these kinds of manifestos about the importance of having and using technological knowledge, the text is permeated with instructions about how to perform specific feats, like building one's own laptop and creating an independent network. As the novel progresses, Marcus becomes an anonymous rebellion leader through the Xnet and through further technological antics such as jamming Homeland Security's monitoring of electronic subway passes.

Little Brother illustrates Selber's notions of functional, critical, and rhetorical literacies in that Marcus is a suave user of technology as well as a critical citizen aware of the role that technology plays in his society. Marcus is functionally literate because he understands how technology works and has resources to learn about what he doesn't know. His functional literacy includes knowing about security systems, wireless infrastructures, computer hardware, encryption details, and more. Although he is a gamer, his use of and interest in technology extends beyond recreational uses into critical literacy. He is a critical user of technology because he questions authorities who use

Technology and Models of Literacy in Young Adult Dystopian Fiction • 153

technology to invade personal freedom and uses his intelligence to fight back against that invasion. In fact, this critical approach to technology is perhaps the largest theme in the novel—young adults can and should use their technological skills to not only have fun, but also to be informed and empowered citizens. The novel is highly political in general, such as including discussions of First Amendment rights and 1960s Vietnam War protestors. The government is highly implicated in its unethical behavior and violation of individual rights. But by being informed, taking initiative, and working together, young adults can fight to maintain certain freedoms.

Marcus also demonstrates rhetorical literacy by the way he uses technology. As a leader of the resistance movement, Marcus is constantly thinking about the best way to communicate with young adults and adults. He goes to great lengths to create a "circle of trust" with a group of friends for a private version of the Xnet after authorities infiltrate the wider Xnet. He convinces them to attend a party by offering beer and then solidifies their trust by destroying the laptop he built to facilitate building the electronic circle after they are done with it. He uses blogs to anonymously post "real" information that traditional news sources fail to disseminate about a variety of events. For example, when Marcus attends a protest concert that is broken up by police who pepper spray the attendees, area newspapers inaccurately report that the attendees were violent. Marcus sets up a blog for attendees to upload photos, videos, and written narratives of their actual experiences. A foreign news outlet picks up the story and the alternate reports receive some recognition (203–205). In another instance, Marcus once again combines his technological capabilities with rhetorical skill when he sets up a press conference through a video game rather than answer individual journalists' questions about the resistance movement (235). Marcus is an anonymous leader, so conducting a press conference this way maintains his secret identity, allows him to address multiple journalists at once, and forces adults to engage with technology along with the young adult rebels in order to gain access to him. Finally, Marcus's rhetorical skills emerge in the most important way when he agrees to let a particular journalist report on his personal experience of incarceration and leading the rebellion. Because one of his friends is still being detained, Marcus realizes that he has to disclose his identity in order for people to believe his story and fight back against the police state, so he trusts one journalist to investigate and publish the story. Although he is briefly incarcerated again by Homeland Security as a result, the journalist is able to find him and save him from waterboarding torture. His friend needs time to heal and recover, but Marcus enables his release and exposed the wrongful incarceration by using a combination of all these literacies.

Compared to *Matched* and *Uglies*, *Little Brother* involves new literacies as methods of resistance, rather than limiting resistance to traditional literacies like handwriting and canonical literature. However, in *Little Brother*, additional literacies do not come at the expense of traditional literacies. Marcus still consumes

154 • Kristi McDuffie

information, like history and poetry, and produces written texts, like blogs, in his resistance efforts. He narrates that he has "always loved just learning stuff for its own sake. Just to be smarter about the world around me," and this applies to politics and literature as well as technology (219). When he is suspended from school for arguing about First Amendment rights, he is assigned to write papers and chooses to write about Beat poets, Jack Kerouac's *On the Road*, and historical resistance movements. Marcus finds inspiration for rebellion in poetry, specifically Allen Ginsberg's work, much like Cassia finds inspiration in Dylan Thomas's work in *Matched*. Although these passages about traditional literacies are brief compared to the extended passages about digital literacies, it is notable that traditional literacies are still important for agency and social change. In fact, digital literacies as a means of agency and change could not be fully realized without being used in tandem with traditional literacies.

Marcus is extremely smart, as are most of the young adults in the novel, and exemplifies a positive alternative to the "dumbest generation" attacks of Bauerlein; in fact, it is adults who are largely censured in this text for being complacent, controlling, and egocentric. The text is heavy-handed in educating young adults about technology and encouraging them to fight for freedom and privacy, in large part through pages-long passages explicating technology like encryption (150). (The text also includes asides on topics such as bathroom stall choice and urban planning.) The narrator as educator and lecturer can become tiring, but the message is that young people should be educated users of technology and should not shy away from the details. By taking ownership and finding agency with technology, young adults can avoid being manipulated and controlled by authorities. There are also two afterwords in the novel, one by a security technologist and another by an Xbox hacker. These are teachable moments; the first afterword's purpose is to tell readers that security is fun and the second's is to discuss hacking's role as a public service. A bibliography follows with recommended texts on hacking for readers who want to learn more. Outside of this novel, Doctorow is an ardent advocate for freedom in technology issues, such as open-source publishing and copyright law. Thus, discussions of technology are often framed in political discussions. These strong lessons might not appeal to all readers, nor might the inclusion of casual drinking and sex. Nonetheless, the novel presents a productive forum for inquiry due to its complicated view of technology, literacy, and agency. The novel celebrates young adults who are innovative and intelligent and offers a constructive way for them to consider the effects of technology and literacy in society.

Conclusion

This exploration of four popular young adult dystopian novels demonstrates a variety of models of literacy that emerge in this genre. Novels like *Feed* that

Technology and Models of Literacy in Young Adult Dystopian Fiction · 155

present young adults as materialistic and illiterate in a way that mirrors critiques about young adults found in popular non-fiction texts provide complaints and warnings rather than critical interrogations of literacy and technology. Other novels, such as *Matched* and *Uglies*, offer more nuanced views of technology and literacy by featuring young adults who gain agency and fight against authoritarian control by learning and using traditional literacy tools. These texts often frame traditional literacy within nostalgia and romance; however, even more progressive models are available. Digital literacies, including functional, critical, and rhetorical approaches to technology, can expand positive depictions of young adults' technological and literate capabilities. Productive approaches to technology and literacy include both old and new literacies and respect young adults as valued citizens and agents of change capable of mastering a variety of forms of communication and technology. This respectful view is likely to be more effective for reaching and engaging with an audience that is anything but dumb.

Notes

1 Nicholas Carr, *The Shallows: What the Internet Is Doing to Our Brains* (New York: W.W. Norton, 2010), 4–5. See also John Brockman, ed, *Is the Internet Changing the Way You Think?: The Net's Impact on Our Minds and Future* (New York: Harper, 2011).

2 Carr, *The Shallows*, 51.

3 N. Katherine Hayles, "Hyper and Deep Attention: The Generational Divide in Cognitive Modes," *Profession* (2007): 187, 188.

4 See Mark Bauerlein, *The Dumbest Generation: How the Digital Age Stupefies Young Americans and Jeopardizes Our Future* (New York: Jeremy P. Tarcher, 2008), ix.

5 Ibid., 10.

6 M.T. Anderson, *Feed* (Cambridge, MA: Candlewick Press, 2002), 163. Subsequent references will be cited parenthetically in the text.

7 Ally Condie, *Matched* (New York: Penguin, 2010), 170. Subsequent references will be cited parenthetically in the text.

8 Scott Westerfeld, *Uglies* (New York: Simon Pulse, 2005), 197–198. Subsequent references will be cited parenthetically in the text.

9 See Dennis Baron, "From Pencils to Pixels: The Stages of Literacy Technologies," in *Literacy: A Critical Sourcebook*, ed. Ellen Cushman et al. (Boston: Bedford St. Martin's, 2001), 72–78.

10 Ibid., 82.

11 New London Group, "A Pedagogy of Multiliteracies: Designing Social Futures," *Harvard Educational Review* 66.1 (1996): 61.

12 Ibid., 64.

13 Stuart A. Selber, *Multiliteracies for a Digital Age* (Carbondale: Southern Illinois University Press, 2004), 9.

156 · Kristi McDuffie

14 Ibid., 24, 25.

15 Cory Doctorow, *Little Brother* (New York: Tom Doherty Associates, 2008), 88, italics original. Subsequent references will be cited parenthetically in the text.

Works Cited

Anderson, M.T. *Feed*. Cambridge, MA: Candlewick Press, 2002.
Baron, Dennis. "From Pencils to Pixels: The Stages of Literacy Technologies." In *Literacy: A Critical Sourcebook*, edited by Ellen Cushman, Eugene R. Kintgen, Barry M. Kroll, and Mike Rose, 70–84. Boston: Bedford St. Martin's, 2001.
Bauerlein, Mark. *The Dumbest Generation: How the Digital Age Stupefies Young Americans and Jeopardizes Our Future*. New York: Jeremy P. Tarcher, 2008.
Brockman, John, ed. *Is the Internet Changing the Way You Think?: The Net's Impact on Our Minds and Future*. New York: Harper, 2011.
Carr, Nicholas. *The Shallows: What the Internet Is Doing to Our Brains*. New York: W.W. Norton, 2010.
Condie, Ally. *Matched*. New York: Penguin, 2010.
Doctorow, Cory. *Little Brother*. New York: Tom Doherty Associates, 2008.
Hayles, N. Katherine. "Hyper and Deep Attention: The Generational Divide in Cognitive Modes." *Profession* (2007): 187–199.
New London Group. "A Pedagogy of Multiliteracies: Designing Social Futures." *Harvard Educational Review* 66.1 (1996): 60–92.
Selber, Stuart A. *Multiliteracies for a Digital Age*. Carbondale: Southern Illinois University Press, 2004.
Westerfeld, Scott. *Uglies*. New York: Simon Pulse, 2005.

Part Four

Biotechnologies of the Self

Humanity in a Posthuman Age

Chapter Ten
Dystopian Sacrifice, Scapegoats, and Neal Shusterman's *Unwind*

Susan Louise Stewart

Dystopian fiction offers a vision of a future train wreck, but one that provides temporal safety: "We haven't quite reached that point," we say with relief. "Not yet. And maybe we won't with due diligence." Fredric Jameson refers to dystopia as "a 'near future' novel [that] tells the story of an imminent disaster—ecology, overpopulation, plague, drought, the stray comet or nuclear accident—waiting to come to pass in our own near future, which is fast-forwarded in the time of the novel."[1] Lyman Tower Sargent offers a similar definition. "The traditional dystopia," writes Sargent, "was an extrapolation from the present that involved a warning.... The dystopia ... says if you behave thus and so, this is how you will be punished."[2] Sargent continues with what has become a frequently quoted definition. He characterizes the dystopia as "a non-existent society ... normally located in time and space that the author intended a contemporaneous reader to view as considerably worse than the society in which that reader lived."[3] For Jameson, Sargent, and many other scholars, dystopias are cautionary tales set in a future with recognizable features.

The recognizable feature in Neal Shusterman's dystopian vision in *Unwind* (2007) is the controversy between proponents of pro-choice and pro-life, who become embroiled in the Heartland Wars. In the process, an unsettling dilemma arises: what does a culture do with its unwanted, troublesome, sometimes inconvenient or imperfect children who aren't quite good enough to become adults? In Shusterman's "modest proposal," those unwanted, troublesome, imperfect children are "unwound." According to the Bill of Life, an agreement reached to end the Heartland War, "Between the ages of thirteen

160 · Susan Louise Stewart

and eighteen, a parent may choose to retroactively 'abort' a child" as long as "the child's life doesn't 'technically' end."[4] Thus, in order to satisfy these conditions, almost every part of the body, including the brain, is recycled into the body of someone else—someone who might need an arm, ear, eye, lung, heart, temporal lobe, and so on. In short, the young "donors" are Dr. Frankenstein's "monster" in reverse. Such a proposition is not considered a stretch or unusual in dystopian fiction, for it is a genre of extremes. As will be demonstrated, however, *Unwind* is situated within a specific type of dystopia wherein children become sacrifices and scapegoats and are eventually cannibalized through their whole-body "donations" or rather, mandatory conscriptions.

To fully illustrate the points above, it is necessary to briefly historicize the role of child sacrifice, for sacrifice, as René Girard explains, is part of scapegoating. Following that is a discussion of other young adult dystopian novels wherein children serve as sacrificial means to adult needs and ends, which helps contextualize Shusterman's novel. *Unwind*, however, encourages a different reading of dystopian circumstances in that it transforms Mosaic Law's conceptualization of holocausts and burnt offerings into a contemporary Holocaust narrative of scapegoating, particularly when considering several elements that echo descriptions of the work camps of WWII. That is, the culture depicted in *Unwind* constructs children as scapegoats, after which it deconstructs them through unwinding; in the process, the novel establishes itself as a revised Holocaust narrative. And last, although Kay Sambell has already visited the role of inadequate, even malevolent adults and parents in young adult dystopian fiction, a deconstruction—unwinding—of some of the underlying ideologies associated with childhood, adulthood, and the nature of young adult dystopian fiction further extends her discussion and provides another possibility regarding the past and future of young adult dystopian fiction.

Sacrificing the Young: Past and Present

Human beings and human sacrifice are seemingly inseparable. As told by the Greeks, Poseidon commanded that the beautiful Andromeda be sacrificed to a sea monster because of her mother's—Cassiopeia's—vanity. In 1981, Harry Hamlin, playing the role of Perseus in *Clash of the Titans*, acquainted contemporary culture with a romanticized variation of the myth.

The biblical tradition, too, tells its own stories of sacrifice. According to the Old Testament, God commands Abraham to sacrifice his only son, Isaac, as a burnt offering. Thus, Abraham and Isaac travel to the place designated by God with Isaac carrying the wood on his back that will be used for the fire that will consume him (similar to the way Christ will later carry his own cross). Abraham builds the altar, places the wood on it, and then places a bound Isaac on top of the wood. Knife in hand, Abraham prepares to sacrifice Isaac, but

Dystopian Sacrifice, Scapegoats, and Neal Shusterman's *Unwind* • **161**

an angel stops him. Abraham has sufficiently proven that he fears God. While Abraham replaces Isaac with a sacrificial ram, Abraham's intent is nevertheless unmistakable. More monumental and most well known in the Christian tradition is God's sacrifice of his son to save humanity from itself. Christ was not a child in terms of age when crucified—he is purported to have been in his thirties—but Christ's crucifixion has long maintained the standard of sacrifice: one individual is designated to alleviate all humanity's sins.

Considering that Greek mythology and biblical history constitute perhaps two of the most influential narratives in western literature and culture, it should not be surprising that remnants of human sacrifice become part of young adult dystopian fiction, though they are not always as obvious as Andromeda, Isaac, or Christ. Rather, human sacrifice becomes more of a subtext, a way of emphasizing the dreadful nature of the dystopian culture. Thus, when the titular character in Lois Lowry's *The Giver* (1993) encourages Jonas to leave his community and he does so, Jonas, like Christ, saves humanity from itself. Jonas's sacrifice does not result in his death, but it was a very real possibility until the publication of *Messenger* (2004), the third novel of the Giver trilogy. While Jonas makes the decision to leave the safety of the community, what happens once he does so is not that different from the excommunications of the medieval Church wherein people were cast out of their communities and left to survive in the wilderness: a formidable prospect. Jonas is just as much at risk as he journeys to Elsewhere as the unfortunate individuals cast out of the medieval Church and community.

In Gemma Malley's *The Declaration* (2007), scientists find a way to prolong life indefinitely. Not surprisingly, the desire to vanquish death results in overpopulation. As a solution, people are not allowed to have children unless they "Opt Out." That is, they would not take the treatments to prolong their lives in exchange for having a child. In general, having children is a crime, and as part of the indoctrination, Surpluses—illegally born children—are convinced that they are to blame. While parents who have children illegally are sent to prison, the children pay a high price for decisions made by adults. Anna, the protagonist who lives in Grange Hall where children learn how to be servants, believes herself "very lucky":

> *I've got a chance to redeem my Parents' Sins, if I work hard enough and become employable. Not everyone gets that kind of chance. . . . In some countries Surpluses are killed, put down like animals.*
>
> *They'd never do that here, of course. In England they help Surpluses be Useful to other people, so it isn't quite so bad we were born. Here they set up Grange Hall because of the staffing requirements of Legal people, and that's why we have to work so hard—to show our gratitude.*[5]

Adults make bad decisions or they "sin" in this instance; children pay the price.

162 • Susan Louise Stewart

In Suzanne Collins's recent and very popular The Hunger Games trilogy (2008–2010), the Capitol, where all decisions are made for each district, televises child sacrifice every year. As a way to remind and punish the people for their rebellion against the Capitol, a girl and a boy between the ages of twelve and eighteen are chosen from each district to be "tributes" or warriors on behalf of their districts. Engaging in guerilla warfare, the children must battle until only one survives. The narrative surrounding *The Hunger Games* is as follows:

> Taking the kids from our districts, forcing them to kill one another while we watch—this is the Capitol's way of reminding us how totally we are at their mercy. How little chance we would stand of surviving another rebellion. Whatever words they use, the real message is clear. "Look how we take your children and sacrifice them and there's nothing you can do."[6]

Notably, the Capitol is marked by excesses—food, riches, luxury—and by its enjoyment of the Hunger Games and annual child sacrifices.

Thus, the sacrifice of the young, whether explicit or implicit, is frequently woven into novels of dystopia; in fact, it is often part of what makes them dystopian narratives. Sacrificing the young for the good of the community—frequently the adult community—makes these kinds of narratives simultaneously striking and horrifying. The contemporary cultural narrative surrounding the death of a child is that of tragedy. According to the narrative, the child has done nothing to deserve to die young—a lamb, an innocent—and the child does not have the chance to fulfill his or her potential. As a result, sacrificing the young—sometimes because they *are* purportedly innocent and because of their unfulfilled promise—translates into an economy of tragedy and is one method of illustrating precisely how unacceptable the dystopian world is. The ideological nature of the dystopia becomes even more reprehensible when the sacrifice results from adults' mistakes, benefits adults, or is enforced by adults. In *Unwind*, adults, as with many dystopian narratives, constitute the governing body; adults make the decisions; adults benefit.

In novels such as *The Giver, The Declaration, The Hunger Games*, and the focus of this essay, *Unwind*, the dystopia applies to a select segment of people—children—who serve a specific purpose: sacrifice. That is, adults sacrifice the young—those who are considered the future of humanity—in order to teach the young a lesson about the future. In *Unwind*, sacrificing children serves to quell the violence between two factions, who are determined to destroy each other. To end the conflict, the two sides strike a bargain wherein the youth will pay the price. This solution is the basis of the violence that leads to sacrifice and the creation of the scapegoat.

Young Scapegoats

Sacrifice is a term that is frequently at odds with itself and in biblical terms, always has been. On one hand, "sacrifice pays," writes Dennis King Keenan: "One gets a return on one's investment."[7] On the other hand, sacrifice "involves selflessness, giving without reserve. Sacrifice has to be beyond calculation and hope of a reward, so as not to be construed as self-serving (and, therefore, not a genuine sacrifice). Sacrifice must necessarily be a sacrifice *for nothing*, a sacrifice for no reason, no goal."[8] Thus, as Keenan reminds us, Christ tells his disciples, who must forego many comforts, that their sacrifices "must be done in *secret*: 'do not let your left hand know what your right hand is doing.'"[9] *Unwind*, as I illustrate below, demonstrates the fluidity and the contradictions associated with sacrifice.

The principle of unwinding occurs as a compromise to end the Second Civil War between pro-life and pro-choice advocates. The constitutional amendments, or "Bill of Life," state that "human life may not be touched from the moment of conception until a child reaches the age of thirteen" (n.p.).[10] Once the child reaches the age of thirteen, though, "a parent may choose to retroactively 'abort' a child" as long as "the child's life doesn't 'technically' end" (n.p.). When a child reaches eighteen, or "the age of reason," the child, now technically an adult, is safe from being unwound (223). Notably, adults, who have surpassed "the age of reason," make a most unreasonable decision when they enter into the Unwind Accord and Bill of Life. Indeed, "Everyone was so happy to end the war, no one cared about the consequences" (224). Thus, unwinding becomes a normalized process soon to be motivated by greed. What would be for contemporary readers a horrific speculation becomes standard practice and "big business" (224). Unwanted children between the age of thirteen and eighteen, particularly "problem" children and thus inconsequential for this community, become sacrificial fodder: their sacrifice maintains peace between two factions that cannot find a better resolution.

Their sacrifice also serves as a communal glue, for as Nancy B. Jay explains, "Sacrifice joins people together in community, and conversely, it separates them from defilement, disease, and other dangers"; war in *Unwind* is equivalent to "other dangers."[11] However, a contradiction exists in *Unwind*, for most adults seem unperturbed at the prospect of retroactively aborting children. Indeed, the reasons given for unwinding are quite shallow. One character whose parents are "ridiculously wealthy" enter into a "brutal custody battle over him. Two years and six court dates later, it still wasn't resolved. In the end the only thing his mother and father could agree on was that each would rather see Hayden unwound than allow the other parent to have custody" (99). Risa, a ward of "Ohio State Home 23," isn't a good enough piano player, not when her school has to cut "5 percent of our teenage population" to make room for more wards (23). The reasons have to be shallow, of course,

164 · Susan Louise Stewart

to effectively manipulate readers so that they have no doubt as to the wrong and ridiculous nature of the adults, who initially go to war instead of finding a reasonable solution to the conflict. And, since adults (and children, too, but mostly adults) benefit because they are the recipients of organs taken from the unwinds, one might wonder if adults are actually sacrificing anything—a paradox of sacrifice. Additionally, the initial decision to make this sacrifice benefits everyone who doesn't have to be unwound because it brings an end to the violence. Perhaps, then, the communal glue is one of complicity as adults, who know better, send children to their deaths as a way to end the violence. If all participate, all are guilty and paradoxically, none are guilty.

Sacrifice to end violence serves as the cornerstone of scapegoating. The Admiral, a former military man who now harbors escaped unwinds, explains, "A conflict always begins with an issue—a difference of opinion, an argument" (223). His descriptions pinpoint the beginning of the violence that will lead to sacrifice (223). The Admiral then further asserts that once a conflict "turns into a war, the issue doesn't matter anymore, because now it's about one thing and one thing only: how much each side hates the other" (223). The violence, an outgrowth of anger, has grown from an argument into a war. In the process, the cause of the war becomes irrelevant. And once the capitalist machine begins churning, for organs from unwinds are in high demand, contemplating a different solution is no longer economically feasible: "People wanted parts" (224).

Girard explains the roles of violence, sacrifice, and the scapegoat, which he finds in Greek plays and mythology as well as biblical history. Girard does more than personify violence; he treats it as an instinctive if not an actual conscious presence when he writes, "If left unappeased, violence will accumulate until it overflows its confines and floods the surrounding area. The role of sacrifice is to stem this rising tide of indiscriminate substitutions and redirect violence into 'proper' channels."[12] In other words, violence tends to multiply if nothing intervenes, a result of what Girard (drawing from Freud) calls "mimetic desire," which Robert G. Hamerton-Kelly explains "is infectious on the group level; we catch it from one another. Fashion, the arms race, the markets are driven by mimesis. . . . Mimesis . . . generates violence in groups through the competition for objects and for prestige."[13] One need only know about mob mentality to understand that until something redirects the anger and violence elsewhere, it grows until the mob finds something to do with its anger and violence—a lynching, for instance. "The mob," writes Hamerton-Kelly, "makes the victim the cause and by so doing obscures its own violence from itself and transfers it to the victim."[14]

Girard also posits that "any community that has fallen prey to violence or has been stricken by some overwhelming catastrophe hurls itself blindly into the search for a scapegoat," which leads the members of the community to "strive desperately to convince themselves that all their ills are the fault of a lone individual who can easily be disposed of."[15] Potentially, then, the

Dystopian Sacrifice, Scapegoats, and Neal Shusterman's *Unwind* • 165

scapegoat is simply a convenient solution to a community's problem, for the violence is "transferred to the victim" but "under controlled circumstances."[16] Theoretically, the scapegoat contains the violence—makes it manageable.

The scapegoat does not have to be an individual. It can be a group of people. For instance, Viktor Karády explains that one "model of anti-Semitism is represented by the set of ideas which deflects the blame for all ills in society to the Jews. In this mechanism of the scapegoat, Jews are absolutely deleterious elements in society, and therefore it is possible to project onto them everything that is not working, disagreeable or judged to be bad."[17] Hitler identified the Jews and other groups as "the problem" with Germany. If he could eliminate the Jews, he could eliminate the problem. The "unwanteds," children who would under other circumstances be aborted, are transformed into "the problem" in *Unwind*. They are not the problem, of course, any more than the Jews were. Nevertheless, instead of being shocked by the proposition of unwinding unwanteds, the two sides refuse to "blink" when faced with the ghastly compromise before them (224). In this way, the children become a solution to the problem.

The scapegoat apparatus is not at first evident in *Unwind* in that no one blames the children, at least not explicitly. That adults make sacrifices of their youth to end the violence does suggest a type of blame, though. The adults do not seem to have an issue with sending children away for unwinding, thus nullifying a sense of sacrifice, except for tithes like Lev. However, since this culture identifies children who just don't quite meet arbitrary expectations as potential unwinds, the children are themselves to blame. They could, after all, be well behaved, or get better grades in school, or so seems the logic. Additionally, adults have identified not just children, but conveniently adolescents and young adults who are between the age of thirteen and eighteen—the most challenging age for many parents—as potential unwinds. Thus, "rather than blame themselves, people inevitably blame either society as a whole, which costs them nothing, or other people who seem particularly harmful for easily identifiable reasons."[18] Adolescents and young adults, then, are in some sense the problem, even if they aren't. Adults in Shusterman's novel, though, have discovered a way to alleviate much of their potential guilt, for "Unwinds aren't really dead. They're still alive . . . sort of" (167).

That life is continued after death is emphasized when the Admiral brings a group of people together toward the end of the novel. As a whole, this group represents his son, Harlan, whom the Admiral permitted to be unwound, for each person at this gathering has received some part of his son. Apparently memories of Harlan's life are embedded at the cellular level resulting in the recipients of various parts of his body possessing Harlan's memories. Thus, when the Admiral meets a man who has Harlan's hand and explains that the scar on the hand is the result of a prior fishing incident, another man who overhears the conversation remembers the accident. Strangers know about Harlan through his cellular memory. Something, indeed everything except

166 · Susan Louise Stewart

a unified consciousness (if a consciousness can ever be unified), remains of Harlan even if he isn't contained in one body. One has to wonder, however, who contains the memory of his father's betrayal, for Harlan's unwinding was a result of Harlan's "troubled" youth and the Admiral's military position. The Admiral explains, "As one of the fathers of the Unwind Accord, I was expected to set an example" (225). The Admiral trades his role as father to his son for one of the fathers of a terrible solution. While the Admiral immediately regrets the decision and tries to stop the process, Harlan has already been unwound.

It is appropriate that Harlan, one of the first scapegoats, one of the first to be unwound, is made almost whole again—rewound, so to speak. That is, the Admiral initially helps quell the mob mentality generated by his role in the Unwind Accord, an act that disperses his son across the country. At the end of the novel, however, and in direct opposition to the underlying violence of the Unwind Accord and the Admiral's previous role, he brings another crowd together in order to bring his son together. This act serves as compensation for his guilt, but it also represents the potential for healing as Harlan is symbolically sutured in place.

From holocaust to Holocaust

Harlan has served at least two purposes: he is one of the first scapegoats of the war, and he is held up as an example, as are his father's actions. The nature of unwinding, however, will eventually assume different meanings and significance. For instance, some religious groups will transform unwinding into tithing, though it is a gesture that simply absolves adults of their guilt. *Unwind* offers another layer of meaning, however, for it is a Holocaust novel, but not in the traditional sense.

The sacrifices that take place in *Unwind* are associated with both the Mosaic notion of burnt offerings—holocaust—and the Holocaust of WWII. Indeed, the Holocaust is associated with ancient rituals including the Old Testament's connections to burnt offerings. Jay explains that in the Old Testament, some sacrificial victims "were destroyed in a variety of ways (including holocaust, meaning 'burnt whole')."[19] Jan G.J. van den Eijnden describes the nature of burnt offerings, a term he eventually uses to replace holocaust because of its painful recent history and its causal connection to the Holocaust of WWII. The term "holocaust," explains van den Eijnden,

> was chosen because of the totality of this extermination. Therefore, what happened to the Jews had some similarity with which happened to the victim of the holocaust or burnt-offering as described in the books of Moses. In a holocaust nothing of a victim may remain. It has to be burnt completely in honour of God. This is not the case with all biblical

Dystopian Sacrifice, Scapegoats, and Neal Shusterman's *Unwind* • 167

offerings. . . . Therefore, only the word "holocaust" or "burnt-offering" can express what happened to the Jews in the concentration camps.[20]

Jay explains that the burnt offering of the Old Testament functioned as both a "peace offering" and a "sin offering."[21] As one of the first to be unwound after the Accord has been signed, Harlan is most certainly a peace offering, but he is also a sin offering, for he and others who follow will serve as absolution for adults not capable of coming to a better solution than murder—or semi-murder since something still remains of the victims. Jay also explains that sacrifices were to be wholly consumed, but not necessarily by fire. Rather, the person offering the sacrifice and the priest conducting the sacrifice would consume designated parts of the sacrificial victim. Harlan and other unwinds are "consumed" by their numerous hosts and become part of their hosts' bodies just as nourishment becomes part of any human's body. Harlan and other unwinds represent a sanitized version of cannibalization and a thinly disguised form of genocide. Unwinding is a form of organ "donation." It is part sacred sacrifice as explained above and part secular conscription. While the "chosen" aren't actually ingested and then digested by their hosts, they are nevertheless consumed until nothing (no less than 99.44%, a percentage that makes allowance for useless body parts such as the appendix) remains. The young donors ultimately become part of their hosts as the body parts are sutured in place.

Unwind also represents a shortened journey from a narrative of holocaust to a Holocaust narrative. Granted, none of the characters are Jewish. During his tithing celebration, which precedes his anticipated and welcome unwinding, Lev "has people lift him up in a chair and dance with him around the room, because he had seen them do that at a Jewish friend's bar mitzvah" (28). That is the only explicit reference to Jewish practices. The novel does not mention WWII or the concentration camps associated with the Holocaust. No mass incinerations or gassings occur. It is, nevertheless, a symbolic Holocaust narrative in its imagery and many allusions to the Holocaust. Only a select group of people, children from thirteen to eighteen, can be unwound. They are taken to "harvest camps" like Happy Jack Harvest Camp to be unwound, rather than concentration and death camps that announce "Work Will Set You Free," but the end is the same. Harvest camps do differ to some degree from death camps such as Auschwitz. Happy Jack, for instance, is not a work camp. No one is starved or harmed. That would be counter-productive, for people need healthy donors. The dormitories are painted in cheerful colors and the staff members wear shorts and Hawaiian shirts. Nevertheless, "There's a barbed-wire fence, but it's hidden behind a towering hibiscus hedge—and although the Unwinds in residence see the crowded buses arriving at the front gate each day, they are spared the sight of departing trucks. Those leave the back way" (265–266). The buses are reminiscent of the trains that took millions to their deaths.

168 · Susan Louise Stewart

The unwind process itself seems like a procedure designed by Joseph Mengele, the notorious SS officer who experimented on inmates at Auschwitz. Although not painful—unwinds only experience a tug here and there while being dismembered—they experience the unwinding process fully conscious. As a nurse explains, "By law, we're required to keep you conscious through the entire procedure . . . [Unwinds] have a right to know everything that's happening . . . every step of the way" (288). The unwinding process takes around three hours and is an incredibly haunting and chilling vision as the donor is relieved of everything from the foot to the medulla—a barbaric practice disguised as democratic process.

The short journey into the unwinding facility, also known as the Chop Shop, further offers a reminder of the death camps. Yitzhak Arad explains that at Auschwitz and other extermination camps, to assure that "the victim's screams on their way to the gas chambers . . . would not be heard throughout the camp—the SS arranged an orchestra," which consisted of other concentration camp prisoners.[22] Similarly, at the Happy Jack Harvest Camp, prisoner-musicians sit at the opening of the unwinding facility and play music as the victims/donors enter the unwinding chamber. The process works. As Roland, who is being taken to the Chop Shop, fights his demise, "above him, the band plays. He wants to scream, but here, so close to the Chop Shop, his screams will be drowned out by the band" (287). The narrative, then, has moved from scapegoating to holocaust to full-blown Holocaust. *Unwind* also serves as a reminder as to how easy it is agree to and even embrace insane propositions such as final solutions, for the Unwind Accord is nothing less than what Hitler proposed.

Ultimately Unwound

Traditionally, conclusions should represent some kind of dénouement wherein loose ends and questions are taken care of and the audience leaves with the satisfaction of finality, certainty, and closure. Conclusions are the final chapter of the novel, the closing scene of the film, the end of the article: the last word. Dystopian narratives, however, frequently reject totalizing conclusions and tend toward ambiguity; otherwise, the didactic lessons of dystopias become easily dismissed. Meaningful and successful novels of dystopia won't let us forget them—they haunt us.

Unwind does offer some satisfaction in that Harlan, the Admiral's unwound son, is brought together through the Admiral's efforts. As a result of the Admiral's regret in having his son unwound, he eventually gathers everyone who has benefitted from Harlan's body. However, the satisfaction is limited. Harlan will never be "himself" again. Once unwound, he lives "in a divided state" (24). In postmodern terms, humans always exist in a divided state, a mosaic of time, place, culture, and circumstances, but because we're contained in one

Dystopian Sacrifice, Scapegoats, and Neal Shusterman's *Unwind* • 169

body, it is relatively easy to deny the division and to participate in the illusion of wholeness. Harlan is even less known than a corporeally contained human being, and when separated from others who carry his organs and cellular memory, he—we—cannot deny that division, which under contemporary conditions would be a very unsettling proposition. A sense of wholeness generally makes us happy.

If the preceding conveys a sense of ambivalence, the role of organized religion as practiced by Lev's family does not. *Unwind* is quite unkind, for it critiques the use of religion as one way of disguising the ugly truth of unwinding and resounds of Marx's declaration that religion "is the opium of the people," and Lenin's later condemnation that "religion is a kind of spiritual intoxicant, in which the slaves of capital drown their humanity and blunt their desires for some sort of decent human existence."[23] Early in the novel, when Lev wonders "why it has to be me," Lev's religious leader, Pastor Dan, tells him that God doesn't ask for the "first fruits but best fruits," to which Lev responds, "Thank you," and, "I'm ready for this" (33). Lev needs to be comforted and uplifted—not spiritually destroyed—by his impending demise and needs to believe that his death means something; he cannot afford to ask what God's role was in the Unwind Accord in the first place, or what God is supposed to do with a tithed, unwound body. He cannot ask who benefits. Lev, then, represents the perfect sacrifice. However, Pastor Dan's comment that "everyone who raised you to be a tithe . . . [is] as guilty as the people who pumped that [explosive] poison into your blood" suggests that adults have created an untenable solution (328). It is only toward the end of the novel—after Pastor Dan has left the church—that Lev discovers he has alternatives. The former pastor tells Lev, "I still very much believe in God—just not a god who condones human tithing" (329). Even if it comes too late in the novel to be truly meaningful and influential, this is a stunning and revelatory prospect for Lev. "I never knew that was a choice," says Lev (329). Lev's attention has previously been diverted elsewhere: toward the responsibilities to his religion, to tithing, and to obeying his parents, who are, according to Pastor Dan, "the kind of people who can't bend without breaking" (328). Lev has been trained to be an obedient son, one who trusts his parents and adult authority and believes that they know what is good for him. He does not question his parents' motives, for they are disguised in the form of a tithe. Not until Connor kidnaps Lev, which leads to Lev's exposure to different perspectives, does he understand adult complicity and that other possibilities exist. In other words, at least for Lev, knowledge of adult failure is not inherent; it is learned through experience and context.

Pastor Dan's response is symptomatic of the inadequacy of adult solutions in young adult fiction. His reaction reflects a tradition born in the 1970s that illustrates the impossibility or rejection of parenthood and adulthood. Although Peter Pan's perennial childhood stands as the ultimate example, the problem novel of the 1970s wherein parents and adults are frequently demonized is the most evident example. Anne Scott MacLeod identifies the

170 · Susan Louise Stewart

problematic parents and adults depicted in the problem novels. "The literature of the 1970s," she explains, "reveals an astonishing hostility toward parents, making parental inadequacies a central theme, especially (though not exclusively) in books written for the teen market. In story after story . . . writers . . . paint devastating portraits of parents."[24] The 1970s also saw what Kay Sambell calls "a dark literature of emergency and despair . . . expressing deep-rooted fears for the future of those children being addressed" in the form of young adult dystopian fiction.[25] As with the problem novel identified by MacLeod, young adult dystopian fiction could not be more hostile toward adults; contemporary dystopian fiction features intolerable and contemptible parents and adults. Sambell identifies the ways in which adults inflict just about every possible cruelty on the youthful characters depicted in young adult dystopias. In some dystopian narratives, "we are introduced to future schools in which children are systematically drugged, brainwashed, or otherwise forced by adult tutors to become docile and compliant," and in others, they "actually die in order to highlight the negligence and corruption of the adult-created world they have inherited."[26] In short, in young adult dystopian narratives, it is wise to avoid childhood at all costs. However, one of the few alternatives—reaching adulthood—is no better. In fact, one has to wonder why the young protagonists even try, for what lies ahead of them is the picture of human imperfection, cruelty, greed, and every other possible negative human characteristic, the very same attributes associated with adults in problem novels. That is, young adult dystopian novels are nothing less than the problem novels of the past reframed as dystopian fiction of the future.

Sambell identifies a potential antidote to the problem parents and awful adults of young adult dystopian fiction in "Carnivalizing the Future: A New Approach to Theorizing Childhood and Adulthood in Science Fiction for Young Readers." She looks to Philip Reeve's *Mortal Engines* (2001) and his innovative and imaginative use of humor "to gently undermine and redefine commonly held theories about the essential differences between childhood and adulthood, which in turn pave the way for a radical reinvention of the potential roles that may be performed by his child."[27] She identifies this as a form of Bakhtin's carnivalization or reversal of hierarchies and roles. I suspect, however, that few authors will follow Reeve's lead.

As imaginative as fiction writers can be, the story of the scapegoat, young sacrifices, and complicit adults resonates on some level—perhaps because the story is too compelling, too old, or too deeply embedded in cultural history and memory to abandon. Authors seem to prefer to cannibalize, rather than carnivalize, the future as well as the youth that would signify hope. Only when the youth depicted in these narratives assume control of their futures can they provide any sense of hope. Unfortunately, more often than not, the future is controlled by adults in the form of authors who write these narratives or the fictional adults who serve as obstacles to a better future.

Dystopian Sacrifice, Scapegoats, and Neal Shusterman's *Unwind* · 171

"At their best," writes Thomas Morrissey in this volume, "today's YA dystopias are invitations to action." Morrissey is absolutely correct. Several authors of young adult dystopias, however, do not meet Morrissey's standard, and instead seem to strive for some kind of sensationalized despair only slightly mitigated by hope. At the conclusion of *Unwind*, Shusterman allows for some degree of hope when Congress, a governmental entity, contemplates lowering "the legal age of adulthood from eighteen to seventeen. That'll save a full fifth of all the kids marked for unwinding" (325). However, the promise of a better future is diminished. Governmental entities suggested unwinding in the first place and cannot be trusted. The government is also frequently inadequate on numerous other levels, yet it controls the future.

Another factor that tempers hope is that not all children in dystopian novels are by any means entirely virtuous. In *Unwind*, for instance, Roland serves as antagonist and foil for Connor, Lev, and Risa. He thrives on violence and control and is the worst kind of survivalist. He is duly punished and pays the price, however, for readers witness his unwinding, which is nothing less than chilling. Few of the characters of this novel, though, are entirely virtuous or without their faults. They are human and follow the imperative to survive.

Ultimately, survival in young adult dystopian novels, then, is an existential pursuit that is frequently mitigated by both hope and despair. When the tensions between hope and despair have easy solutions or solutions at all, readers should perhaps be suspicious. After all, the need to resolve the tension and conflict between two factions in *Unwind* results in compromise, child sacrifice, and the impossibility of both childhood and adulthood.

Notes

1 Fredric Jameson, *The Seeds of Time* (New York: Columbia University Press, 1994), 56.
2 Lyman Tower Sargent, "The Three Faces of Utopianism Revisited," *Utopian Studies* 5.1 (1994): 8.
3 Ibid., 9.
4 Neal Shusterman, *Unwind* (New York: Simon and Schuster, 2007), n.p. Subsequent references will be cited parenthetically in the text.
5 Gemma Malley, *The Declaration* (New York: Bloomsbury USA Children's Books, 2007), 9, italics original.
6 Suzanne Collins, *The Hunger Games* (New York, Scholastic, 2008), 18–19.
7 Dennis King Keenan, *The Question of Sacrifice* (Bloomington: Indiana University Press, 2005), 1.
8 Ibid., italics original.
9 Ibid., 2, italics original.
10 The Bill of Life is offered as a preamble to the text and as such the pages are unnumbered.

172 • Susan Louise Stewart

11 Nancy B. Jay, *Throughout Your Generations Forever: Sacrifice, Religion, and Paternity* (Chicago: University of Chicago Press, 1992), 17.
12 René Girard, *Violence and the Sacred*, trans. Patrick Gregory (Baltimore: Johns Hopkins University Press, 1977), 10.
13 Robert G. Hamerton-Kelly, "Religion and the Thought of René Girard: An Introduction," in *Curing Violence*, ed. Mark I. Wallace and Theophus H. Smith (Sonoma, CA: Polebridge Press, 1994), 9.
14 Ibid., 11.
15 Girard, *Violence and the Sacred*, 84.
16 Hamerton-Kelly, "Religion," 11, 15.
17 Viktor Karády, *The Jews of Europe in the Modern Era* (Budapest: Central European University Press, 2004), 320.
18 René Girard, *The Scapegoat*, trans. Yvonne Freccero (Baltimore: Johns Hopkins University Press, 1986), 14.
19 Jay, *Throughout*, 22.
20 Jan G.J. van den Eijnden, *Poverty on the Way to God: Thomas Aquinas on Evangelical Poverty* (Leuven, Belgium: Peeters, 1994), 156.
21 Jay, *Throughout*, 24–25.
22 Yitzhak Arad, *Belzec, Sobibor, Treblinka: The Operation Reinhard Death Camps* (Bloomington: Indiana University Press, 1987), 86.
23 Quoted in Franklin Le Van Baumer, *Main Currents of Western Thought: Readings in Western European Intellectual History from the Middle Ages to the Present* (New Haven: Yale University Press, 1978), 729.
24 Anne Scott MacLeod, *American Childhood: Essays on Children's Literature of the Nineteenth and Twentieth Centuries* (Athens: University of Georgia Press, 1994), 200.
25 Kay Sambell, "Presenting the Case for Social Change: The Creative Dilemma of Dystopian Writing for Children," in *Utopian and Dystopian Writing for Children and Young Adults*, ed. Carrie Hintz and Elaine Ostry (London: Routledge, 2003), 163.
26 Kay Sambell, "Carnivalizing the Future: A New Approach to Theorizing Childhood and Adulthood in Science Fiction for Young Readers," *The Lion and the Unicorn* 28.2 (2004): 251, 250.
27 Ibid., 257.

Works Cited

Arad, Yitzhak. *Belzec, Sobibor, Treblinka: The Operation Reinhard Death Camps*. Bloomington: Indiana University Press, 1987.
Baumer, Franklin Le Van. *Main Currents of Western Thought: Readings in Western European Intellectual History from the Middle Ages to the Present*. New Haven: Yale University Press, 1978.
Collins, Suzanne. *The Hunger Games*. New York, Scholastic, 2008.
Eijnden, Jan G.J. van den. *Poverty on the Way to God: Thomas Aquinas on Evangelical Poverty*. Leuven, Belgium: Peeters, 1994.

Dystopian Sacrifice, Scapegoats, and Neal Shusterman's *Unwind* · **173**

Girard, René. *The Scapegoat*. Translated by Yvonne Freccero. Baltimore: Johns Hopkins University Press, 1986.

———. *Violence and the Sacred*. Translated by Patrick Gregory. Baltimore: Johns Hopkins University Press, 1977.

Hamerton-Kelly, Robert G. "Religion and the Thought of René Girard: An Introduction." In *Curing Violence*, edited by Mark I. Wallace and Theophus H. Smith, 3–24. Sonoma, CA: Polebridge Press, 1994.

Jay, Nancy B. *Throughout Your Generations Forever: Sacrifice, Religion, and Paternity*. Chicago: University of Chicago Press, 1992.

Karády, Viktor. *The Jews of Europe in the Modern Era*. Budapest: Central European University Press, 2004.

Keenan, Dennis King. *The Question of Sacrifice*. Bloomington: Indiana University Press, 2005.

MacLeod, Anne Scott. *American Childhood: Essays on Children's Literature of the Nineteenth and Twentieth Centuries*. Athens: University of Georgia Press, 1994.

Malley, Gemma. *The Declaration*. New York: Bloomsbury USA Children's Books, 2007.

Sambell, Kay. "Carnivalizing the Future: A New Approach to Theorizing Childhood and Adulthood in Science Fiction for Young Readers." *The Lion and the Unicorn* 28.2 (2004): 247–267.

———. "Presenting the Case for Social Change: The Creative Dilemma of Dystopian Writing for Children." In *Utopian and Dystopian Writing for Children and Young Adults*, edited by Carrie Hintz and Elaine Ostry, 163–178. London: Routledge, 2003.

Sargent, Lyman Tower. "The Three Faces of Utopianism Revisited." *Utopian Studies* 5.1 (1994): 1–37.

Shusterman, Neal. *Unwind*. New York: Simon and Schuster, 2007.

Chapter Eleven
The Soul of the Clone
Coming of Age as a Posthuman in Nancy Farmer's *The House of the Scorpion*

Erin T. Newcomb

Introduction

Nancy Farmer's 2002 text *The House of the Scorpion* is a typical young adult novel in its emphasis on the coming-of-age narrative of its protagonist, Matteo "Matt" Alacrán. What differentiates Farmer's text, as well as her protagonist, is that Matt is a clone, created so that his organs can prolong the life of his benefactor and parent El Patrón. In their land of Opium, clones share the same status as cattle, meaning that Matt is regarded as property whose value extends only as far as the usefulness of his body parts. Coming of age, in this context, requires a different framework—one that accommodates the biotechnical possibilities of cloning humans as well as the theological questions Farmer threads throughout her narrative. As Francis Fukuyama argues in *Our Posthuman Future: Consequences of the Biotechnology Revolution* (2002), "The most significant threat posed by contemporary biotechnology is the possibility that it will alter human nature and thereby move us into a 'posthuman' stage of history." This concept is critical, Fukuyama asserts, "because human nature exists, is a meaningful concept, and has provided a stable continuity to our experience as a species. It is, conjointly with religion, what defines our most basic values."[1] Matt, cloned as an instrument of another's will instead of a person in his own right, exists as part of a posthuman, subhuman class. Yet establishing Matt's coming of age as posthuman raises the stakes because, in his case, becoming adult means claiming humanity—and its attendant values of human uniqueness, dignity, and agency. The only cure for the inhumanity of the posthuman condition, Farmer's text suggests, is to balance biotechnology with a philosophy that asserts the *de facto* value of all life. That position

176 · Erin T. Newcomb

alone allows Matt to move from instrument to agent and from a collection of spare parts to a whole creature with a body and soul; the soul is a critical component of Farmer's text because, unlike his body, Matt's soul is all his own, and his spiritual life becomes the place where he can establish his individual identity and worth. Only a position that encompasses body and soul, Farmer's text suggests, allows biotechnological possibilities to be embraced while still valuing humans over machines. In this essay, I discuss the ways that Farmer's text uses posthuman concepts in a way that is both compatible with and unique within young adult literature. Finally, I argue that Farmer's text disrupts dichotomous thinking about biotechnology and theology by asserting Matt's identity as a new kind of creature—a clone with a soul.

Posthumanism

In *Cyberculture, Cyborgs and Science Fiction: Consciousness and the Posthuman* (2006), William S. Haney describes posthumanism generally "as a human-technology symbiosis."[2] That definition encompasses a range of biotechnical possibilities but points to the central feature of the movement, where humans no longer simply use technology but incorporate technology into the most intimate aspects of humanity (such as reproduction) and within the human body itself. Robert Pepperell depicts posthumanism more broadly as a time period after the rise of humanism during which occurs a "general convergence of biology and technology to the point where they are increasingly becoming indistinguishable" and where "our traditional view of what constitutes a human being is now undergoing a profound transformation."[3] Pepperell's quote in particular deals with the posthuman as a transitional period (like adolescence itself), where human ontology and epistemology stand poised between paradigms with no clear method of determining what constitutes humanness.

It is the indistinguishableness of biology and technology, child and adult, that is most disconcerting for the characters in *The House of the Scorpion*. On one level are the eejits, whose brains are modified by computer chips that remove their sense of self-preservation as well as their freewill; that fate belongs to border-crossers and enemies, and the process creates a human subclass completely subservient to El Patrón's demands.[4] Technology defines the eejits' role in Opium and relegates them to an inhuman, objectified position. Typical clones face a similar scenario; their intellects are destroyed at birth. Matt's encounter with another clone leaves him with the impression not of humanity but of monstrosity:

> At first Matt thought it was some kind of beast, so alien and terrible was its face. It had doughy, unhealthy skin and red hair that stuck up in bristles. It seemed never to have been in the sun, and its hands were twisted like

The Soul of the Clone • 177

claws above the straps that held it down. It was dressed in green hospital pajamas, but these had been befouled by its terror . . . It was as though invisible snakes were rippling beneath the skin and forcing its arms and legs to move in a ceaseless bid for freedom (119–120).

The use of technology strips the clone of humanity, creating animalistic conditions that help Matt identify the clone not as kin but as other—animal, beast, creature, monster. These examples of biotechnology are not posthuman because they eliminate the clone's conscious awareness of humanity, but they illustrate by contrast the significance of the singular example of the posthuman in Farmer's text: Matt himself. Matt is also destined for organ donation, yet El Patrón's hubris requires that Matt receive an excellent education and the idyllic childhood denied to his family of origin (233).[5] Further, Matt, unlike El Patrón, develops a gift for music, and his talents emphasize his humanity and differentiate him from his parent while still underscoring the oddity of an artistic clone (90–91).

Both Matt and those around him struggle with what kind of clone he is; in his first encounter with other children, Matt is revealed as a clone only by the incriminating text "Property of the Alacrán Estate" tattooed onto his leg (23). Only that marking differentiates him from the other children. Later in the text, Matt learns that he is not a machine but a "photograph" taken from the genetic material encoded on a piece of El Patrón's skin (80). Matt's bodyguard Tam Lin later explains that Matt was not born, but harvested (189). The photographic metaphor defines Matt not as a machine but as the product of a machine, yet with the appearance of a biological human. Being harvested as opposed to being born follows a similar line of thinking in which Matt comes into being through technological means, but the circumstances of his birth are not visible the way his tattoo is. Even that tattoo, a clear indication of Matt's position, is obscured by an injury Matt sustains, making the textual evidence of his ontology indistinct. Further, the bodyguard asserts, "No one can tell the difference between a clone and a human. That's because there *isn't* any difference. The idea of clones being inferior is a filthy lie" (245, italics original). The bodyguard refers to difference in terms of inherent value and deserved social position, yet there are clearly differences in the inchoate stages of a human clone and a non-cloned human. What this quotation points to is not the lack of difference but the invisibility of those differences—the seamless and invisible merger of biology and technology that defines the posthuman. Matt's ability to pass enhances the fear of the posthuman among us, indistinguishable from ordinary humans and thus calling into question the uniqueness of the human species.[6]

As feminist critic Donna Haraway famously states, "We are all chimeras, theorized and fabricated hybrids of machine and organism; in short, we are cyborgs. The cyborg is our ontology."[7] Haraway's claim of cyborg as human ontology fits precisely within the posthuman framework and also explains the

178 • Erin T. Newcomb

threat that Matt poses to the order of Opium. If all of humanity moves toward the posthuman, then the categories that denigrate Matt as less-than-human become even more artificial, and even more meaningless. El Patrón himself is a cyborg, patched together with organs from multiple clones; he not only provides his skin and genetic material to create clones, but he also reabsorbs the clones' organs back into his body to prolong his unnatural lifespan. Yet while the methods and means (the cultivation of human clones for his personal usage) of El Patrón's cyborg status are particularly sadistic, it is not the cyborg-drug lord who embodies the anxiety-inducing aspects of the posthuman in Farmer's text. As Daniel Dinello explains in *Technophobia!: Science Fiction Visions of Posthuman Technology* (2005), "While robots and cyborgs destabilize the boundaries between human and machine, the clone counters our sense of possessing a unique identity—it's another created-by-technology being that potentially can replace us."[8] The clone, especially the indistinguishable clone, is vastly more dangerous to the concept of humanity than the cyborg; a cyborg can hybridize human and machine without losing individuality, and thus can usher in the posthuman era without calling into question the fundamental tenets of human ontology. Meanwhile, the clone walking unknown in our midst challenges the very notion of human uniqueness and leads to speculations about what actually makes up a human identity—genetics, bodies, memories, choices, souls, or some combination of these.

Young Adult Literature and the Posthuman

The questions raised by posthumanism infiltrate young adult literature in ways that are unique to younger audiences. Farmer's text fits within an emerging market of young adult science fiction that grapples with biotechnological ethics; as Elaine Ostry writes in "Is He Still Human? Are You?" (2004), such texts "use biotechnology as a metaphor for adolescence."[9] That metaphor raises fundamental questions of coming of age but also problematizes the transition from childhood to adulthood. If one of the primary concerns of adolescence is figuring out one's self and one's identity, the posthuman context complicates those questions by casting species identity into doubt as well. In a sense, humanity itself is in the midst of coming of age, with no mentorship, as it grapples with the shift from humanism to posthumanism. Posthumanism, too, can serve as a metaphor for adolescence: humanity mingles with technology until the two are indistinguishable, and humanity, like the youths who can no longer see themselves as the center of the universe, wonders what makes it so special. In the case of cloning, the issue of individual (and species) uniqueness comes to the forefront, as is the case in *The House of the Scorpion*. Discussing clones specifically, Ostry asserts that "the feeling of being different from others and estranged from oneself is particularly strong. Their sense of identity is confused as they must judge whether they even have

The Soul of the Clone • 179

a separate self."[10] Such claims certainly apply to Matt in *The House of the Scorpion*, as does Ostry's concluding remark that "most writers for young adults simplify the argument [about biotechnology's ambivalent ethics] in favor of making an ideological point about the fixed quality of human nature and values."[11] Farmer's conclusion expresses the permanence of human nature, yet at the text's end, Matt takes over El Patrón's identity—still a clone, but also a human. This dual position (in conflict through most of Farmer's text) expresses the conviction that Matt the clone was always-already human, yet it also realizes the human fear of being replaced by a clone. At the text's end, it is not in spite of, but because of being a clone that Matt gains the power to right the injustices of Opium; thus as Matt comes into his own identity, property, and power as the new El Patrón, the source of his original disenfranchisement becomes the means by which he, and he alone, rules the land. Coming of age, at the conclusion of Farmer's text, does not alter Matt's isolated position, but it does move him to a position of privilege, fully human and fully clone—a posthuman ruler for a posthuman world. His subject position simultaneously reaffirms the values of human nature while transcending the biological limits of "natural" humanity.

Certainly Farmer's text wrestles with these issues, yet the cause is not biotechnology itself but the one who wields its powers; as so much of science fiction indicates, it's not science we ought to fear but humanity. Initially, Matt is like all clones, "classified as livestock because they're grown inside cows. Cows can't give birth to humans" (226). Yet Matt's paternity also sets him apart from other clones; as El Patrón explains, "I would have had your brain destroyed at birth. Instead, it pleased me to give you the childhood I never had" (232). This gift represents El Patrón's vanity and pride more than his beneficence, but the resulting education and experiences elevate Matt above other clones and prepare him to usurp his biological benefactor. El Patrón always intends to sacrifice Matt, and that theme of the untrustworthy adult who uses a child for self-advancement fits within the larger framework of young adult science fiction. Critic Hilary Crew explains, "The moral and ethical reasons against cloning-to-produce-children are made clear in Farmer's story, including the unjustified dehumanization of life by viewing and treating a child as a product to be used, the violation of a child's most basic rights, and a child's lack of biological parents."[12] Susan Stewart's essay in this collection discusses child sacrifice as "simultaneously striking and horrifying," and she articulates how a world based on "sacrificing the young—sometimes because they *are* purportedly innocent and because of their unfulfilled promise—translates into an economy of tragedy and is one method of illustrating precisely how unacceptable the dystopian world is." El Patrón's insistence that he is "owed" his clones' childhoods (233) highlights the injustice not of cloning but of instrumentalism, a form of objectification that El Patrón practices (often with the assistance of biotechnology) throughout Opium's class system. Matt's status as a clone does not inspire the instrumentalism, though it does underscore

180 · Erin T. Newcomb

it because El Patrón sees Matt as a sort of pet and a physical extension of himself, whereas the eejits are regarded impersonally as inhuman machines. Crew also states, "Encoded into young adult texts are the fears about the risks, mistakes and failed experiments that have been documented in the stories of the research on cloning."[13] El Patrón exemplifies this argument and so many of the concerns that cloning means "playing God." The "risks, mistakes and failed experiments" Crew describes carry high stakes precisely because biotechnology involves altering human lives and perhaps humanity itself. Both posthuman theory and literature struggle to come to terms with the potential to modify humanity without dehumanization. The irony of Farmer's conclusion is that Matt reveals himself as more human(e) than El Patrón; it is Matt's moral and spiritual coming of age, wherein he feels compassion and reels at injustices, that makes him mature enough for leadership—not the circumstances of his birth. As the editors of *The Cyborg Handbook* (1995) emphasize, the "artificial-natural, human-machine, organic and constructed, were dualities just as central to living, but the figure of the cyborg has revealed that isn't so." Instead, they assert, "There are, after all, more important distinctions to make, between just and unjust, between sustaining and destroying."[14] Matt, the cyborg citizen, synthesizes the dualities of artificial and natural, reminding readers that the ambivalence of biotechnology lies with those who use it.

Farmer represents that uncertainty about the future of humans and biotechnology in the conclusion of her text. After the death of El Patrón, the law defining Matt as cattle shifts:

> You can't have two versions of the same person at the same time . . . One of them—the copy—has to be declared an *unperson*. But when the original dies, the copy takes his place. . . . It means you really are El Patrón. You have his body and his identity. You own everything he owned and rule everything he ruled. It means you're the new Master of Opium (367, italics original).

The narrative leading up to this point defies the logic of these legal acrobatics. Matt's character development distinctly leads the reader to believe that he is not a copy and not "the same person" as El Patrón because of the different choices Matt makes. What sets Matt apart from his biological parent are his humanity and his personal moral development, yet his body (genetically and materially) has not changed, nor has his name. What changes here are human laws that do not know how to manage the complexities of biotechnology. By the novel's end, Matt comes of age but his cultural context fails to keep pace. The only reason to expect Matt will be treated differently upon his return to Opium is that most of his enemies were killed by El Patrón. The elimination of opposition does not stem from a social maturation with regard to the status of clones, but from a convenient plot maneuver. Matt as "the new Master of Opium" signals a new reign—the compassionate clone who inherits power

The Soul of the Clone · 181

only to dismantle the system that brought him into being. Again Matt embodies the tension of the posthuman society: not human or clone but human and clone; not master or slave but master and slave. Matt reaches moral maturity at the critical moment in the text, when his adolescent society, born of biotechnological tyranny, needs leadership to usher in an age of wisdom; here Matt serves as the medium, the human clone and "Master of Opium" who owes his life to science and his soul to God. Farmer's text begins with both an adolescent Matt and an adolescent society, yet only Matt comes of age by the conclusion. The society is biotechnologically advanced—using computer implants to control the eejits and cloning to prolong the elites' lifespan—but the ethical and legal considerations surrounding those issues are controlled by the whims of the powerful. Even the law that thrusts Matt into power is nonsensical, as it disregards the natural possibility of genetically identical humans (as in some twins) and reduces identity to genetic determinism. Matt's entire coming-of-age narrative works against the principles of genetic determinism, affirming the humanness of moral choice, but the society cannot complete the same journey without guidance from outside the realm of biotechnological potential.

Theology and the Posthuman

Matt's mastery of Opium (and its attendant hopes for the redemption of his biotechnological world) requires the legal shift just discussed, yet Matt realizes his own personhood earlier outside of the law. Farmer incorporates theology into her text as an alternative ontology, one outside the boundaries of science and technology. By offering Matt a religious narrative of transcendence, the body becomes less significant as the focus turns toward the soul, and the concept of the soul reinforces what sets humans apart from all other creatures—regardless of their biotechnological origins. Farmer's emphasis on the soul highlights that Matt, even as clone, is always-already human. Through his spiritual maturation, Matt wrestles with the possibility of possessing a soul, and it is a religious narrative that gives meaning to his life and future before there is ever hope of a sociocultural or legal transformation in the treatment of clones. Matt's embracing of the spirit as a human component that transcends the body—and the limitations imposed on it by human (mis) use of biotechnology—provides him with supernatural value unrestrained by any of his earthly circumstances. It gives him an alternative ontology. In the Catholic framework that Farmer uses for the text, the clone can gain theological status as human without regard to law or culture. As Pope John Paul II describes in his "Message to the Pontifical Academy of Sciences" (1997), the Catholic Church accepts the theory of evolution based on scientific evidence and posits an "ontological leap" that ultimately differentiates humans from other animals.[15] The difference, according to the pope, is the spirit; the

182 · Erin T. Newcomb

papal message further states: "The human individual cannot be subordinated as a pure means or a pure instrument, either to the species or to society; he has value *per se*. He is a person."[16] These messages, while based on evolution instead of cloning, certainly affirm Matt's position, not in relation to his benefactor's desires or the usefulness of his body, but in his own right as a spiritual being. Based on the same source, Fukuyama concludes, "It is this leap from parts to a whole that ultimately has to constitute the basis for human dignity, a concept one can believe in even if one does not begin from the pope's religious premises."[17] With or without the "ontological leap," the soul remains an intangible and elusive concept, one that is impossible to define with the precision for which the pope commends the theory of evolution. Yet the key point, as Fukuyama explains and Matt seems to understand, is the existence of a qualitative factor that separates humanity from other species; that factor exists regardless of origin from other primates or a cow used as a surrogate for breeding human clones. That factor distinguishes Matt as human with an inherent worth and dignity that surpass his situation as a tool of El Patrón.

Yet Matt's own desire for a coming-of-age narrative that values him is at odds with an established culture that denies his humanity and refuses him a place in its theological account. When Matt tries to enter the church for a family wake, the priest rejects the clone's presence: "*This* does not belong here! . . . This unbaptized limb of Satan has no right to make a mockery of this rite! Would you bring a *dog* to church?" (153–154, italics original). Maria, Matt's only non-servant friend and the object of his (unrequited) affection, protests, "Saint Francis would take a dog to church. . . . Saint Francis took a wolf to church" (154). The priest counters, insisting, "Saint Francis spoke to the wolf *outside* the church" (154, italics original). Both Maria and the priest reference the legend of Saint Francis and the wolf of Gubbio, wherein the twelfth-century saint rescues a village from a ravaging wolf by establishing a pact of peace and friendship between the two parties.[18] But the priest is correct— that pact takes place *outside* the church. Matt, as clone, also exists *outside* the church, literally expulsed from the building and metaphorically beyond the reach of the church's rituals. Within the theological framework sanctioned by the priest, there is simply no known sacred space for a clone. In this way, Matt represents the outsider typical of so many young adult texts; he is superior to most clones because his intellect was left intact, but other humans regard him legally as cattle and socially as a "bad animal" (27). At the text's end, Matt remains a species of one, not an insider but an outsider embraced because his peripheral perspective and (perhaps most importantly) genetic makeup suit him to rule Opium. Matt's leadership destabilizes the standard theological and biotechnological narratives of his society, and in doing so, creates an alternative and independent story: the clone who gains a soul.

Yet Maria, who leaves the wake along with Matt, interprets the story of Saint Francis and the wolf differently than the priest. Reassuring Matt after the confrontation, she compares her cloned friend to "Brother Wolf," to whom

The Soul of the Clone · 183

Saint Francis offers forgiveness and an opportunity for redemption. Further, Maria muses:

> You don't have a soul, so you can't be baptized. All animals are like that. I think it's unfair and sometimes I don't believe it. After all, what would heaven be without birds or dogs or horses? And what about trees and flowers? They don't have souls either. Does that mean heaven looks like a cement parking lot? I suppose that is what the nuns call a theological problem (159).

Maria does indeed pose a theological problem as she applies her knowledge of church lore and tradition to the contemporary issue of cloning. Later in the text, Maria conducts further research on Saint Francis and concludes, "He preached to animals because they had little souls that could grow into big ones. With work, even a sparrow or a cicada could make it into heaven" (207). Her position shifts from regarding Matt as having no soul to having a small soul with potential for growth, reflecting her desire to legitimate Matt within the church. By drawing the comparison between "Brother Wolf" and "Brother Clone," Maria works within the limitations of her culture's perspective on clones as "bad animals" to secure an eternal place for Matt. In Catholic theology, the expectation of that eternal place sets humans apart and warrants not just an eschatology, but also a sense of worth and justice in mortal life. The priest and Maria illustrate that there is tension within Catholicism (because no theology is monolithic), but Farmer attempts to carve out a theological space that considers the clone as brother.

Matt expresses less optimism, wavering between the hope of heaven, the fear of hell, and the conviction that animal theology cannot apply to clones. As Ostry explains, "The characters in these posthuman science fiction books for young adults are faced with a choice that determines the level of their humanity."[19] Again, Matt's story follows that path but with a theological twist; the potential to go to hell indicates Matt's recognition of himself as a moral human being, one who is responsible for his choices and his actions. At one point, Matt confesses to Maria, "If I had a soul, I'd probably wind up in hell anyway" (159). Accepting the burden of a soul and the full humanity it entails means that both heaven and hell are open to him. Even with that knowledge, Matt struggles to escape the animalistic language that has always defined him and his place in the world. He wonders, "Would Saint Francis have said *Brother Clone?*" and his "warm feelings evaporated. He wasn't part of the natural order. He was an *abomination*" (167, italics original). But at another point, Matt admits that he "saw nothing wrong with being born in a stable. Jesus had found it perfectly acceptable" (188). In both of these instances, Matt removes himself from the natural order, vacillating from an unnatural abomination to an analogy with a supernatural figure. One position renders him unsavable, while the other sets him up as Savior. Indeed, Matt exists outside

184 · Erin T. Newcomb

the natural order, because his society—from a legal or theological or cultural standpoint—does not know how to integrate the clone-as-human; Farmer's conclusion ultimately suggests that the outsider knows best how to rehabilitate society, to draw the culture out of its tumultuous adolescence, with the wisdom that comes from a peripheral position.

Matt's outsider status speaks to the larger context of theology and the posthuman by mingling the narratives of religion and biotechnology as opposed to seeing them as oppositional. For instance, Leon Kass represents a typical anti-cloning argument when he states: "Human cloning would also represent a giant step toward turning begetting into making, procreation into manufacture (literally, something 'handmade')."[20] Kass's point holds weight, particularly given the fictional case of El Patrón, whom Farmer uses in typical science fiction fashion to represent the monstrosity not of the experiment but of the experimenter. There are any number of secular and religious objections to non-traditional procreation, but the end result in *The House of Scorpion* seems to speak against these fears. Matt, with the assistance of characters like Celia, Tam Lin, and Maria, defies his role as El Patrón's instrument and redefines his place in the world. It is unsurprising from a young adult literature standpoint that the protagonist is exceptional, that he rises above his circumstances, and that his coming of age ushers in a new era of hope. At the same time, Matt's exceptionality undermines many of the fears regarding cloning. Author George Johnson compares modern anxieties about cloning to aboriginal uncertainties about photography: "The most fundamental fear is that the soul will be taken by this penetrating new photography called cloning. And here, at least, the notion is just as superstitious as the aborigines'. There is one part of life biotechnology will never touch. While it is possible to clone a body, it is impossible to clone a brain." Johnson continues: "We each carry in our heads complexity beyond imagining and beyond duplication. Even a hard-core materialist might agree that, in that sense, everyone has a soul."[21] Certainly readers bring vastly different conceptions of the soul to Farmer's text, yet both Pope John Paul II and Johnson agree on the absolute uniqueness of each human being. Johnson may never consent to the "ontological leap," yet his broadest meaning aligns with the position that humans are a species set apart, with each member an irreplaceable and irreproducible specimen.

What unites the biotechnological and the religious, beyond Matt himself, are the shared concerns regarding eschatology, for the body, the soul, or both. As Brent Waters articulates, "The cyborg, like its human predecessor, can still fear death, and such a fear is a deadly constraint against its will. So long as any finite or temporal limits remain, however feeble they may have been rendered, the posthuman vision remains but a dream because the will remains shackled by external constraints."[22] In Farmer's novel, this distinction manifests most clearly in the relationship between El Viejo and El Patrón; though El Viejo is actually El Patrón's son, the former refuses biotechnological intervention for his cancer and lives out the end of his life as a frail and sickly old

The Soul of the Clone • 185

man. As Matt's caregiver Celia attests, "El Viejo was the only good man in this family. . . . He accepted what God gave him, and when God told him it was time to go, he did it" (234). Earlier, El Viejo's son remarks, "He's deeply religious. He thinks God put him on earth for a certain number of years and that he mustn't ask for more" (106). El Patrón, of course, resides on the other end of the eschatological spectrum; he laughs at his son and calls him a fool (234), expected behaviors from the man who built an empire to support his biotechnological pursuit of earthly immortality. The divide between these characters, father and son, exemplifies the point Waters makes, that "it is the differing perceptions of time that most deeply divide the ontology of technology from that of creation, for in confronting time the question of an anticipated destiny cannot be avoided. Consequently, the ontologies of technology and creation incorporate contrasting and sharply contending eschatologies."[23] Whereas El Viejo contents himself with a theological explanation of his finitude, El Patrón manipulates biotechnology to compensate for his past and ensure his future. Matt, meanwhile, is encouraged by his benefactor to scoff at El Viejo and regard his own existence as a gift from El Patrón—meaning Matt is granted neither eschatology because he exerts no control over his future. That initial position is childlike, but in Matt's coming of age, he once again breaks down the dichotomies of biotechnology and science by incorporating a religious eschatology into a clone's future. Chapter 23 of Farmer's text is entitled "Death," yet the book's final section is called "La Vida Nueva," suggesting that Matt's realization of his own instrumentality and mortality is a symbolic death that leads him to greater maturity and, ultimately, a new beginning.

Unlike El Viejo, that new life involves a return to Opium with the help of characters named Fidelito and Esperanza (faith and hope). El Patrón's death is real, but Matt's is only symbolic, and his new opportunities as ruler, combined with his allegorical friends who represent spiritual maturity, suggest a new kind of eschatology, where clones have a future on earth and beyond. Given the reluctance of Matt's society to come of age alongside him, there's no telling what that future will hold; the same law that provides Matt's inheritance could provide motivation for clones to usurp their masters, and identity remains fundamentally genetic—with no consideration for the markers of humanity that are not encoded on DNA. Even Matt expresses some hesitation during his mission at the novel's conclusion that he has moved from being an instrument of El Patrón to an instrument of Esperanza: an ostensibly good agent but not one who considers Matt's freewill as primary. Matt remains useful, yet the measure of his own maturity and his society's will most likely manifest in the response to and relationship with the eejits, whose usefulness to the Opium empire diminishes if they cease to be eejits. Religion, like biotechnology, can take the fearful aspects of cloning and unleash a narrative of abomination, but in Farmer's narrative, a theological story that incorporates the *de facto* value of all human life (regardless of its biotechnological origins

186 · Erin T. Newcomb

or social utility) offers a maturity to both Matt and his society. Matt seems to embrace that "Vida Nueva," and in doing so becomes an adult human clone; his society sidesteps that offer, and the open-ended conclusion of Farmer's text leaves the readers wondering if Matt's hope and faith will be sufficient to bring forth a new life for Opium and its posthuman inhabitants.

Notes

1   Francis Fukuyama, *Our Posthuman Future: Consequences of the Biotechnology Revolution* (New York: Farrar, Straus, and Giroux, 2002), 7.
2   William S. Haney, *Cyberculture, Cyborgs and Science Fiction: Consciousness and the Posthuman* (Amsterdam: Rodopi, 2006), 2.
3   Robert Pepperell, *Posthuman Condition: Consciousness Beyond the Brain* (Bristol: Intellect, 2003), iv.
4   Nancy Farmer, *The House of the Scorpion* (New York: Atheneum, 2004), 142, 197. Subsequent references will be cited parenthetically in the text.
5   Hubris seems a particularly apt word to describe El Patrón's use of biotechnology and his treatment of Matt; ultimately, El Patrón is so blinded by his self-aggrandizement that the clone meant to grant him immortality serves, in tragic form, as his undoing.
6   Matt is unique in his ability to pass because the other clones and the enslaved eejits have their intellects destroyed, making their oppression absolute and permanent. The concept of passing, taken to this extreme in Farmer's text, references practices of racial passing in contexts of slavery, racism, and racial conflict. In a racial sense, passing reveals race not as static but as socially constructed. Although difference in *The House of the Scorpion* is marked by biotechnology instead of biology, passing serves much the same role, helping those who can practice it gain privilege and avoid oppression. Further, passing destabilizes hierarchies based on physical difference by showing that such power structures are as artificial and vulnerable as the distinctions on which they are based.
7   Donna J. Haraway, *Simians, Cyborgs, and Women: The Reinvention of Nature* (New York: Routledge, 1990), 150.
8   Daniel Dinello, *Technophobia!: Science Fiction Visions of Posthuman Technology* (Austin: University of Texas Press, 2005), 216.
9   Elaine Ostry, "Is He Still Human? Are You?: Young Adult Science Fiction in the Posthuman Age," *The Lion and the Unicorn* 28.2 (2004): 223. Ostry, for instance, also mentions K.A. Applegate's Remnants series; Marilyn Kaye's Replica series; Ann Halam's *Taylor Five: The Story of a Clone Girl*; Rhiannon Lassiter's *Ghosts, Hex*, and *Shadows*; Nicole Lukien's *Silver Eyes* and *Violet Eyes*; Carol Matas's *Cloning Miranda* and *The Second Clone*; Garth Nix's *Shade's Children*; Rodman Philbrick's *The Last Book in the Universe*; Philip Reeve's *Mortal Engines*; Malcolm Rose's *Clone*; Ann Schlee's *The Vandal*;

The Soul of the Clone · **187**

Neal Shusterman's *The Dark Side of Nowhere*; and L.J. Singleton's Regeneration series.

10 Ibid., 226.

11 Ibid., 242–243.

12 Hilary S. Crew, "Not So Brave a World: The Representation of Human Cloning in Science Fiction for Young Adults," *The Lion and the Unicorn* 28.2 (2004): 207.

13 Crew, "Not So Brave a World," 213.

14 Chris Hables Gray, Steven Mentor, and Heidi J. Figueroa-Sarriera, eds. *The Cyborg Handbook* (New York: Routledge, 1995), 13.

15 John Paul II, "Message to the Pontifical Academy of Sciences," *The Quarterly Review of Biology* 72.4 (1997): 383.

16 Ibid., italics original.

17 Fukuyama, *Our Posthuman Future*, 170.

18 Regis J. Armstrong, *Francis of Assisi—The Prophet: Early Documents*, vol. 3 (New York: New City Press, 2001).

19 Ostry, "Is He Still Human?" 240.

20 Leon Kass, "The Wisdom of Repugnance," in *Flesh of My Flesh: The Ethics of Cloning Humans*, ed. Gregory E. Pence (New York: Rowman and Littlefield, 1998), 29.

21 George Johnson, "Don't Worry: A Brain Still Can't Be Cloned," in *Flesh of My Flesh: The Ethics of Cloning Humans*, ed. Gregory E. Pence (New York: Rowman and Littlefield, 1998), 9–10, 11.

22 Brent Waters, "From Human to Posthuman: Theology and Technology," in *Human Identity at the Intersection of Science, Technology and Religion*, ed. Nancey Murphy and Christopher C. Knight (Burlington, VT: Ashgate, 2010), 200–201.

23 Ibid., 209.

Works Cited

Armstrong, Regis J. *Francis of Assisi—The Prophet: Early Documents*. Vol. 3. New York: New City Press, 2001.

Crew, Hilary S. "Not So Brave a World: The Representation of Human Cloning in Science Fiction for Young Adults." *The Lion and the Unicorn* 28.2 (2004): 203–221.

Dinello, Daniel. *Technophobia!: Science Fiction Visions of Posthuman Technology*. Austin: University of Texas Press, 2005.

Farmer, Nancy. *The House of the Scorpion*. New York: Atheneum, 2004.

Fukuyama, Francis. *Our Posthuman Future: Consequences of the Biotechnology Revolution*. New York: Farrar, Straus, and Giroux, 2002.

Gray, Chris Hables, Steven Mentor, and Heidi J. Figueroa-Sarriera, eds. *The Cyborg Handbook*. New York: Routledge, 1995.

Haney, William S. *Cyberculture, Cyborgs and Science Fiction: Consciousness and the Posthuman*. Amsterdam: Rodopi, 2006.

Haraway, Donna J. *Simians, Cyborgs, and Women: The Reinvention of Nature*. New York: Routledge, 1990.

John Paul II. "Message to the Pontifical Academy of Sciences." *The Quarterly Review of Biology* 72.4 (1997): 381–383.

188 • Erin T. Newcomb

Johnson, George. "Don't Worry: A Brain Still Can't Be Cloned." In *Flesh of My Flesh: The Ethics of Cloning Humans*, edited by Gregory E. Pence, 9–11. New York: Rowman and Littlefield, 1998.

Kass, Leon. "The Wisdom of Repugnance." In *Flesh of My Flesh: The Ethics of Cloning Humans*, edited by Gregory E. Pence, 13–37. New York: Rowman and Littlefield, 1998.

Ostry, Elaine. "Is He Still Human? Are You?: Young Adult Science Fiction in the Posthuman Age." *The Lion and the Unicorn* 28.2 (2004): 222–246.

Pepperell, Robert. *Posthuman Condition: Consciousness Beyond the Brain*. Bristol: Intellect, 2003.

Waters, Brent. "From Human to Posthuman: Theology and Technology." In *Human Identity at the Intersection of Science, Technology and Religion*, edited by Nancey Murphy and Christopher C. Knight, 197–213. Burlington, VT: Ashgate, 2010.

Chapter Twelve
Parables for the Postmodern, Post-9/11, and Posthuman World
Carrie Ryan's Forest of Hands and Teeth Books, M.T. Anderson's *Feed*, and Mary E. Pearson's *The Adoration of Jenna Fox*

Thomas J. Morrissey

Dystopian fiction for young adults celebrates the potential for personal and species advancement without sugarcoating the very real dangers we and our progeny face in the postmodern and posthuman environment. YA dystopias are fictive versions of the contemporary world that promote reflection and critique. Their enormous and growing popularity suggests that we live at a pivotal moment in human history just as the members of the intended youth audience are experiencing pivotal moments in their own development. The phrase "brave new" in the title of this collection is an intertextual invocation of Shakespeare and Aldous Huxley, those literary bookends between whom the modern world rises and falls. Eighty years after *Brave New World* (1931), we live and raise our children in what Paul Crutzen and Eugene Stoermer have dubbed the Anthropocene,[1] the geo-historical moment of uncertain duration in which humans wave with abandon a wand more awesome than any stick Prospero or even Huxley could have fashioned. Like Prospero, we want something better for our children; like John the Savage, we fear it doesn't exist. I have called the YA dystopias under discussion parables not because they are short, straightforward didactic analogies—far from it. They are, however, imaginative and encouraging extrapolations that offer ethical pathways to better futures than current behavioral paradigms are likely to produce. All of these pathways require that we stop expecting

190 · Thomas J. Morrissey

different results from the same behaviors and adopt what I am calling a posthuman perspective.

The novels discussed here are postmodern in outlook rather than form. All of them speak to the contemporary anxieties that Veronica Hollinger captures so succinctly: "To be postmodern is to sense that we have become separated from the past by the ruptures and crises of ever more quickly receding recent history and also to recognize that we do not yet have much of an idea about where we are headed."[2] All of these books question why if we don't know where we're going we are in such a hurry to get there. As the speed of our dash into the future accelerates, our ability to get a fix on where we are wanes, and the opportunities for fatal mistakes multiply. Living from crisis to crisis affords little space for reflection. That events quickly disappear into a nebulous, ahistorical past makes contextualizing the present very difficult. In the U.S. the September 11, 2001 terrorist attacks, a decade of inconclusive war, and the financial collapse of 2008 have taken their toll. For Americans at least, the post-9/11 environment is redolent of fear of the Other and economic uncertainty. Writers of YA dystopias have as a backdrop an unpleasant present and a dubious future. We live in dystopian times, and young readers know it, which is why the subgenre is so popular.

Although their specific concerns and fictional methodologies differ, Carrie Ryan, M.T. Anderson, and Mary E. Pearson have written novels that capture the dystopian zeitgeist, offer hope in hard times, and challenge young readers to understand that there are ways to make sense out of our times and to salvage the future. The question of whether and how humans will survive and prosper in centuries to come is inextricably tied to the question of who or even *what* we will become. If posthumanity does not describe our extinction, then it must describe new ways of managing or even becoming one with our technology. Hollinger's definition of the postmodern concludes with this observation: "In the context of technoculture, it is the feeling that we now live science fictional lives, that we have been precipitated into time-future before we were quite ready for it."[3] Ready or not, the age of posthumanity is upon us. Two decades ago in her "Cyborg Manifesto" Donna Haraway proclaimed the potential benefits of merging with our technologies and "taking seriously the imagery of cyborgs as other than our enemies." She goes on to say that "taking responsibility for the social relations of science and technology means refusing an anti-science metaphysics, a demonology of technology, and so means embracing the skillful task of reconstructing the boundaries of daily life, in partial connection with others, in communication with all of our parts."[4] N. Katherine Hayles assures us that "it is important to recognize that the construction of the posthuman does not require the subject to be a literal cyborg. Whether or not interventions have been made on the body, new models of subjectivity emerging from such fields as cognitive science and artificial life imply that even a biologically unaltered *Homo sapiens* counts as posthuman."[5] Understanding how complex systems work, biological and cybernetic, actually

Parables for the Postmodern, Post-9/11, and Posthuman World • 191

facilitates a state of mind. "In the posthuman view," Hayles goes on to say, "conscious agency has never been 'in control.'"[6] It is the illusion of human control that has led to the gross social injustice and environmental destruction so common in dystopias whether written for YA or adult audiences.

First of all, then, posthumanity implies contesting the meaning of human agency. In different ways and to different degrees all of the novels featured here do this. Crises generated by attempts to impose personal or partisan will over others or nature—whether with hi-tech or lo-tech instrumentality—is the root of the dynamic tension in each of these fictions. Furthermore, all of the books show a way out, whether that means Ryan's heroines envisioning a more egalitarian and ecologically sound society, Anderson's readers opting out of mindless consumerism, or Jenna Fox's family, friends, and society learning to recognize that true humanity can flourish in a posthuman being whose body is only 10% biological. It is possible, even imperative, that we imagine a new, harmonious, and productive relationship with our tools.

Secondly, and more dramatically, posthumanity describes the advent of mechanical or biological augmentations that could turn us into the marching morons of *Feed* or give each of us the long, illness-free life that Jenna Fox has and could enjoy if only she were fully accepted as human. It is easy to imagine the neural implants of *Feed* enhancing our access to knowledge and bringing us closer together through instantaneous non-verbal communication, if only those were really the goals of their inventors or the collective will of their human hosts. At this point in our history we are figurative cyborgs whether or not we know it or accept it. None of the texts in question advocates our transformation into literal cyborgs, but all of them link our happiness and survival to attitudes which, if adopted, would pretty much guarantee that we would prevail even if we eventually choose literal cyborghood.

Finally then, I am using the term posthumanity to denote a system of values that embodies attitudes essential to our survival. Whether we augment ourselves so much that we become a new species or simply develop more powerful tools, we would do well to think of ourselves as a new species. In *Beyond Religion* (2011), His Holiness the Dalai Lama asks, "Is it possible that our responsibilities are now growing too fast for our natural capacity for discernment to keep pace? Can we trust ourselves with the power that science and technology have brought us?"[7] These questions are implicit in all YA dystopias. Treating one another and the Earth with respect and using our tools to enrich our lives have always been good ideas, but choosing to do otherwise is no longer a viable option. To be posthuman is to recognize that we and our technology are inseparable and that technology shapes us even as we shape it. We are already augmented beings; now we need to augment our behavior. It seems indisputable that the three authors treated here—and many others as well—hope to make a positive impression on their readers and to inspire them to act not only with intelligence but with wisdom.

192 • Thomas J. Morrissey

YA dystopias with postmodern and posthuman sensibilities critique the behaviors and institutions built by those who think of themselves as in control. The five texts under discussion here—Ryan's Forest of Hands and Teeth books (2009–2011), Anderson's *Feed* (2002), and Pearson's *The Adoration of Jenna Fox* (2008)—expose and confront individual and species vulnerability in the postmodern and posthuman world. Each of these novels is about individual development, and each in different ways interrogates the fate of the human species. Regardless of what megatext they invoke, the level of technology they feature, their mode of narration, or the tropes and icons of science fiction they employ, their protagonists' fates depend on the degree to which they respond to dystopia flexibly and ethically with behaviors that resist the paradigms that brought about the dystopian settings.

The texts under discussion in this essay embody three distinct varieties of literary response to the Anthropocene in YA dystopia. Taken together, they show how diverse YA dystopia can be. Carrie Ryan's books are similar in form to most contemporary YA critical dystopias. These novels are what I call macro critiques. They reflect negatively on our times by positing besieged postapocalyptic societies in need of radical change lest the human race fall even further. Though *Feed* is also a macro critique and cautionary tale, it is first and foremost a sophisticated satire aimed directly at the shortsightedness of monolithic late capitalism and its potential co-option of mind-augmenting technology. Like Jonathan Swift's *A Modest Proposal* (1729), it is a merciless, over-the-top treatment of a pervasive evil. Although accessible to a YA audience, as a narrative *Feed* has more in common with the work of satirists like Kurt Vonnegut, Jr., Norman Spinrad, Max Barry, or Sean Murphy, all of whom are writers for adults.

The odd text out in this discussion is *The Adoration of Jenna Fox*. It is a micro dystopia in that it focuses primarily on the immediate impact on its protagonist of technological innovations with which the society at-large is uncomfortable and ambivalent. Jenna is not in rebellion against corrupt postapocalyptic forces. Rather, she is a once relatively normal teen forced to lead a challenging science fictional life. Jenna is an involuntary, illegal cyborg whose angst stems from the ultimate identity crisis: living in a society in which one is not regarded as a real person.

Awash in Carrie Ryan's Lo-tech Sea of Zombies

This dystopian trilogy requires on the part of its heroines paradigmatic ethical moves that could be described as posthuman even though the hi-tech explored in "The Cyborg Manifesto" died with the old civilization that went down in the zombie tsunami that Ryan dubs the Return. The science behind the plague that has turned the mass of humanity into the Unconsecrated or Mudo (the term "zombie" is never used) is never explained, which makes sense since

Parables for the Postmodern, Post-9/11, and Posthuman World · 193

scientific investigation has ceased. Moreover, the swiftness and mysterious nature of zombie apocalypses speak to the pervasive sense of insecurity that lurks in the minds of many post-9/11 Americans. In recent incarnations of the zombie megatext, the absence of science is more important than a scientific explanation of the catastrophe's cause. D. Harlan Wilson explains that "in the postmodern era, the zombie has often served as a vehicle for expressing social and political anxieties," and that the zombies in Danny Boyle's film *28 Days After* "are produced by a virus and can signify contemporary post-9/11 fears of bioterrorism."[8] Today's teen readers are too young for 9/11 to be their formative traumatic event, but they live in an environment shaped by the terrorist attacks and the wars that followed.

Ryan's heroines not only must avoid or fight the ubiquitous living dead, but must also survive and ultimately resist the corrupt postapocalyptic civil authorities for whom the zombie threat is a license for oppression and cruelty. This is consistent with Kim Paffenroth's observation that in George Romero's films, "Living humans are more of a threat to one another than zombies are to them."[9] Civil authority in Ryan's novels is vicious, self-serving, and, ultimately, ineffectual. Unlike the Mudo, leaders have *chosen* to live inhumanely. The parallel behaviors of the Mudo and the ruling elites is consistent with Henry Giroux's contention that "the new zombies are not only wandering around in the banks, investment houses, and death chambers of high finance, they have an ever-increasing presence in the highest reaches of government and in the forefront of mainstream media."[10] The three women narrators and their allies reject the zombie-like cruelty and corruption rampant among their societies' political and military rulers.

The pressures on the settlement in *The Forest of Hands and Teeth* (2009) are both external and internal. The Unconsecrated beyond the fence are the external threat that surrounds the village whose leaders tell the people that theirs is humanity's last bastion. The torture of seeing loved ones turned to monsters is the internal threat that is too much for some to bear. Surviving angst is almost as hard as surviving the encroachment of the Unconsecrated, a reality that should resonate with many a teen reader.

However, it is the women who rule the besieged village that pose the greater threat to the meaning of humanity. The image of the habited Sisterhood invokes simultaneously iconic nuns and witches. In order to keep their village in quarantine, they hide by any means necessary the fact that other towns exist. Like any good YA dystopian heroine, Mary, the book's narrator, has subversive tendencies from the start, but the discovery that the Sisters have sacrificed to the Unconsecrated a girl her own age from another settlement who had the misfortune to drop in for a visit destroys whatever faith she retains in the ruling elite. When the village finally falls, Mary, inspired by a childhood memory of the seaside, assumes agency by escaping and taking up a new life as the keeper of a lighthouse—appropriate for a person whose character is a beacon of hope.

194 • Thomas J. Morrissey

The second and third volumes portray the destruction of what remains of more traditional patriarchal government. Mary raises her daughter Gabrielle in Vista, a coastal bastion under the sway of the Protectorate, a regime that requires its tributary towns to provide youths to become soldiers in the never-ending war against Mudo terrorism. Conscripts who survive their tours of duty get full citizenship and the right to reside in the Dark City, a place with the imagined aura of Oz but which is, in fact, the rotting carcass of New York City. An era ends when the Recruiters (the army of the Protectorate) seize power. The military coup essentially decapitates government. Instead of a force that tries to maintain order and promote the rebirth of civilization, the new regime has no plans other than enjoying the spoils and terrorizing civilians. In the final volume, even as the Mudo hordes advance on the Dark City, the brutes in power continue to enjoy watching caged human captives ravaged by Mudo. As Kim Paffenroth observes, "Zombies are us—not the mysterious or reviled 'other,' however that is constructed—but us, in all our hungry, grasping, mindless simplicity."[11]

Ryan's novels are *YA* dystopias: nihilism is not an option. The corrupt governments are fictional projections of how *not* to run a polity. The inhuman behavior of the oppressors is not a species imperative but a choice. The novels serve the high purpose of dystopian fiction: showing us the worst so that we can learn to build the better. Ryan's sister-heroines Gabrielle and Annah literally rise above the ethically challenged Recruiters when they take to the air in improvised hot air balloons. Readers are invited to imagine that the escapees and their followers will try to build a new society based on humane values. Here is Annah's utopian dream: "There would be these beautiful buildings all connected with bridges—everything would be off the ground. It would be part of nature—not trying to change it but to meld to it . . . It would be safe. We wouldn't ever have to worry again."[12] There is room to hope that these young women will grow into an agency as powerful as any in the traditional masculine *Bildungsroman*, a feminist coup accessible to a generation of readers for whom gender issues are more out in the open and less troublesome than ever before. The voracious and stupid hunger of the Mudo is challenged by irrepressible youthful hope and exuberance driven by the desire for posthuman liberation.

Feed: Food for Thought or Cure for Undue Optimism?

M.T. Anderson's *Feed* straddles the narrow but crucial divide between absurdity and existential horror. A scathing send-up of the evils and suicidal short-sightedness of late capitalism and its senseless, ceaseless production of the day's great American novelty, *Feed* speaks for and to those whose personal growth has been stunted by the consumer society. Darko Suvin tells us, "Adolescents have normal age-bound fears about affirmation, sex, identity and so

Parables for the Postmodern, Post-9/11, and Posthuman World • 195

on. But in capitalism without a human face, the anxieties grow deeper than ever."[13] *Feed* is a subversive text, a virtuoso performance by a writer who trusts that his young adult audience will grasp the gravity of the subject matter but also appreciate and maybe even be inspired by the novel's grace and wit. The book celebrates literacy and critical thinking as the only antidotes for terminal consumerism. Although the *novum*—that teens' minds are permanently open to the Feed's endless stream of advertising via neural implants—requires a technology that does not yet exist, imagining such a breakthrough is easy given the extent to which young people live in virtual venues and the extent to which they are targeted by advertisers.

The key to Anderson's satire is the humorous banality of his narrator. Titus speaks to the young adult audience in a language they will understand, even though any teen who would actually read the book would have Titus's number from the outset. No-Speak replaces Newspeak. Like Beavis and Butthead, Titus and most of his peers amuse readers with their language deficits. There is no prestige dialect. No sharp reader could possibly miss the significance of Titus and his friends having to resort to the Feed's "English-to-English workbook."[14] School™ gives corporations a captive audience whose ignorance of the past allows them to be lured into buying clothes from the Kent State collection, Stonewall Clogs, or, most ironically, WTO riot Windbreakers. The ineffectual government is headed by a George W. Bushesque president whose gaffes are rationalized by a captive media: "It has to be understood that when the President referred to the Prime Minister of the Global Alliance as a 'big shithead,' what he was trying to convey was, uh—this is an American idiom used to praise people, by referring to the sheer fertilizing power of their thoughts" (119). This is Orwell in the age of idiocy.

Anderson's novel is dedicated "to all those who resist the Feed," the very teens who can appreciate his satire and survive unscathed his message of doom. He trusts his readers with a glimpse at the possible death of our biosphere, which is rendered by means of nullification. The novel nullifies great stories we tell ourselves—the Garden of Eden, the concept of the sea as life's amniotic origin, and the notion that love, especially young love, conquers all. In fact, the novel is nothing short of a *de*-creation myth. As a fictive construct, it is a consciously sterile re-enactment of Genesis: a first-magnitude, urgent warning to a new generation that there is no viable alternative to resistance. This is what makes this novel stand out in the world of YA fiction. Given the pressure to conform, young people need encouragement to follow the road not taken, and they need to know that there are those among older generations who are not as blind or unscrupulous as are the perpetrators in the presidential palaces and boardrooms of the world.

In *Feed's* revisioning of creation, Titus and Violet are Adam and Eve. They do not have sex, and she dies a virgin, so we can forget about Cain and Abel. But in its early stages their relationship does provide some hope that they will become a dynamic duo. On a junket to the Moon, the two teens behold a

196 · Thomas J. Morrissey

garden that is emblematic of the anti-Edenic Earth: "Outside the window, there had been a garden, like, I guess you could call it a courtyard or terrarium? But a long time ago the glass ceiling over the terrarium had cracked, and so everything was dead, and there was moon dust all over everything out there. Everything was gray" (62). The lunar garden has died because technology has failed. The terrestrial biosphere is dying because technology has been misused. Thus the garden that was intended to remind lunar visitors of the homeworld's bounty instead tells a tale of misapplied creative zeal. The pleasure dome is cracked; Eden is sterile.

The amniotic sea is dead too. Titus's total inability to understand that nature will get its revenge for our tampering is evidenced in one of the book's most telling comments. When he and Violet behold the dead ocean, Titus attempts to comfort her: "I was like, *I don't think you have to worry. Science is like, they're always discovering things*" (179, italics original). Science may dis-cover, but the powers that be simply cover up. They have covered up their sins by hooking the populace on their products, and they have covered up the world in a shell under which humans are perishing in ignorance and hopelessness. Violet has tasted the fruit of the tree of knowledge; Titus and his peers starve.

The time-honored trope of young love conquering all fares as poorly as the memory of Eden. Violet's slow decline as her feed fails offers Titus a chance to show his humanity and maybe even vow to avenge her or to at least give meaning to her death. It does not happen. Titus retires into the world of insatiable longing for stuff. Reviewer Lauren Adams succinctly captures Titus's lack of development in the face of Violet's illness and death: "He fails her utterly, heartbreakingly, by closing himself off. Right there, Anderson hands us the worst of ourselves—erecting blinders to the pain and suffering of others in order to protect our own way of life."[15] No one in this novel is a brother's or sister's keeper. In a book in which teens mutilate themselves to be accepted, there is so little love of self that there isn't much left over for anyone's neighbors.

The ultimate satirical nullification is its close: on the final pages, the phrase *"Everything must go"* appears five times in successively smaller fonts; the human going-out-of-business sale is underway (299–300, italics original). Abbie Ventura claims that the novel's one significant act of defiance offers adolescent readers a way out of unconscious conformity: "Teenage Violet stops buying goods in her commodity-driven society."[16] Yes, Violet dies, but as bad as things are in our world, *Feed*, like *A Modest Proposal*, is over-the-top. Unless or until the fictive world of the novel becomes reality, surrender is not an option.

Like the best of YA writers, Anderson respects young people. In an interview in *Voya*, Anderson tells Joel Shoemaker, "People underestimate the intelligence of teen readers. We do them a disservice by talking down to them."[17] Like any good satirist, he knows that "humor is not about trivialities." And what are the heavy matters he wants to convey to his astute young readers? He

Parables for the Postmodern, Post-9/11, and Posthuman World • 197

tells Shoemaker, "I conceive of *Feed* as a novel that uses images from an imagined future in an almost allegorical way to discuss things we're dealing with now."[18] This intent heeds Hayles's call: "The best possible time to contest for what the posthuman means is now, before the trains of thought it embodies have been laid down so firmly that it would take dynamite to change them."[19] *Feed* portrays a route to the future in which the blame for technological irresponsibility lies squarely with the totalizing late capitalist machine that is the product of the same mindset that brought us colonization, slavery, and Auschwitz. The best insurance against such a future is youthful resistance. It is not the technology that is at fault; rather, it is the fact that all information goes one way—from the admen to those who are fed. Stop the top-down flow of knowledge (if one can call what the Feed gives knowledge) and new vistas of a decentralized, democratic, and non-commercial communication open. The future belongs to the destroyers or to those who resist the Feed. To lose faith in the young is to lose hope. Now that I am a grandparent of four boys to whom this new century really belongs, I simply cannot allow myself to do that.

Jenna Fox, Soulful Cyborg

The world does not have to collapse in order for some individuals to suffer in the crossfire of ever-new scientific agency and slow-to-change moral beliefs. In the first novel of what will be the Jenna Fox Chronicles, Mary E. Pearson adapts the coming-of-age tale to the era of posthumanity. Intimate first-person revelation of hard-won personal growth is a tried and true formula for novels of teen angst, but Jenna's primary rite of passage is anything but familiar: she awakens to find herself a cyborg. Her body, and therefore identity, was altered without her consent by parents whose grief at the loss of their only surviving child was so great that they had to have "her" back at all cost. She is, in a sense, Jenna 2.0, the existence of whom/which prompts other characters and readers to consider whether she is a biotechnological abomination or the first beneficiary of a human-made miracle. She is the first of her kind, a being composed of 90% artificial parts and only 10% human tissue, but is she also the last of our kind, a harbinger of our transition to posthumanity?

Pearson deftly co-opts tropes of the novel of development. For example, Jenna struggles with adult power. When her grandmother Lily stares down Gabriel, the first boy Jenna sees in her postaccident brave new world, the granddaughter tells herself: "I am immediately angry with myself for being so quick to please Lily and Mother. It won't happen again."[20] When Jenna's mother Claire drops her off on the first day of school in her new life, Jenna observes that, "It is like we are both fighting for control of Jenna Fox" (65). Teen readers would understand Jenna's rage at discovering that she has been programmed to cease and desist rebellion when a parent says, "go to your room." Amending the parental program is essential for true individuation whether it rests on learned behavior or software code. As in so many YA fictions, Jenna must become her own person to become an active agent.

At the same time, in order to act ethically she must learn to understand others' perspectives, forgive others' shortcomings, and empathize with their suffering. As Jenna comes to terms with what her parents have done for and to her, she must imagine their grief in order to be able to forgive their actions. Her anger with her father for forcing her conscious mind to live for a time in a computer, in constricted, bodiless cyberspace ("That environment was my hell," [124]) is not so different from many adolescents' reactions to well-intended but nonetheless traumatic parental actions. Jenna observes parental love in Lily's behavior towards her daughter, Jenna's mother: "There is nothing she wouldn't do for Claire" (84). When she discovers that Lily's devotion to her daughter caused her to break her own moral and religious codes, Jenna asks herself the now rhetorical question, "How far will a parent go for a child?" (189). This is, of course, a central question in the novel, but Jenna's asking it of herself is a key to understanding why her parents felt compelled to save her at all costs.

Healthy development is hard enough for a flesh and blood teen, but it is even harder when one is an illegal cyborg whose humanity is in question. YA readers who have ever felt rejection will empathize with Jenna when her Catholic grandmother, convinced that Jenna is not a person but an affront to creation, utters one of the book's most shocking sentences: "They should have let you die" (117). When her friend Allys learns the truth about Jenna, she reports her and her family to the authorities, who she believes are "trying to preserve our humanity" (96). The implication is clear: Jenna is not human.

Since there is no question about what Jenna's body is made of, her potential humanity must reside in her consciousness. First, there is ample proof that biological humanity does not guarantee socially acceptable behavior. She says of Dane, the young sociopath who assaults her, "He's shown me how empty a one hundred percent human can be. Percentages can be deceptive" (216). Fortunately for Jenna, her Catholic grandmother Lily comes to a similar conclusion with respect to her cyborg granddaughter. Near the end of the book, Jenna relates one of the novel's most evocative moments: "She reaches out. I fold into her arms, and she holds me tight, stroking my head. Neurochip to neuron, it doesn't matter, I am weak with her scent and touch" (256). The rapprochement between the two marks their mutual transformation into posthumans. One is augmented, the other is not, but both make ethical judgments informed by a deep familiarity with the mixed moral results of blending human being and machine.

The novel raises one of the most important issues facing a society with advanced technology, that is, how to decide which technologies are ethically acceptable. In one succinct sentence, Allys stakes out a moral position that informs this novel: "But just because we *can* doesn't mean we should" (95, italics original). Jenna and Lily apply this precept when they join together to

Parables for the Postmodern, Post-9/11, and Posthuman World · **199**

subvert Jenna's father's work by releasing the consciousnesses of her two dead friends from the computers in which they are trapped. Whether recreating Jenna was morally right, it is clear in her mind that keeping human consciousness in cyber limbo is not. The damage that Dr. Fox has done to one of these minds is the subject of the sequel *The Fox Inheritance* (2011).

The Adoration of Jenna Fox explores the unintended dystopian potentiality of the heedless application of advanced technology by focusing on the impact on one individual and those closest to her. Jenna suffers because her controlling father manipulates nature in order to soothe his own broken heart without considering the ethical or global implications. At the same time, Jenna is a 90% artificial being whose personal growth is as palpable and compelling as that of many young protagonists in novels of development. She has her whole life ahead of her, and it will be a longer and more physically comfortable life than any of us will have.

Conclusion

YA dystopias are selling so well in part because they touch upon complex and frightening issues in a manageable format. How to adjust to postmodern indeterminacy and posthuman selfhood are two of the more troublesome and timely issues. The books discussed here, in one way or another, fit N. Katherine Hayles's concept of posthuman narratives: "Although some current versions of the posthuman point toward the anti-human and the apocalyptic, we can craft others that will be conducive to the long-range survival of humans and of other life-forms, biological and artificial, with whom we share the planet and ourselves."[21] The lo-tech Return trilogy shows us a dystopian world of technological loss and a potential utopian future in which any revived technology will be applied using new criteria. *Feed* satirizes the apocalyptic fate of a postliterate, purposeless, totalizing late capitalist culture but leaves room for and encourages resistance in its young readers. *The Adoration of Jenna Fox* illustrates the high-stakes pitfalls of selfish behavior but also celebrates the ability of people of good will to adapt to change, even if that means swapping out neurons for neurochips. These books show respect for and faith in their intended audience as they invite them to experience versions of the future with profound import for the present. Thinking about these novels affords us an opportunity to witness the developing kinship between literature and science as we ponder the developing kinship between people and machines.

At their best, today's YA dystopias are invitations to action. What Laura Chernaik observes about the inspirational potential of science fiction is equally true of the YA dystopian form. She tells us that reading SF can "call us, as agents and as ethical beings, to responsibility."[22] This is precisely what Anderson does when he dedicates his book "to all those who resist the Feed," and it is reasonable to assume that many YA dystopian writers are hoping for

200 · Thomas J. Morrissey

the same efficacy; social activism is a viable and desirable reader response to utopian/dystopian SF. As Prospero tells Miranda and Ferdinand, "We are such stuff as dreams are made on."[23] Let us keep dreaming along with YA writers and the young readers who will inherit the Earth.

Notes

1 "The Anthropocene: A Man-Made World," *The Economist*, May 26, 2011, http://www. economist.com/node/18741749.

2 Veronica Hollinger, "Apocalypse Coma," in *Edging into the Future: Science Fiction and Contemporary Cultural Transformation*, ed. Veronica Hollinger and Joan Gordon (Philadelphia: The University of Pennsylvania Press, 2002), 161.

3 Ibid.

4 Donna Haraway, "A Cyborg Manifesto: Science, Technology, and Socialist-Feminism in the Late Twentieth Century," in *Simians, Cyborgs and Women: The Reinvention of Nature* (New York: Routledge, 1991), 180, 181.

5 N. Katherine Hayles, *How We Became Posthuman: Virtual Bodies in Cybernetics, Literature, and Informatics* (Chicago: University of Chicago Press, 1999), 4.

6 Ibid., 288.

7 The Fourteenth Dalai Lama, *Beyond Religion: Ethics for a Whole World* (Boston and New York: Houghton Mifflin Harcourt, 2011), 85.

8 D. Harlan Wilson, *Technologized Desire: Selfhood and the Body in Postcapitalist Science Fiction* (Hyattsville, MD: Guided Dog Books, 2009), 95.

9 Kim Paffenroth, "Zombies as Internal Fear or Threat," in *Generation Zombie: Essays on the Living Dead in Modern Culture*, ed. Stephanie Boluk and Wylie Lenz (Jefferson, NC: McFarland and Company, 2011), 20.

10 Henry Giroux, *Zombie Politics and Culture in the Age of Casino Capitalism* (New York: Peter Lang, 2011), 2.

11 Paffenroth, "Zombies," 24.

12 Carrie Ryan, *The Dark and Hollow Places* (New York: Delacorte Press, 2011), 321.

13 Darko Suvin, "Afterword: With Sober, Estranged Eyes," in *Learning from Other Worlds: Estrangement, Cognition, and the Politics of Science Fiction and Utopia*, ed. Patrick Parrinder (Durham, NC: Duke University Press, 2001), 263.

14 M.T. Anderson, *Feed* (Cambridge, MA: Candlewick Press, 2002), 23. Subsequent references will be cited parenthetically in the text.

15 Lauren Adams, Review of *Feed*, by M.T. Anderson, *The Hornbook Magazine* 78.5 (2002): 564.

16 Abbie Ventura, "Predicting a Better Situation? Three Young Adult Speculative Fiction Texts and the Possibilities for Social Change," *Children's Literature Association Quarterly* 36.1 (2011): 89.

Parables for the Postmodern, Post-9/11, and Posthuman World · **201**

17 Joel Shoemaker, "Hungry for M.T. Anderson . . . An Interview with M.T. Anderson," *Voya* 27.2 (2004): 99.
18 Ibid., 100.
19 Hayles, *Posthuman*, 291.
20 Mary E. Pearson, *The Adoration of Jenna Fox* (New York: Henry Holt and Company 2008), 39. Subsequent references will be cited parenthetically in the text.
21 Hayles, *Posthuman*, 291.
22 Laura Chernaik, *Social and Virtual Space: Science Fiction, Transnationalism, and the American New Right* (Madison and Teaneck, NJ: Fairleigh Dickinson University Press, 2005), 190.
23 Shakespeare, *Tempest*, IV, i, 156–157.

Works Cited

Adams, Lauren. Review of *Feed* by M.T. Anderson. *The Hornbook Magazine* 78.5 (2002): 564.
Anderson, M.T. *Feed*. Cambridge, MA: Candlewick Press, 2002.
"The Anthropocene: A Man-Made World." *The Economist*, May 26, 2011. www.economist.com/node.18741749.
Chernaik, Laura. *Social and Virtual Space: Science Fiction, Transnationalism, and the American New Right*. Madison and Teaneck, NJ: Fairleigh Dickinson University Press, 2005.
Dalai Lama, Fourteenth. *Beyond Religion: Ethics for a Whole World*. Boston and New York: Houghton Mifflin Harcourt, 2011.
Giroux, Henry A. *Zombie Politics and Culture in the Age of Casino Capitalism*. New York: Peter Lang, 2011.
Haraway, Donna J. "A Cyborg Manifesto: Science, Technology, and Socialist-Feminism in the Late Twentieth Century." In *Simians, Cyborgs and Women: The Reinvention of Nature*, 149–181. New York: Routledge, 1991.
Hayles, N. Katherine. *How We Became Posthuman: Virtual Bodies in Cybernetics, Literature, and Informatics*. Chicago: University of Chicago Press, 1999.
Hollinger, Veronica. "Apocalypse Coma." In *Edging into the Future: Science Fiction and Contemporary Cultural Transformations*, edited by Veronica Hollinger and Joan Gordon, 159–173. Philadelphia: The University of Pennsylvania Press, 2002.
Paffenroth, Kim. "Zombies as Internal Fear or Threat." In *Generation Zombie: Essays on the Living Dead in Modern Culture*, edited by Stephanie Boluk and Wylie Lenz, 18–26. Jefferson, NC: McFarland and Company, 2011.
Pearson, Mary E. *The Adoration of Jenna Fox*. New York: Henry Holt and Company, 2008.
Ryan, Carrie. *The Dark and Hidden Places*. New York: Delacorte Press, 2011.
Shoemaker, Joel. "Hungry for M.T. Anderson. . . An Interview with M.T. Anderson." *Voya* 27.2 (2004): 98–102.
Suvin, Darko. "Afterword: With Sober, Estranged Eyes." In *Learning from Other Worlds: Estrangement, Cognition, and the Politics of Science Fiction and Utopia*, edited by Patrick Parrinder, 233–271. Durham: Duke University Press, 2001.
Ventura, Abbie. "Predicting a Better Situation? Three Young Adult Speculative Fiction Texts and the Possibilities for Social Change." *Children's Literature Association Quarterly* 36.1 (2011): 89–103.
Wilson, D. Harlan. *The Technologies of Desire: Selfhood and the Body in Postcapitalist Science Fiction*. Hyattsville, MD: Guided Dog Books, 2009.

Contributors

Balaka Basu has a PhD in English literature from the Graduate Center of the City University of New York and a BA in English from Cornell University. Recent publications include essays in Sherlock *and Transmedia Fandom* (McFarland, 2012) and *Peregrinations, Ruminations, Regenerations: A Critical Approach to* Doctor Who (Cambridge Scholars Press, 2010). Currently, she is working on a monograph, *Neverending Stories: Unauthorized Continuations, Fictional Realities, and the Long-Form Narrative from 1590–2011,* and teaching children's and YA literature, early modern literature, film and television studies, and nineteenth-century fiction at Queens College.

Katherine R. Broad holds a PhD in English from the Graduate Center, CUNY, and a BA in English and Political Science from Wellesley College. She has essays in *Tulsa Studies in Women's Literature, The Postnational Fantasy: Nationalism, Cosmopolitics, and Science Fiction,* and forthcoming in *Janus Head.* She is currently working on a monograph, *Courting Utopia: The Persistence of the Romance Plot in Contemporary Utopian Fiction,* as well as a YA science fiction novel called *The Columbus Experiment.*

Mary J. Couzelis is currently working towards her PhD focusing on children's literature at Texas A&M University-Commerce. She received her MA in children's literature from Hollins University in 2009, and a second MA in literature with an emphasis on Native American fiction from the University of North Carolina at Charlotte in 2008. Her research interests include young adult historical fiction, the Gothic in adolescent literature, and multiethnic American literature. Her published research centers on cultural representations of gender and race in children's literature.

Claire P. Curtis is Associate Professor of Political Science at the College of Charleston. She is the author of *Postapocalyptic Fiction and the*

204 · Contributors

Social Contract: "We'll Not Go Home Again" (Lexington, 2010). She teaches classes in the history of political thought, contemporary liberalism, utopia/dystopia, and sexual harassment. Her research interests include the intersections between postapocalyptic, utopian, and dystopian thought with political philosophy. She coedited a special edition of *Utopian Studies* on Octavia Butler and has also published essays on Octavia Butler, Ursula Le Guin, and Marge Piercy. She regularly presents papers at the annual Society for Utopian Studies conferences and recently published an advice piece in the *Chronicle of Higher Education.*

Carrie Hintz is Associate Professor at Queens College/CUNY and the Graduate Center, CUNY. She is the author of *An Audience of One: Dorothy Osborne's Letters to Sir William Temple, 1652–1654* (University of Toronto Press, 2005) and the coeditor, with Elaine Ostry, of *Utopian and Dystopian Writing for Children and Young Adults* (Routledge, 2003). With Eric Tribunella, she coauthored a college textbook in the field of children's literature: *Reading Children's Literature: A Critical Introduction* (Bedford St. Martin's, 2013). She served as President of the Society for Utopian Studies from 2006 to 2010, and she continues to write about the politics and aesthetics of speculative fiction for children and young adults.

Emily Lauer majored in English and religious studies at New York University and then obtained a PhD in English and an interdisciplinary certificate from the Graduate Center, CUNY. She is now Assistant Professor of English at Suffolk County Community College in New York, where her research interests include visual and cultural literacy as well as world-building in children's and young adult fiction. Dr. Lauer frequently presents at regional and national conferences on these topics.

Kristi McDuffie is a PhD student in English studies at Illinois State University with a focus on rhetoric and composition. Her research interests center on digital literacies, rhetorics of race, and language ideologies. Her publications to date have explored writing center pedagogy and narrative discourse in television.

Thomas J. Morrissey is University Distinguished Teaching Professor and Chair of the English Department at Plattsburgh State University of New York. He is coauthor of *Pinocchio Goes Post Modern: The Perils of a Puppet in the United States* (2002) and coeditor of *When Genres Collide* (2007). He is also the author/composer of musical comedies for young people, including *Puppet Song*, a play inspired by *The Adventures of Pinocchio.*

Contributors • 205

Erin T. Newcomb earned her PhD in literacy education and women's studies at the Pennsylvania State University. She specializes in religion and literature as well as theories of writing. Currently, she teaches literature and composition courses in the SUNY New Paltz Department of English, including a course on young adult literature.

Elaine Ostry is Associate Professor of English at SUNY-Plattsburgh. She is the author of *Social Dreaming: Dickens and the Fairy Tale* (2002) and the coeditor, with Carrie Hintz, of *Utopian and Dystopian Literature for Children and Young Adults* (2003). She has published articles on young adult science fiction, conduct literature, and *Harry Potter*.

Carissa Turner Smith is Assistant Professor of English at Charleston Southern University, where she teaches American literature and literary theory. She has published articles in *African American Review*, *Literature and Belief*, and *Renascence*. While revising her dissertation on American women writers and spiritual geography, she is pursuing other projects involving spatial approaches to literature. She also is writing about recent American YA novels' interaction with the works of Phillis Wheatley, Benjamin Franklin, and Mark Twain.

Susan Louise Stewart is Associate Professor of English at Texas A&M University-Commerce. The bulk of her work has been focused on the role of race, ethnicity, gender, and religion in young adult literature. Through her articles and conference presentations, she has examined invisibility as experienced by African American young adults, the role of white privilege, the rhetoric and ideology embedded in religious discourse in young adult literature, and the way in which some American authors characterize and represent adolescents and young adults from other countries. Her work has appeared in journals like *The Lion and the Unicorn* and *Children's Literature in Education*.

Alexa Weik Von Mossner is Assistant Professor of American Studies at the University of Klagenfurt in Austria and an affiliate at the Rachel Carson Center for Environment and Society in Munich, Germany. She earned her PhD in literature at the University of California, San Diego in 2008 with a dissertation on literary cosmopolitanism. Her essays on transnationalism, cosmopolitanism, and various eco-critical issues in Anglophone literature and film have appeared in journals such as the *African American Review, English Studies, Environmental Communication, Ecozona*, and in the *Journal of Commonwealth and Postcolonial Studies*. Her current research focuses on the imagination of global ecological risk in American popular culture.

Index

ability, 25, 26, 37–40, 43; and worth, 38, 47
activism, 5, 46, 200; and civil disobedience, 78; and political action, 43, 79, 93
Adams, Lauren, 196
adults, 87, 91, 94; and inadequacy, 4, 7, 160, 169. *See also* family; adolescents (and adults)
adulthood, 7, 21, 46, 126. See also *Bildungsroman*; coming of age; growing up
adolescents: and adults, 45–46, 101, 162; and agency, 46, 109, 110, 194; and change, 70; and identity (*see* identity); and literacy, 146–147, 153–155; and maturation, 37, 103, 106, 109; and the posthuman, 178; as protagonists (*see* young adult protagonists); as readers (*see* young adult readers); and responsibility for the future, 73, 79, 97, 108, 111; and sexuality, 21; and technology, 146, 152–154; and typical concerns, 19, 22, 30–31, 72–78, 88–89, 121; and youth culture, 101, 102, 111 (*see also* culture)
adventure, 7–8. *See also* genre
Africans: stereotypical representations of, 133
African Americans, 133, 138–141; representations in children's literature, 140
Agee, Jane M., 127
agency, 124, 175; and cataclysmic events, 93–94; and coming of age, 46; and critical dystopias, 70; and literacy, 154; and unmediated experience,

106–107. *See also* adolescents (and agency)
Alcott, Louisa May, 5
Anderson, M.T., 102, 110, 111. See also *Feed* (Anderson)
Anthropocene, 189, 192
anxiety. *See* fear
apocalypse, 3, 6, 86, 93, 96, 109. *See also* postapocalypse
Arad, Yitzhak, 168
Atwood, Margaret: *Handmaid's Tale, The*, 37

Babb, Valerie, 133
Babbitt, Natalie, 109
Baccolini, Raffaella, 7, 70, 86, 136, 138. *See also* critical dystopia; Moylan, Tom
Bacigalupi, Paolo, 8; *Ship Breaker*, 3, 71
Baron, Dennis, 150
Barry, Max, 192
Baudrillard, Jean, 58
Bauerlein, Mark, 146, 154
Baum, L. Frank: *Master Key, The*, 20–21
Beck, Ulrich, 10, 70, 77–79. *See also* world risk society
Bell, Derrick: "Space Traders, The," 140
Bentham, Jeremy, 52
Bertagna, Julie. *See* Exodus series (Bertagna)
Bildungsroman, 6–7, 36, 44–47; and women, 194. *See also* coming of age; growing up
biotechnology: and bioterrorism, 193; as combination of biology and technology, 176; relationship to nature, 104, 108; and theology, 175, 184. *See also* environment;

208 · Index

posthuman, the; technology (and biology)
Bitch magazine, 117
Black, Holly: Curse Workers series, 9, 36–48
Blade Runner, 53
Bloch, Ernst, 70, 78. *See also* hope
Bould, Mark, 137
Boyer, M. Christine, 52–53, 55–56, 58–59, 62
Boyle, Danny, 193
Bradford, Clare, *et al*, 86
Braithwaite, Elizabeth, 97n2
Brockman, John, 146
Brink, Carol Ryrie: *Caddie Woodlawn*, 127
Brown, Joanne, 127
Buell, Frederick, 79
burnt offerings, 160, 166–167

capitalism, 35, 111, 192, 194–195, 197, 199; and sacrifice, 164. *See also* consumption
carceral archipelago, 52–55, 59–60, 62
Carr, Nicholas, 146
Cawelti, John G., 7
Chambers, Iain, 56
change: apocalyptic, 88, 93; avenues of, 41; environmental, 69–73, 77–78; future, 73, 124; personal, 40, 43, 77–78, 80, 101; political, 2, 70, 76; resistance to, 29, 44, 91; social, 8, 27, 70–73, 91, 101, 127; utopian, 3, 70, 79, 96–97, 110, 120, 125; and young adults, 72, 109. *See also* transformation
children, 121–122, 125–126. *See also* reproduction
cities, 96, 101–106, 108, 111; and the body, 59, 62; and urban/suburban divide, 53. *See also* nature; postmetropolis; Simcity; space (urban); technology
Chernaik, Laura, 199
class, 38, 41, 88, 90; and inequality, 38, 92; and racial identity, 138–139; and social structures, 90–91
classification, 20–27, 31. *See also* stratification
clones, 175–186; and biotechnology, 180; compared to cyborgs, 178, 180, 184; opposition to, 184; and racial passing, 186n6
Cocalis, Susan, 45, 46
cognitive estrangement, 86

Collins, Suzanne. *See* Hunger Games series, The (Collins)
coming of age: and narrative, 182; personal and political, 37, 40, 43, 46, 78, 175; and the posthuman, 178–180, 197. *See also Bildungsroman*; growing up
community: as group membership, 24–25, 164–165; in postapocalyptic fiction, 85, 89, 94–97; and sacrifice, 162–163; and technology, 108; as transnational and global, 70; young adult participation in, 85
conclusions, 168; "cop out", 154–155. *See also* endings
Condie, Ally. See *Matched* (Condie)
conformity, 3, 57, 195–196; and rebellion, 4
conservatism: and genre, 8, 9, 27, 44; and an idealized past, 28–29, 57; and identity, 31, 45; and passivity, 46, 85, 90–91, 125–127; political (*see* right-wing dystopia, objectivism); social, 11, 31, 47, 120–122, 125–127; and young adult dystopias, 2. *See also* retrofuturism
consumerism. *See* consumption
consumption, 101, 102, 104–106, 119; and youth culture, 74, 102
counter-narrative, 85–87, 90, 95. *See also* rebellion; resistance; revolution
courtship. *See* romance
Crew, Hilary, 179, 180
crisis, 73, 75–76
critical dystopia, 70, 78; critical eco-dystopia, 10, 70, 71, 78, 79
Crutzen, Paul, 189
culture: young adult, 101, 103; popular, 106, 111
Crowe, Chris, 2
Curtis, Claire P., 79
cyborgs, 177, 190–192, 197–199; compared to clones, 178, 180, 184

darkness: in young adult dystopias, 69, 71–72, 78, 81–82n14
Deleuze, Gilles, 53
desire: readerly, 75, 86–87, 92, 95, 97; and teens, 74–78, 89; utopian, 70
despair, 2, 71, 95, 109, 111, 170–171. *See also* hope
didacticism, 154; in postapocalyptic texts, 10, 87; use of humor to mitigate, 80; and young adult dystopias, 2, 5–6, 72, 79, 189. *See also* warnings

Index • 209

digital literacies, 145; 150–154
Dinello, Daniel, 178
disaster. *See* apocalypse; environment (disaster/degradation); postapocalypse
discipline: constructive, 61; as deprivation of quality of life, 38; as enslavement, 4; and Foucauldian discipline, 61; and geography, 53, 55, 56; as isolation, 24, 55; as prison, 52; as surveillance, 52, 55, 56; as technological deprivation, 56, 57; and violence, 37–38; with bodies as prisons, 54, 59. *See also* Foucault, Michel
Doctorow, Cory: and digital literacies, 152–154. See also *Little Brother* (Doctorow)
domesticity. *See* home; family
Donawerth, Jane, 70
dystopia: acceptance of, 26–28, 31, 44–45; adult, 72, 85; and ambiguity, 168; causes of, 20, 39; and catastrophe, 72 (*see also* postapocalypse); and change, 121; children as scapegoats within, 160; and critique of parenting, 170; definition of, 159; dystopian regimes, 35, 119; as extrapolation from the present, 159; and genre, 40, 45, 72, 86, 87 (*see also* critical dystopia); and geography, 53; and history, 133, 136; and immanent disaster, 159; negotiating life within, 36; purpose of, 61, 85, 194; and the status quo, 133; and utopia, 2, 54; and white privilege, 132–133, 135

eco-dystopia. *See* critical dystopia
ecology, 101–105; and Eden, 110. *See also* environment
education. *See* didacticism
Eisenstadt, Oona, 28–29
Ellis, Lorna, 125
enclosure, 52, 53, 55
endings: ambivalence in, 61–62, 72, 78, 101, 108–111; bleakness of, 72, 73, 109; 196; hopeful, 72, 79, 109, 194; open, 78; problematic, 27–28, 92; representations of the future in, 79, 92, 110; and utopia, 43–44, 78, 125. *See also* conclusions; hope
end of the world. *See* apocalypse
environment: biophilia, 105, 107; catastrophe/ecological crisis 70–80, 87, 88, 93; climate change, 3, 69–79, 92–95, 101; degradation/destruction, 3, 11, 105, 109; sustainability, 107, 109, 111

escape, 5–6, 54, 59–61, 96
ethics, 71, 78, 95. *See also* justice
equality, 91, 92, 95; and ability, 38–39; in dystopia, 36, 37; and gender, 125. *See also* class
Exodus series (Bertagna), 2, 10–11; and adults in, 94; and *Aurora*, 109; and environmental change, 3, 86, 92–94, 101; fear and anxiety in, 86, 107; and nature, 103–107; and the postapocalypse, 93, 96; and resistance, 95, 97; and survival, 8, 93–96; and technology, 94, 96, 104–107; utopia, 86, 87, 93, 95, 107–108; and *Zenith*, 3

family: in critical eco-dystopias, 75–76, 80; and heterosexual reproduction, 120–122, 125; and parental abandonment, 128n12, 169; in postapocalyptic fiction, 88, 89–90; and protection of children, 102; resistance to, 197; and retreat from political involvement, 127; role of parents within, 74–76, 94–95
fantasy, 9. *See also* genre
Farmer, Nancy. See *House of the Scorpion, The* (Farmer)
fear, 3, 13, 36–37, 55, 61, 190; and utopia, 86
Feed (Anderson), 2, 4–5, 12; as allegory, 197; and critique of capitalism, 102, 104–107, 192, 194–195; as encouraging resistance, 110, 195, 197; ending of, 108–110, 196; and the environment, 101–102, 105, 107, 196; and *Genesis*, 195; and love, 196; and posthumanism, 191–192; as satire, 192, 194–196; technology, 101, 104, 106, 145, 147–148; and youth illiteracy, 145, 147–148
feminism, 117, 118, 124–127, 194; and activism, 127
film, 1, 72, 73, 98n11
Fisher, Catherine: Incarceron series, 4, 10, 51–62
fitting in, 22, 42
Fitting, Peter, 35
freedom, 4, 9, 59–61; and free will, 185. *See also* rebellion; resistance

210 · Index

frontier, 8, 27
Foucault, Michel: and discipline, 61; *Discipline and Punish*, 51, 52; post-Foucauldian, 31; and prison, 53, 56–57, 61. *See also* discipline
Fraiman, Susan, 126
Fukuyama, Francis, 175, 182
future: fear of, 159, 190; future societies, 70–71, 80, 92; hope for, 78, 96, 189, 197; multiple races in, 138; new world, 97, 109; representations of, 74, 79, 80, 95, 170; twenty-first century, 73. *See also* change; retrofuturism

Garforth, Lisa, 108–109
Gary, Alison, 117
gender, 11, 85; female protagonists, 117; gender roles, 126–127; stereotypes, 117, 125–127; tomboys, 127. *See also* feminism; heroines
genre, 5–9; hybridity, 10, 47; problem novel, 169–170; science fiction, 51, 131, 137, 140, 141; young adult, 20. *See also* dystopia; postapocalypse; utopia
Geus, Marius de, 102
Ginsberg, Allen, 154
Girard, René, 160, 164
Giroux, Henry, 193
Giver, The (Lowry), 2, 3, 4, 11; and critique of modern society, 131; and murder, 133; and race, 133–134; and sacrifice, 133; and sameness 132. *See also* Lowry, Lois
Goodall, Jane, 110
government, 36–40, 42, 76–78, 89–90, 193–194; breakdown of, 85; overthrow of, 47, 118, 123. *See also* totalitarian regime
Green, John, 1, 123
Green, Martin Burgess, 7–8
Gross, Melissa, 121
growing up: and acceptance of dystopian conditions, 37; and ecological utopias, 102–104, 106–108; and growth of agency, 46; and personal growth, 43, 110; and stabilization of identity, 21–22. *See also* adolescents; *Bildungsroman*; change; coming of age
Gurdon, Meghan Cox, 2n5, 81–82n14

Hamerton-Kelly, Robert G., 164
Hamlin, Harry, 160
Haney, William S., 176
Hansen, James, 69
Haraway, Donna, 177–178, 190
Hayles, N. Katherine, 146, 190–191, 197, 199
heroines, 54, 117–118, 125–126
heroism, 88, 121–123; and anti-heroism, 88–89. *See also* heroines
heterosexuality, 117–118, 123–124. *See also* romance
high concept narrative, 19–20
Hillcoat, John, 72
Hines, Maude, 20–21
Hinton, S.E: *Outsiders, The*, 2
Hintz, Carrie: on adolescent political voice, 121; on the *Bildungsroman*, 44; on definition of young adult dystopia genre, 40; on dystopias as cautionary tales, 110; on intergenerational tension, 46; on the political potential of young adult dystopias, 133–134; on post-disaster dystopias, 71. *See also* Ostry, Elaine
Hitler, Adolf, 165, 168
Hollinger, Veronica, 190
Holocaust, the, 166
holocaust. *See* burnt offerings
home, 120, 121, 125, 127. *See also* family
hooks, bell, 134
hope: and adolescent readers, 109–111; and Ernst Bloch, 70, 78; for utopia, 41; and radical hope, 70 (*see also* Moylan, Tom); and young adult dystopias, 2, 13, 72, 79, 109–111, 171. *See also* despair
House of the Scorpion, The (Farmer), 175–188; and cloning, 175–188; and coming of age, 175, 182; and posthumanity, 175, 178
Hubler, Angela, 127
Hughes, Monica, 71–72
Humor, 73–74, 80
Hunger Games series (Collins), 4, 5, 8, 9, 11, 22; *Catching Fire*, 120–122, 124; and child sacrifice, 140–141, 162; and critique of modern society, 131; film, 1; and history, 141; *Hunger Games, The*, 92, 119–122; *Mocking-jay*, 122–126; and race, 138–141
Huxley, Aldous: *Brave New World*, 105–106, 189
hyper-reality, 52, 58

identity, 9, 19, 178–181; classification of, 20–23; fixed, 20, 21, 30; as group membership, 21–25; labels, 27; legibility of, 20, 21. *See also* coming of age; community; stratification
Incredibles, The, 35–36, 47
inequality. *See* equality
injustice. *See* justice

James, Edward, 135–136
Jameson, Fredric, 9, 159
Jay, Nancy B., 163, 166, 167
John Paul II, Pope, 181–182
Johnson, Elana: *Possession*, 4
Johnson, George, 184
justice, 78, 86, 87, 90–97, 118

Karády, Victor, 165
Kass, Leon, 184
Keenan, Dennis King, 163
Kerouac, Jack, 154
King, Stephen, 5, 119
Kingsley, Charles: *Water Babies, The*, 5
Konner, Melvin, 110

Lane, Robert E., 39, 44, 46
Lavender, Isiah, 139, 140
Lavoie, Chantel, 23
Lawrence, D.H., 103
Lea, Susan, 132
LeGuin, Ursula K., 109
lessons. *See* didacticism
Levinas, Emmanuel, 28–29
Levitas, Ruth, 70
Levy, Michael, 110
Lewitt, Meghan, 117
literacy, 12; loss of, 145, 147–148; and multiliteracies, 150–155; and political resistance, 148–150. *See also* digital literacies
Little Brother (Doctorow), 2, 4, 8, 12; and digital literacies, 152–154
Lloyd, Saci: Carbon Diaries series, 3, 10; *Carbon Diaries 2015, The*, 69–71, 73–76, 79; *Carbon Diaries 2017, The*, 69–71, 73, 76–80
Leonard, Elisabeth Anne, 141
Lenin, Vladimir Ilyich, 169
Louv, Richard, 103
love. *See* romance
Lowry, Lois, 72; and critique of modern society, 131; *Gathering Blue*, 3; *Giver, The*, 2, 3, 4, 11; *Messenger*, 161; and murder, 133; and race, 133–134; and sacrifice, 131; and sameness, 132. *See also Giver, The* (Lowry)
Lurie, Alison, 45

MacCann, Donnarae, 140
MacLeod, Anne Scott, 169–170
Malley, Gemma: *Declaration, The*, 161
marketing, 1, 29–31, 195. *See also* consumption
marriage, 125, 127. *See also* heterosexuality; reproduction; romance
Marx, Karl, 169
Matched (Condie), 3–4, 8, 12; and romance plot, 154; traditional literacy and rebellion in, 148–149
McAlear, Rob, 29
McCafferty, Megan: *Bumped*, 8
McCarthy, Cormac: *Road, The*, 72–73, 96, 98n8
McKenna, Laura, 117
McKibben, Bill, 69
Mengele, Joseph, 168
messages. *See* didacticism
Miles, David H., 44
Miller, Laura, 6–7, 119, 122, 126
Mills, Charles, 97n1
Morse, Samuel F. B., 150
motherhood. *See* reproduction; family
Moylan, Tom, 7, 86; on critical dystopia, 70, 78; on history, 136; on ideology, 141; radical hope, 70
multiliteracies, 150–154; and pedagogy, 151. *See also* digital literacies
Murphy, Sean, 192

nature, 73, 101–108, 111; and fake nature, 57–58, 96, 104, 106. *See also* ecology; environment
Ness, Patrick: Chaos Walking series, 4, 8
New London Group, the, 151
normalcy, 74, 75–76, 78, 86, 88–91; rejection of, 45
North, Phoebe, 29–30
nostalgia, 20, 28, 57, 155. *See also* conservatism
Nussbaum, Martha, 97n1

obedience, 126, 169. *See also* discipline; rebellion; resistance
objectivism, 35, 47
O'Brien, Robert C.: *Z for Zachariah*, 3, 71
O'Keefe, Deborah, 125
Olalquiaga, Celeste, 59

212 · Index

Oliver, Lauren: *Delirium*, 2, 4
O'Quinn, Elaine, 125
Orwell, George: *1984*, 3
Ostry, Elaine: and cloning, 178–179; on dystopias as cautionary tales, 110; on the political potential of young adult dystopias, 133–134; and post-disaster dystopias, 71; and posthumanity, 183. *See also* Hintz, Carrie

Paffenroth, Kim, 193, 194
pain, 60–61
panopticism, 51–53, 55, 58
parents. *See* family
Pateman, Carole, 97n1
Patterson, Katherine: *Jacob Have I Loved*, 127
Pearson, Mary E.: Jenna Fox Chronicles, The, 197–199
Pepperell, Robert, 176
Pfeffer, Susan Beth: *Dead and the Gone, The*, 1, 88–90; Last Survivors series, 10, 71, 79, 87–88, 97; *Life as We Knew It*, 85–86, 88; *This World We Live In*, 88, 90–92
Piranesi, Giovanni Battista, 52, 62
Plato, 150
politics: political theory and philosophy, 85, 96. *See also* activism; agency; change (political); coming of age (personal and political)
postapocalypse: compared to near-future eco-dystopian novels, 79; and education of desire, 87, 92, 95; as fresh start, 85, 96, 109; and genre, 86–89, 96; and justice, 51, 90–92, 95–97; and political engagement, 10, 85–86, 96, 193
posthuman, the, 12, 176, 189, 192; and cloning, 175–176, 178, 181; and cyborgs, 197–199; and indeterminacy, 199; and selfhood, 199; and technology, 190, 198–199; and theology, 181–185
postmetropolis, 10, 52–56, 59–62
postmodern, the, 52, 189, 192; and contemporary anxieties, 190
power, 3, 90–91; and embodiment, 61–62; as pain, 60–61. *See also* discipline
Pratt, Annis, 125
privilege: class, 41, 95; heterosexual, 11; and specialness, 35; and utopianism, 41–42, 44; white, 11, 132–133, 135–136, 138

Pullman, Philip: His Dark Materials series, 21–22

Quealy-Gainer, Kate, 51

race, 11, 85, 127, 131; and futuristic texts, 132; and ideology, 134; and science, 134–135
racism, 135–136. *See also* privilege (white); white privilege
radicalism, 85–86, 90; and political activism, 76–78. *See also* conservatism
Rand, Ayn: *Atlas Shrugged*, 35–36. *See also* objectivism
rebellion, 4, 11, 118, 121, 125–126, 192; and literacy, 149, 154. *See also* resistance; revolution
Reeve, Philip, 27; *Mortal Engines*, 3; 170
refugees, 77, 95, 106. *See also* global impact
repression, 3, 4; by criminalization, 37–40; of labor and productivity, 38–39; and motherhood, 127 (*see also* heterosexuality; romance); by policing specialness, 37–38, 47; as regulation, 35–36; and reproduction, 120–122, 124–127. *See also* discipline; totalitarian regime
resistance, 25, 86–87, 95–96, 148–149, 150, 152–153, 193; absence of, 89, 90–92; and readers, 195; and revolutionary figures, 120–121, 123; and revolutionary potential, 85. *See also* freedom; rebellion; revolution
retrofuturism, 9, 27, 57
revolution, 85, 108, 117–118, 120–123, 125. *See also* freedom; rebellion; resistance
revolutionary figures, 120–121, 123
Rheingold, Howard, 58
right-wing dystopia, 35, 37, 47
risk, 70, 93, 96. *See also* safety; world risk society
Robinson, Kim Stanley, 109
romance, 8, 45, 118–124, 148–149, 195–196; conventions of, 119, 127; queer, 8
Rosoff, Meg: *How I Live Now*, 2, 3
Roth, Veronica: *Divergent*, 3, 9, 19–20, 22–31; *Insurgent*, 32n10
Rowling, J.K.: Harry Potter series, 22–23, 40, 45–46, 47; 125
Ryan, Carrie: *Forest of Hands and Teeth, The*, 3, 12, 193–194

Index · 213

Sackin, Jacob: *Islands*, 71
sacrifice: of children, 140, 160, 164, 165, 179; in the Christian tradition, 161, 163; as critique of dystopian culture, 161; in Greek Mythology, 160, 164; in the Old Testament, 160, 164; in young adult dystopian fiction, 161
safety: absence of, 37–38, 87, 95; access to, 91; and class, 41; in dystopian societies, 74, 76, 90, 92; and privilege, 38, 70, 91; and rescue, 93–96, 122; and security, 36, 41, 57. *See also* class; risk
Sambell, Kay, 72, 79, 109, 160
Sargent, Lyman Tower, 37, 41, 47, 159
Satrapi, Marjane: *Persepolis*, 37
scapegoating, 164; of adolescents, 165; and the Holocaust, 165, 168; and violence, 165
science: and the history of racism, 135–136. *See also* technology
science fiction, 9, 176, 178; and contemporary fears, 131; and race, 137, 140, 141. *See also* genre
Scott, A.O., 35
Selber, Stuart, 151
Seltzer, Sarah, 117
Shoemaker, Joel, 196–197
Shusterman, Neal. See *Unwind* (Shusterman)
Simcity, 52–54, 58–60, 62. *See also* virtual reality
social contract, 97n1
Soja, Edward, 10, 52, 54–56
space: embodied, 60–62; disembodied, 54, 59, 60; and geography, 55, 91; historied, 53, 62; and place, 62; urban, 52, 53, 56; utopian and dystopian, 53
Spinrad, Norman, 192
Stafford, Barbara, 62
status quo, 125–126. *See also* conservatism
Stephens, John, 86
Stoermer, Eugene, 189
St. Clair, Nancy, 127
Stoutenburg, Adrien: *Out There*, 71
Stewart, Susan, 132, 133–134
Stracher, Cameron: *Water Wars, The*, 71
stratification, 20, 23, 26, 27, 37, 57; eroded, 60; and pleasure, 30–31; rigid, 30. *See also* classification
Sullivan, Shannon, 132, 137, 138, 139
survival, 88–90, 93–96, 121, 165, 171

Suvin, Darko, 194
Swift, Jonathan: *Modest Proposal, A*, 192, 196
Swindell, Robert: *Brother in the Land*, 71, 86–88

Taylor, Charles, 61
teaching. *See* didacticism
technology, 94–95, 101–109, 111; and biology, 12; and bodies, 57, 104, 108; and ethics, 12; and literacy, 12, 152–154; and nature, 11; and pedagogy, 151; and the posthuman, 176, 197–199; and the postmetropolis, 56–58; and spirituality, 12; as tool for resistance, 151
teenagers. *See* adolescents
terrorism, 77–78, 193
Thomas, Dylan, 154
Thompson, Kate: *White Horse Trick, The*, 71
Thoreau, Henry David, 150
tomboys, 127
totalitarian regime, 4, 19, 36–38, 54; and *Divergent*, 23; and *Forest of Hands and Teeth, The*, 193; and *Hunger Games, The*, 118, 162; and *Little Brother*, 152, and *Matched*, 148; and *Uglies*, 134, 149
Totaro, Rebecca Carol Noël, 45
time, 53, 57, 61–62
transformation, 87, 121, 125, 127. *See also* change
transnationalism, 70, 76
Trites, Roberta Seelinger, 2, 141

Uglies series (Westerfeld), 101, 109, 111; and critique of modern society, 131; *Extras*, 8; and history, 136; and notions of beauty, 134, 136, 137, 149; *Pretties*, 107–108; and race, 11, 134–137; and sameness, 3, 134–135; and science fiction, 9; and *Specials*, 108; technology, 149; and traditional literacy, 12, 145, 150; *Uglies*, 2–4, 102–107
uncertainty, 96. *See also* risk
United Nations, 69
Unwind (Shusterman), 12, 159–173; and cannibalism, 167; and family, 169; and genocide, 167; and religion, 169
urban areas. *See* cities; space (urban)
Ure, Jean: *Plague 99*, 3

utopia, 2, 3, 10; Anti-Dystopia, 29; Anti-Utopia, 28–29; building a better world, 3, 6, 41, 118, 189, 200; choice of, 46, 118; definition of, 41; as dystopia, 23, 28, 53–54; and genre, 78, 86; right-wing, 35; and social critique, 131; transformation, 71, 79, 121; utopian hope, 79; utopian impulse, 87; visions of, 42, 54
utopianism, 41

van den Eijnden, Jan G. J., 166
Ventura, Abbie, 196
violence, 38, 89, 91, 122, 124. *See also* discipline
virtual reality, 24, 25, 57–59, 61. *See also* Simcity
Vonnegut, Kurt, 192

war. *See* violence
warnings, 71, 86, 93 (*see also* didacticism); and caution, 72
Waters, Brent, 184, 185
Welsh, Alexander, 109
Westerfeld, Scott, 5–6. *See also* Uglies series (Westerfeld)
Weyn, Suzanne, *Empty*, 71
white privilege, 132–133, 135–136; and science, 135–136, 138. *See also* privilege
Wilson, D. Harlan, 192
Wilson, Edward O., 105

world risk society, 10, 70, 74, 76–79. *See also* risk

young adult dystopias: and activism, 200; compared to the problem novel, 169–170; darkness in, 69, 72, 78, 81–82; and fears of the future, 170, 191, 199; and postmodernity, 192; and the posthuman, 192; and technology, 191; themes in, 3, 4, 13
young adult literature, 2, 4, 20, 53–54, 175
young adult readers: and desires, 19–20, 61–62, 86–87, 92; as fans, 23, 117–118; and hope, 71; and identity, 19; infantilized, 107; narratives for, 5, 6–7, 79, 82n14, 101; and political agency, 70, 93, 95, 97; and the problem novel, 169; questioning, 92; and reader's expectations, 70, 92; and response to text, 75, 93, 110–111, 197, 200; versus protagonists, 191
young adult culture. *See* culture
young adult protagonists, 4, 7, 19–20, 45, 109–110, 184; and readers, 87; and vulnerability, 85. *See also* gender (female protagonists); heroines

Zipes, Jack, 54, 71, 131
Zipp, Yvonne, 123
zombies, 3, 193, 194